Self and Nature in
Kant's Philosophy

Self and Nature in Kant's Philosophy

EDITED BY

ALLEN W. WOOD

Cornell University Press

ITHACA AND LONDON

Copyright © 1984 by Cornell University

All rights reserved. Except for brief quotations in a review, this book, or parts thereof, must not be reproduced in any form without permission in writing from the publisher. For information, address Cornell University Press, 124 Roberts Place, Ithaca, New York 14850.

First published 1984 by Cornell University Press.
Published in the United Kingdom by
Cornell University Press Ltd., London.

International Standard Book Number (cloth) 0-8014-1610-8
International Standard Book Number (paper) 0-8014-9268-8
Library of Congress Catalog Card Number 84-76781
Printed in the United States of America
*Librarians: Library of Congress cataloging information
appears on the last page of the book.*

*The paper in this book is acid-free and meets the guidelines
for permanence and durability of the Committee on Production
Guidelines for Book Longevity of the Council on Library Resources.*

Contents

Preface

Anyone familiar with Kant's thought knows the famous passage from the conclusion of the *Critique of Practical Reason*: "Two things fill the mind with ever new and increasing admiration and awe, the oftener and more steadily we reflect on them: the starry heavens above me and the moral law within me" (161g 166e). The passage identifies two important focuses of Kant's philosophy: the natural or sensible world in its "unbounded magnitude" ("the starry heavens") and the rational personality or "invisible self" (with whose reality the moral law acquaints us). These two focuses, however, are also related. Not only are they alike objects of admiration and awe, but they are involved with one another: the self is for Kant the point of origin, the "lawgiver of nature," just as its freedom is "the keystone of the whole architecture of the system of pure reason and even of speculative reason" (320g 62e; 3g 3e). Further, the two focuses are united in the direct certainty Kant says we have of them: "I do not merely conjecture them and seek them as though obscured in darkness or in the transcendent region beyond my horizon; I see them before me, and I associate them directly with the consciousness of my own existence" (161fg 166e).

Yet both these relationships between the invisible self and sensible nature (the self as lawgiver of nature and the immediate certainty of self and nature) have seemed to Kant's readers to raise troubling questions for him. How does the world that—as Kant insists—exists independently of us come to be governed by

7

laws arising a priori from the understanding? What is nature if it is posited—or at least legislated to—by the human self? Does not Kant's transcendental idealism, like all idealism, reduce the sensible world or nature to a mere illusion? How can Kantian transcendental idealism be consistent with his insistence, in his "refutation" of dogmatic and problematic idealism, that a nature outside of me is given along with my consciousness of myself?

Do we, on the other hand, have any real certainty, as Kant claims, of the free, active self in his theory? Indeed, can we even form a coherent conception of this self? In any case, how is the noumenal self posited by Kant's "two worlds" theory related to the practically free self, which is the subject of Kantian morality? How is it related to the thinking, unifying self, which is the source of the categories and the "lawgiver of nature"? And how are any of these selves related to the empirical self, which is the subject of sensible desires and the result of its own self-affection?

It would be absurd to claim that any essay in this volume definitively answers any of these questions, for the questions will probably divide and perplex Kant's readers for as long as Kant has any readers. But the essays do address these questions, and each scholar has something both original and responsible to say about them. The essays are based on papers and commentaries presented in November 1981 at a colloquium sponsored by Cornell University's Society for the Humanities, commemorating the two hundredth anniversary of the first publication of Kant's *Critique of Pure Reason*. The aim of the colloquium was not so much to focus on a specific theme or themes in Kant's philosophy as to bring together for thoughtful exchange some of the best philosophical scholars now working on Kant's philosophy. The essays display some common concerns, with Kant's conception of nature and natural science, with Kant's theory of moral autonomy and free will, and with Kant's conception of the thinking self.

Philip Kitcher finds some strongly anti-empiricist yet realist elements in Kant's philosophy of science and argues that this side of Kant's philosophy, so interpreted, is more central to Kant's philosophical project than has usually been thought. Charles Parsons has reservations about Kitcher's way of interpreting

Kant's conception of pure natural science, but notes a similarity between this interpretation and recent German scholarship on the topic. Parsons explores the sense in which Kant may have meant that a part of natural science is pure or a priori. He also discusses the relation between pure natural science in the *Metaphysical Foundations* and central parts of the first *Critique*, for example, the Analogies of Experience.

Margaret D. Wilson's essay also considers the Kantian conception of nature; her comparison of Kant and Berkeley portrays Kant as much more of a scientific realist than has been believed. Specifically, Wilson shows that if Kant was both a transcendental idealist and an empirical realist about the spatial, temporal, and causal qualities of nature, he was not even an empirical realist about sensible qualities, such as color, sound, taste, and so on. Instead, she argues, Kant held a scientific realist position about the latter qualities, close to the positions of Descartes and Locke. Elizabeth Potter does not dispute Wilson's reading of Kant so much as her suggestion that Kant's treatment of sensible qualities as empirically unreal is unattractive when compared with Berkeley's defense of their empirical reality.

Several of the essays deal with the troubling question of free will in Kant's philosophy. In "Kant's Compatibilism," I attempt to reconstruct Kant's notorious "two worlds" theory as sympathetically as I can, and to defend it against the objections that seem most natural and most common. Jonathan Bennett perhaps speaks (with uncommon articulateness) for the majority of Kant's readers in finding Kant's theory of freedom (as I reconstruct it) less than compelling and beset with insuperable difficulties. Whereas my essay straddles the gap between metaphysics and moral philosophy in its treatment of free will, Terence Irwin treats the same question from the standpoint of idealist criticisms of Kantian ethics. The idealist he chooses, however, is T. H. Green, who conceived his own moral theory not as a rejection of the Kantian but as an amendment that preserves the core of truth in Kant's own theory. Irwin sees matters the same way, and attempts to separate that core of truth from the errors in Kant's moral psychology that leave his theory open to idealist objections. Ralf Meerbote is unconvinced that the amendments proposed by Green and Irwin are friendly ones, and he defends the view that the amended theory is incompatible with Kant's deepest insights into the distinction between morality and self-interest, between autonomy and heteronomy of the will.

The self is also the central theme of Patricia Kitcher's essay, but she argues that the real hero of the *Critique of Pure Reason* is neither the passive empirical self nor the ghostly transcendent noumenal self but the "thinking self" of the Transcendental Deduction, whose function it is to introduce connectedness among representations through the "synthetic unity of apperception." Kitcher develops her interpretation of this thinking self in a way that is original and yet is also in line with some contemporary developments in the philosophy of mind. Sydney Shoemaker is intrigued by and sympathetic to Kitcher's exegetical project, but he sees some gaps in her account, which he attempts to locate and for which he prescribes some possible remedies.

In the introductory essay, Lewis White Beck attempts to deal in a comprehensive way with Kant's philosophy, encompassing not only natural science but morality, politics, and art as well. His focus, however, is also the self. According to Beck, the Kantian Revolution in philosophy was not only Copernican but also Promethean. Kant conceived of the human self fundamentally as a creator, as seizing the prerogative of the gods in legislating both to nature and morality, but remaining all the while a finite and fallible being who must subject its creativity to the guidance and criticism of reason.

With two exceptions, the essays appear in print for the first time. Philip Kitcher's "Kant's Philosophy of Science" was previously published in *Midwest Studies in Philosophy* 8 (University of Minnesota Press, Minneapolis, copyright © 1983 by the University of Minnesota). It is reprinted here with their permission. Lewis White Beck's "What Have We Learned from Kant?" appears here for the first time in English. Two (slightly different) versions of it have been published in German: "Was haben wir von Kant gelernt?" in *Akten des V. Internationalen Kant-Kongresses* (Mainz, 1981), ii, and in *Kant-Studien* 72 (1981) pp. 1-10. The English version appears here with the permission of Gerhard Funke, editor of both the *Akten* and *Kant-Studien*.

Gratitude is owed to Cornell's Society for the Humanities, which sponsored the colloquium from which this volume is derived, and in particular to Eric Blackall, director of the society, and Anne-Marie Garcia, whose expertise and generosity helped to make the colloquium a success, and thus to make this book possible. My friend and colleague John G. Bennett generously donated both time and expertise to create a computer program that greatly facilitated the compilation of the index. Finally, I owe a personal debt of gratitude to my friend and colleague Norman Kretzmann, without whose benevolent prodding I would have been motivated neither to organize the colloquium nor to edit this book.

A.W.W.

Berlin

Abbreviations Used in Citing Works of Kant

All citations of Kant in German refer to Kant's *Gesammelte Schriften* (Berlin, 1902–), abbreviated *GS*. German pagination is followed by *g* and English pagination is followed by *e*. Abbreviations used in citing particular works of Kant are as follows:

A/B   *Kritik der reinen Vernunft, GS* 3–4
       Critique of Pure Reason, tr. Norman Kemp Smith (London, 1963)

EaD   *Das Ende aller Dinge, GS* 8
       "The End of All Things," in *Perpetual Peace and Other Essays*,
          ed. Ted Humphrey (Indianapolis, 1983)

G   *Grundlegung zur Metaphysik der Sitten, GS* 4
       Foundations of the Metaphysics of Morals, tr. L. W. Beck (Indi-
          anapolis, 1959)

GT   *Über den Gebrauch teleologischer Prinzipien in der Philosophie, GS*
       8

I   *Idee zu einerallgemeinen Geschichte in weltbürgerlicher Absicht, GS*
       8
       "Idea for a Universal History with a Cosmopolitan Intent," in
          Perpetual Peace and Other Essays, ed. Ted Humphrey

KpV   *Kritik der praktischen Vernunft, GS* 5
       Critique of Practical Reason, tr. L. W. Beck (Indianapolis, 1956)

KU   *Kritik der Urteilskraft, GS* 5
        Critique of Judgment, tr. J. H. Bernard (New York, 1951)

L   *Vorlesungen über Logik, GS* 9
       Logic, tr. R. S. Hartman and W. Schwarz (Indianapolis, 1974)

MN   *Metaphysische Anfangsgründe der Naturwissenschaft, GS* 4
       Metaphysical Foundations of Natural Science, tr. J. Ellington (In-
          dianapolis, 1970)

Abbreviations

P *Prolegomena zu einer jeden künftigen Metaphysik, GS* 4
   Prolegomena to Any Future Metaphysics, tr. P. Carus; rev. J. Ellington (Indianapolis, 1977)

Rel *Die Religion innerhalb der Grenzen der blossen Vernunft, GS* 6
   Religion within the Limits of Reason Alone, tr. T. M. Greene and
   H. H. Hudson (New York, 1960)

TL *Die Metaphysik der Sitten: Tugendlehre, GS* 6
   The Doctrine of Virtue, tr. M. J. Gregor (New York, 1964)

VM *Vorlesungen über die Metaphysik*, ed. K. H. L. Pölitz, *GS* 28, 1

VpR *Vorlesungen über die philosophische Religionslehre*, ed. K. H. L. Pöl-
   itz, *GS* 28, 2, 2
   Lectures on Philosophical Theology, tr. A. W. Wood and G. M.
   Clark (Ithaca, 1978)

Wh *Was heisst Sich im Denken Orientiren? GS* 8
   "What Is Orientation in Thinking?" in *Critique of Practical Rea-
   son and Other Writings in Moral Philosophy*, ed. L. W. Beck
   (Chicago, 1949; reprint, New York, 1976)

Z *Zum ewigen Frieden, GS* 8
   "Perpetual Peace," in *Perpetual Peace and Other Essays*, ed. Ted
   Humphrey

Self and Nature in
Kant's Philosophy

I

What Have We Learned from Kant?

Lewis White Beck

The publication of Immanuel Kant's *Critique of Pure Reason* two centuries ago concerns a wider public than the professional philosophical community. Although the *Critique of Pure Reason* was written almost exclusively for the professional philosopher, it was nonetheless the foundation for most of Kant's other writings, nearly half of which were addressed to the general learned public.

Great philosophers such as Kant speak not just to the professoriate, but to all who agree with Socrates that the unexamined life is not worth living. Accordingly, in his own work Kant explicitly distinguished between the "interests of the school" and the "interests of humanity." The interests of the school are those of professional philosophers. Kant believed that the interests of the school were subordinate to the interests of humanity though, in the long run, important to them. As a young man Kant wrote in a private jotting:

By inclination I am an enquirer. I feel a consuming thirst for knowledge, the unrest which goes with the desire to progress in it, and the satisfaction which comes with every advance in knowledge. There was a time when I believed that this constituted the honor of humanity, and I despised the people, who know nothing. . . .[But] I have learned to honor man, and would find myself more useless than the common laborer if I did not believe that this attitude of mine [as an enquirer] can give a worth to all others, in establishing the rights of mankind.[*GS* 20:44].

Kant openly sympathized with both the French and the American revolutions, at a time when expressions of such sympathy were in Germany personally hazardous. When he wrote of "the rights of mankind," he certainly meant political and legal rights of the kind that those revolutions were meant to secure. But Kant's conception of rights was much more than political. Political rights were, he thought, essential to all others; they were conditions for the exercise of other rights—the rights of people to enlighten themselves, to use their talents freely in the discovery of truth, and to develop their moral character. All of these constitute the calling (*Bestimmung*) of man.

To determine the calling of man, philosophy is needed. Around the time Kant wrote the note just quoted, he also remarked, "If there is any science which man stands in need of, it is one which teaches him to occupy properly the place assigned to him in creation, and one from which he can learn what he must be, in order to be a man (*GS* 20:45). *But what is man?* This is the principal question of philosophy, and it epitomizes three preliminary questions: What can I know? What ought I to do? What may I hope? (*L* 25g 29e; cf. *A805/B833*). To each of these questions a great *Critique* is devoted, but only the entire corpus is adequate to answer the principal question. The three preliminary questions have definite answers in their respective *Critiques*; nowhere is there a simple, explicit answer to the principal question. Yet Kant's answers to the first three queries point unmistakably to an answer to the ultimate question, for there is a single common theme running through all the *Critiques* that leads always to the same reply to the question, What is man?

PHILOSOPHY OF SCIENCE

In the philosophy of science Kant effected what has been called (though not by him) the Copernican Revolution. Copernicus found that the phenomena of planetary astronomy can best be understood by taking into account the movements of the earth. The real motion of the astronomer who observes the skies introduces an order into the observations that would not be there if the earth itself stood still, or if the astronomer denied its motion. The movement of every perceiving subject must be reckoned in with the movements observed, in order to discover the real motion of the object one is observing.

Kant drew a fruitful analogy between terrestrial motion and other factors which, from the side of the observer, determine in part both the subjective and the objective (that is, the intersubjective) aspects of what is observed. The knowing subject can understand any phenomenon of the world (whether or not it involves motion) only if he takes account of his own contribution (whether the parallax of his own motion, or some other factor). The observer's contribution is not just the relatively unimportant, that is, nonexplanatory secondary qualities, but the most objective of all properties and structures, the formal characteristics of experience and its underlying laws. These are, as it were, read into experience by the intellectual and operational acts of the observing and explaining mind. Therefore, Kant says, "The understanding derives its laws (*a priori*) not from nature, but rather prescribes them to nature" (*P* 320g 62e). By subsequent experience we are instructed as to what specific generalizations and laws obtain, as specifications of a priori concepts such as cause, substance, magnitude, and position. Nature, says Kant, is "the existence of things so far as it is determined by universal laws" (*P* 294g 38e); accordingly, the human mind can be regarded not only as the legislator or the lawgiver of nature, but as the creator of nature—not of the stuff of nature, of course, for the human mind is finite and must work with material supplied by some unknown source—but of nature considered as a system existing under laws the knowledge of which gives nature whatever intelligibility it exhibits. (When the German idealists denied the limitations Kant placed on our cognitive capacity, they thought of the mind as being the creator of nature in a much more extravagant sense. Kant should not be blamed for their excesses, which in fact he tried to prevent.) Kant stands between the doctrine of Nicolas of Cusa and Vico that *verum et factum convertuntur* (truth is what is made, we can know only what we can make), and Nietzsche's profound aphorism, "Bevor 'gedacht' wurde, muss schon *gedichtet* worden sein" (Before something is 'thought' it must first be *composed*).[1]

The only science Kant knew was Newtonian; the only geometry, Euclidean; the only logic, Aristotelian. Because all of these have been superseded or revised, it is sometimes said that the *Critique of Pure Reason*, which supported them, was a defense of lost causes. Nevertheless, the epistemological foundations Kant supplied to Newtonian physics and Euclidean geometry are reminders that non-Newtonian physics and non-Euclidean geometries also stand on epistemological foundations. The latter are not self-explanatory and self-justifying; they must be, in Kant's language, transcendentally deduced. It is a point of dispute in modern philosophy of science whether the foundations needed for these new disciplines are more like or more unlike those of the Kantian model of classical physics. Whether like or unlike, a treatise analogous to the *Critique of Pure Reason* needs to be written after every scientific revolution. The resemblances between the *Critique of Pure Reason* and modern positivistic, operationalistic, and model theories are striking, for all these contemporary theories emphasize one Kantian theme: the ways in which the mind's own activities in inquiry are projected into and reflected back by nature. Naturally this Kantian theme has been modified, and most of these modifications move in the same direction; that is, away from what Stephan Körner has called Kant's uniqueness-thesis, in other words, the doctrine that there is only one way of organizing experience so that we can make any knowledge-claims, even false ones.[2] No doubt the rigidity of the Kantian transcendental apparatus must be relaxed, alternative category systems must be conceded, knowledge itself must

---

[1]On the equivalence of *verum* and *factum*, see Isaiah Berlin, *Vico and Herder* (London, 1976), pp. 21 and 142 n. The aphorism is in Nietzsche's *Gesammelte Werke*, Musarion Ausgabe (Munich, 1925), vol. 16, p. 115. All quotations in the text, except those from the *Critique of Pure Reason*, are translated by me; those from the first *Critique* are from the Kemp Smith translation.

[2]Stephan Körner, "The Impossibility of Transcendental Deductions," *Kant Studies Today*, ed. L. W. Beck (La Salle, Ill., 1969), p. 233.

be relativized according to changing cultural systems. The creative activity of minds—the central thought in the *Critique of Pure Reason*—is made perhaps even more pervasive by those who undertake these revisions than it was by Kant himself: whereas the creativity in Kant's account is somewhat abstract and transcendental, modern studies of conceptual change emphasize the actual historical, social, and personal factors, and give empirical meaning to the notion of cognitive creations. These changes do not evade the issue that led Kant to write the *Critique*, namely, How can free creations of the mind have objective validity? This question remains, even when the concepts Kant thought of as unique creations of the mind have long since been shown to have alternatives or, indeed, have been replaced by others in the progress of science.

Contemporary sociology of knowledge emphasizes cultural factors in the creation and acceptance of alternative portrayals of the world. Kant, on the other hand, was aware of only one system of grammar. He also thought—perhaps in part for that reason—that there was only one type of cognizing mind, only one system of scientific knowledge. He overlooked the variable social dimensions of thought and was little interested in the philosophy of language (in fact, little interested in language itself, which he seems to have regarded as hardly more than a transparent medium). Because he presented his categorial system as a "transcendental grammar" (*P* 323g 65e), Kant appears to belong to the tradition Noam Chomsky has called "Cartesian linguistics."

But anti-Cartesian linguistics also may have Kantian sources, as seen originally in the work of Kant's disciples Herder and Humboldt and in this century in that of the neo-Kantians Georg Simmel and Ernst Cassirer. Alternative pictures of the universe and of society depend upon the symbol systems in use, which determine the a priori features of experiences accepted into the communication network. Whether or not a single universal grammar exists, the linguistic turn in philosophy a generation ago was an analogue of the Copernican Revolution, with or without the uniqueness-thesis. Whether the epistemological center (like the sun in Copernican astronomy) is a single universal grammar or whether there are at the ultimate depths diverse and irreducible systems of semiotic rules, the a priori forms of experience of the world correspond to the forms in which this experience is articulated and communicated. We see only what we can say.

Each culture, each scientific paradigm, each linguistic system requires something analogous to a *Critique of Pure Reason* in order to understand how its principles and rules are projected into its cosmological and cultural conceptions. It was no surprise to me, therefore, when Ernest Gellner recently counted Kant as chief among the ancestors of structuralism.[3]

MORALITY AND POLITICS

Just as Kant's Copernican Revolution taught that the scientific thinker gives the form of lawfulness to the events in nature, reads the law into nature, as it were, and then specifies the variables by empirical research, an analogous revolution occurs in Kant's moral philosophy, which I call the Rousseauistic Revolution. Rousseau, Kant's favorite modern author, wrote: "Freedom is obedience to a law which man gives to himself."[4] Rousseau meant this primarily in a political sense, and the idea was the basis of his theory of self-government. Only by participation in government and not by mere tacit consent is political authority justified. Kant developed this political theory further than Rousseau did, and he also developed it into a philosophy of morals.

The moral law, which philosophers before Kant had found in what they considered to be the will of God, or the law of nature, or the human desire for happiness, he found (using a political metaphor) in autonomy. Perhaps for the first time, a clear conceptual distinction was drawn between morality and prudence raised to an almost transcendental elevation. Prudence is rea-

[3]Ernest Gellner, "What Is Structuralism?" *Times Literary Supplement*, July 31, 1981, p. 881.
[4]Rousseau, *Social Contract*, 1:8 (Everyman ed., London, 1946, p. 16).

sonable adherence to policies for reaching desired and desirable ends; morality is adherence to a maxim out of respect for its status as a law for rational beings. Respect is a unique feeling evoked only by a law which, having no prudential sanctions, is an expression of one's rational capacity shown both in making and judging knowledge-claims and in reaching and justifying practical decisions. I can *obey* laws out of concern with reward and punishment, and if I am prudent I usually do so; but I can *respect* them only if their origin in my own rational lawgiving capacity humbles my merely prudential concerns.

There is an analogy between moral principles and the categorial principles in the first *Critique*. The only theoretical law or principle I can acknowledge as a priori necessary is one my understanding prescribes to nature. 'Acknowledge as necessary' is the first *Critique*'s epistemological analogue of moral 'respect' in the second *Critique*. Autonomy is a fundamental condition of both cognitive and practical activity; because the *word* did not come into Kant's vocabulary until after 1781, many readers have missed the *thing* in the first *Critique*. Yet the analogies are vivid. Pure practical reason stands in the same relation to the moral realm (the realm of ends) as pure understanding does to the realm of nature. Both are sources of a priori laws. One exacts our obedience in interpreting nature, which we regard as equivalent to nature's own obedience to law. The other exacts our obedience in the pursuit of happiness, human rights, and virtue, regardless of whether nature responds favorably to our efforts, or thwarts them. Whether virtue is rewarded with happiness is something that does not lie with man; what is within his power, and what he ought to undertake, is to be *worthy* of happiness. Obedience to a law given by one's rational nature is a necessary condition of such worthiness, but it is neither necessary nor sufficient for the attainment of other human goals.

Many have objected that Kant held obedience to be so high a virtue—indeed the only virtue—that he regarded the origin and consequences of a law as morally irrelevant. Therefore, it has been held, he could not distinguish between legitimate and illegitimate laws, could not condemn fanaticism devoted to some immoral goal, and could not morally criticize any actual government or resist any actual tyranny. Paradoxically, the friend of the American and French revolutions has been seen as a defender of political absolutism.

I must grant that there are paradoxes in Kant's political philosophy, especially in his adherence to the Lutheran position on the unrighteousness of rebellion, which led him into some not very edifying casuistry. Nevertheless, Kant always clearly distinguished between the moral law, which derives from reason, and the positive law, which arises from empirically determined power-relations. Even in his casuistical accounts of the misadventures of the French Revolution he never failed to give priority to the moral: "Politics," he says, "must always bend its knee to morality" (Z 380g 134e). The law we respect is no arbitrary edict with sanctions of reward and punishment; rather, it is a law of a kind we as impartial lawgivers prescribe, or at least could prescribe, for ourselves. It is a maxim made under the veil of empirical ignorance, with the moral innocence of the dove instead of the political wisdom of the serpent. A law of this kind arises, and is valid, only insofar as it is reasonable. 'Reasonable' here means far more than merely self-consistent; it means constrained by the universal rights and serviceable to the universal interests of mankind. The moral law, then, is not an absolutized positive law, but rather a rational criterion of the legitimacy of statute law. Moral law is the rationalized and secularized form of the law of God or the law of nature, and fulfills much the same functions that these venerable concepts had served as constraints on arbitrary political power.

I have just compared Kant's theory to the traditional doctrines of the law of nature or the law of God, but one might better ask, What is *living* in Kant's moral philosophy? Indeed, there has been a revolution in the moral life just as great as the revolution in the scientific world-picture, and one may well believe that Kant's humanistic ethic with its Jewish, Christian, and Stoic components and Protestant Prussian coloration is as antiquated as the Euclidean geometry and Newtonian physics to which Kant adhered. Nowadays we do not have his faith in the rationality and universality of morality. The very word "rationalization" expresses psychoanalytic suspicions, and the Kantian equation of moral actions with actions done out a punctilious sense of duty or out of pure reason is hardly persuasive today. We see many factors as limitations on human freedom that were morally irrelevant for Kant.

Such reservations appear to me to be legitimate and important, and yet are somewhat superficial, because they misread Kant as a casuist and do not touch the principal points of his moral philosophy. After every moral revolution a new *Critique of Practical Reason* ought to be written, or at least Kant's own ought to be reread. Our present-day ethical views, however far from Kant's they may be, need philosophical foundations not found in clinical psychology or modes and fashions; they need what Kant perhaps misleadingly called a "metaphysics of morals." The foundations of every ethics are to be found in conceptions of an ideal human nature. It is possible that Kant conceived this nature too rationalistically in trying to establish an ethics valid for all rational beings and not for human beings alone, but the metaethical structure of ethical systems based upon quite different ideals of human nature may well be Kantian.

People often indignantly contrast *Kantian* ethics with *human* ethics and say of the former, "It may be right in theory, but will not hold in practice."[5] Against this objection, recall Kant's rejoinder to those who presumed to criticize Plato on the sorry pretext of the impracticality or unfeasibility of his political theory: "Nothing indeed can be more injurious or more unworthy of a philosopher than the vulgar appeal to so-called adverse experience. Such experience would never have existed at all, had history followed the prescriptions of Plato" (*A* 316–17/*B* 373). Per corollary, one ought not object to the Kantian moral philosophy on grounds of its impracticality, but rather one ought to use it as an admonition against actual tendencies that do not aim to establish the kingdom of God on earth (or, in Kantian language, the realm of ends), in which rational beings will be treated as ends in themselves, and not as means only.

[5]See, for example, F. Sartiaux, *Morale kantienne et morale humaine* (Paris, 1917).

PHILOSOPHY OF ART

One of the strangest phenomena in the history of thought is that Kant led a revolution in our conception of art. It is strange because it was so unlikely: in his entire life, Kant probably never had an opportunity to see a fine painting or hear a good performance of great music. His Copernican and Rousseauistic revolutions were historically conservative; they did not revolutionize science or morals but provided new and revolutionary foundations for the science and the moral ideals already current. His aesthetic revolution, on the other hand, was a renunciation of the critical standards of his time. It prepared the way for artistic developments that occurred after he wrote, and, in the case of German romanticism, in part *because* of what he wrote.

Here again we meet with an analogue of the Copernican Revolution. M. H. Abrams, writing of Wordsworth, says that "the Copernican revolution in epistemology—. . . the general concept that the perceiving mind discovers what it has itself partly made— was effected in England by poets and critics before it manifested itself in academic philosophy."[6] But in Germany the revolution in aesthetics came first, in Kant's academic philosophy.

Kant turned against two dominant aesthetic principles that had governed European thought on art, if not art itself: that art is the imitation of nature (*ut pictura poesis*) and that the purpose of art is moral edification. Kant rejected both principles because they confined art and made it parasitic upon either knowledge or morals. Kant is clear and convincing in his rejection of theories that the aesthetic response is a response to the information-content of a work of art. He saw that aesthetic value is attached to the syntactic, not the semantic, dimension of meaning. Only in that way is the artist free to create something "purposive, [but] without purpose." (*KU* 241g, 78e).

One cannot maintain that Kant was completely successful in separating moral from aesthetic interests. Perhaps he was not sufficiently independent of the critical thought of his time to have made a clean break between them. It is not clear whether,

---

[6]M. H. Abrams, *The Mirror and the Lamp* (New York, 1953), p. 58.

given the rest of his theory, he should have, or could have, done so. Historically, however, the principal thrust of Kant's arguments has been in the direction of the emancipation of art from extra-artistic criteria, whether of factual truth or moral value.

Kant replaced the two standard critical principles of his time—the imitation of nature, and the moral edification of the audience—with his theory of genius. Genius is a law unto itself, and it creates a second nature, not just a copy of a first nature. The German romantic movement developed its program from Kant's philosophical emancipation of art through genius. Because the excesses of romantic genius were distasteful to Kant, some may believe that the romantic and other later anticlassical movements in art have made his aesthetic theory as obsolete as they view his defense of Newtonian physics, Christian ethics, and Roman law. After all, Kant's taste was for tulips and arabesques; what could he have seen in Duchamp's *Nude Descending a Staircase*?

Nineteenth- and twentieth-century revolutions of thought about art (perhaps with the exception of the Marxist) appear to be pushing to an extreme what was implicit in Kant's own theory; that is, the doctrine of the autonomy of art, its freedom from nonartistic concerns, or art for art's sake. The creativity of the artist, not the contingent occurrence of beautiful objects and the talent to reproduce them faithfully on canvas, is the decisive condition of aesthetic excellence. If we imagine Kant's coming back to life and visiting our museums and laboratories, I suspect that, after an initial shock and a little time to get his bearings, he might be as much at home in the one as in the other. And I even suspect that in the art gallery he would be more comfortable with *Nude Descending a Staircase* than with Titian's nudes, because his theory of human beauty is not, at least in any obvious way, consistent with his formalistic analyses, which apparently fit arabesques better than they do human portraits.[7] Designs, without

[7]Paul Guyer in "Formalism and the Theory of Expression in Kant's Aesthetics," *Kant-Studien* 68 (1977), 46–70, argues very effectively that the limitation to formal (geometric) elements is not inherent in Kant's theory. "Nothing in this doctrine," Guyer says, "need be seen as excluding concepts, symbols and the like from being *part of the manifold of imagination* which the mind ranges over in its free play" (p. 55).

representational content or moral message, which present or stimulate the free play of imagination were the paradigms of Kant's aesthetic theory, and are especially characteristic of much post-Kantian art.

THE PROMETHEAN REVOLUTION

From the foregoing, a common theme may be seen in Kant's work in science, morals, and art. The same theme underlies his theories of mathematics, history, religion, and politics. All his works lead to the same answer to the question, What is man? That answer is, man is creator. To Kant's Copernican and Rousseauistic revolutions, therefore, I would add a third: his work also represents a Promethean Revolution in philosophy. It was Prometheus who seized the prerogative of the gods and gave it to humankind. Through possession of fire, everything else could be created. Certainly the Prometheus role is not without its mortal danger; the ancient hero suffered martyrdom, and Prometheanism leads to the vice of hubris. Kant avoided both the fate and the vice by never forgetting that man is a finite-all-too-finite being, and that the world created by man is a human-all-too-human world—indeed, a world of appearance, the basic conditions and materials of which lie beyond the limits of human knowledge and power. Man is no god, but in his creativity he may be godlike, and many of the tasks previously assigned to god in the creation and governance of the world are reassigned by Kant to man.

The world man orders, or seeks to order, is only the known part of the unknown all. Kant was the anthropologist of a race that dwelt in "the land of truth"—the "land of truth" is man's realm, man is the lawgiver in it. But the "land of truth" is only an island, surrounded by "a wide and stormy ocean, the native home of illusion, where many a fog-bank and many a swiftly melting iceberg give the deceptive appearance of farther shores, deluding the adventurous seafarer ever anew with empty hopes, and engaging him in enterprises which he can never abandon and yet is unable to carry to completion" (*A* 235–36/*B* 294–95).

The cultivation of this island and the exploration of this ocean is the calling of man. In these dual efforts of *Aufklärung*, the human race stands alone and independent: "Nature has willed that man, by himself, should produce everything that goes beyond the mechanical ordering of his animal existence, and that he should partake of no other happiness or perfection than that which he himself, independently of instinct, has created by his own reason" (*I* 19g 31e).

Were it not for the words "happiness" and "reason" in this quotation, you might have thought that I was quoting a rather prosaic Sartre. The autonomy of the individual in creating out of chaos the world in which one is to live is as characteristic of Kant's teaching as it is of that of the modern existentialist thinker. But "happiness" and "reason" cannot be left out of the quotation. For Kant, only reasonable human beings, in spite of all their errors, can create a world in which there is some chance for well-being and happiness, and only the criticism and discipline of reason can lead toward the requisite wisdom.

Like the present, the Age of Reason had its irrationalists. The German Enlightenment had its Counter-Enlightenment just as we have a counterculture. Kant lived in an age that was changing just as rapidly and violently as ours, in which tradition was under as serious a challenge as now, in which it was just as questionable as it is now what should be saved in established institutions and practices and what should be changed or rejected. There were those in his day, as in our own, who were brought to skepticism by the knowledge explosion and by conflicts in values. There were people, even in Königsberg, who had no faith in the life of reason and took refuge in irrationalistic enthusiasms and superstitions. The Germans had a name for this rebellion: *Sturm und Drang*. (The very name sounds frightening.) Kant saw Storm and Stress as a threat to the progress of knowledge and to civilized life, which depends upon that progress. What Kant said in 1786 is as portentous now, because something like *Sturm und Drang* is still with us. These words were addressed to the people of Storm and Stress, but they may be meant also for us:

Friends of the human race, and of that which is holiest to it!...Do not wrench from reason what makes it the highest good on earth, the prerogative of being the final touchstone of truth. If you do this, you will become unworthy of freedom, and lose it, and bring misfortune to those who want to use freedom in a lawful manner to secure the good of mankind. [*Wh* 146fg 305e]

II

Morality and Personality: Kant and Green

Terence Irwin

IDEALIST CRITICISMS OF KANT

Kant's moral philosophy includes sharp contrasts and dualisms—between form and content, categorical and hypothetical imperatives, moral and nonmoral motives, the rational and sensuous selves, noumenal and phenomenal causes. Kant's critics have attacked one or another of these dualisms. Without the dualisms there is not much Kantian ethics, but how many of them are needed for Kant's main moral principles?

I will discuss here one Kantian dualism, that between the moral and the nonmoral selves. This dualism connects Kant's account of free will with his conception of the moral motive. The proper motive for the moral person, in his view, is the motive that appeals to our rational selves, not our sensuous selves, and our rational selves are the free selves, free from coercion by natural impulses.

I will discuss one critic of this dualism, the idealist T. H. Green. Green's criticism is instructive because he is an unusual idealist.[1]

---

[1] For a brief account of Green's place in idealism see A. M. Quinton, "Absolute Idealism," *Proceedings of the British Academy* 57 (1971), 20.

The translations of Kant in this essay are taken from the versions cited in the list of abbreviations used in this volume.

I have benefited from comments on versions of this essay by participants in the colloquium at Cornell, and by members of the Jowett Society in Oxford. I am especially grateful to Allen Wood, Sydney Shoemaker, and Thomas Arner.

Hegel's sharp and unsympathetic criticism of Kantian ethics forms a common idealist attitude to Kant, forcibly expressed in F. H. Bradley's *Ethical Studies*. For Hegel, Kantian dualisms are both essential to and the ruin of Kantian ethics. The categorical imperative prescribes to a moral self that has no sensuous impulses whatever. It is pure form, abstracting from all content. Nothing is left, in Hegel's view, but some indeterminate general conscientiousness, with no firm conception of what to be conscientious about. When Kant divides the rational from the sensuous self, he leaves us with no intelligible account of the will, or of the relation of the moral motive to other motives.

Green is an unusual idealist because he thinks the destructive dualism is a fault, not in Kantian ethics itself but in Kant's statement of his own doctrine; the doctrine itself can be restated without Kant's errors. Most idealists think Kant presents only a one-sided exaggeration of part of the truth about ethics. Green, however, argues that Kant has grasped the main truth, when he is properly understood and freed from his misleading statements of his view: "As it is, though his doctrine is essentially true, his way of putting it excites the same opposition as his way of putting the corresponding doctrine in regard to the a priori element in knowledge."[2]

It is often wise to be skeptical about "charitable" interpretations of a philosopher that offer to restate his "essential" doctrines in less "misleading" terms. This sort of charity has been lavished on Kant by critics from Schopenhauer to Strawson, and we may not always agree with a critic's view of what is the essential doctrine and what is merely the misleading statement.

Here I will defend some aspects of Green's criticism and reconstruction to show why some Kantian claims need to be reinterpreted and why Green sometimes presents a defensible version of a Kantian claim, not a different claim altogether.

[2]There are two sources for Green's views on Kant: his professorial lectures on Kant in volume 2 of his *Collected Works*, 3 vols., ed. R. L. Nettleship (London, 1885–88), and his *Prolegomena to Ethics* (Oxford, 1883). These are cited hereafter as *LK* and *PE*, by paragraph numbers. The actual extent of overlap is not clear from the published texts, since Nettleship omitted the parts of *LK* that seemed to him to duplicate *PE*. The quotation is from *LK* 105.

THE FREE WILL AND THE RATIONAL WILL

In Kant's view, the morally good, autonomous will achieves a type of freedom that the heteronomous will lacks. This moral freedom, however, presupposes metaphysical freedom, which both the good and the bad will have, and which is necessary and sufficient for moral responsibility. Though these are distinct types of freedom, Kant's views of them are connected. Some mistakes in his view of moral freedom reflect mistakes in his view of metaphysical freedom. However, some of what he says about metaphysical freedom is reasonable, and Green tries to separate the reasonable parts from the rest. Kant explains freedom both by reference to rational self-consciousness and by reference to choice undetermined by earlier events. I suggest, with Green, that the first explanation is right and the second wrong.

Kant rejects Hume's attempt to dissolve the problem of free will. Hume claims that someone has free will, in the only sense of any interest, when his actions are internally caused by his desires. Kant rejects Hume's answer because it obscures the difference between the purely animal will and the free will of a rational agent. For Hume both wills must be equally free. Kant argues, however, that a rational agent has practical freedom that the animal will lacks. Practical freedom is "the will's independence of coercion by impulses of sensibility"; the animal will lacks this independence because it is pathologically necessitated (*A*534/*B*562; cf. *TL* 212g 8e).

A rational will's independence of sensuous impulses is expressed in the form of self-consciousness peculiar to rational agents: "Man, however, who knows all of the rest of nature solely through the senses, knows himself also through pure apperception; and this, indeed, in acts and inner determinations which he cannot regard as impressions of the senses" (*A*546/*B*574).

The contrast between self-consciousness and mere consciousness is familiar and important in the first *Critique*. Kant accepts Leibniz's distinction between the two (*New Essays on Human Understanding*, 2: 9.4) and argues that self-consciousness requires unity of consciousness, without which "there might exist a multitude of perceptions, and indeed an entire sensibility, in which much empirical consciousness would arise in my mind, but in a state of separation, and without belonging to a consciousness of myself, which, however, is impossible" (*A*212).[3] Animals are taken to lack self-consciousness because they lack "that unity of consciousness that is necessary for knowledge of myself."[4] In this nonself-conscious condition "sense-data might have an influence on my feeling and desire, without my being aware of them."[5]

What is the unity that we lack when we lack unity of consciousness? Probably Kant means at least the sort of unity that I am aware of when I regard myself as a single person persisting over time, not merely as an aggregate of states of consciousness.[6] This is the conception of personality that is assumed in the discussion of the Third Paralogism (*A*362); and Kant identifies psychological personality with "the power to become conscious of one's self-identity at different times and under the different conditions of one's existence" (*TL* 222g 21e).

These views on the unity of consciousness and on self-consciousness are the foundations of Kant's argument in the Transcendental Analytic. However exactly the argument goes, the Transcendental Deduction includes an attempt to find the necessary conditions of unity of consciousness and argues that one of the necessary conditions is the belief in the existence of external objects.

I refer to self-consciousness in the Deduction to suggest that self-consciousness may be equally important in Kant's conception

---

[3]The antecedent of "which" in the last clause is unclear. It might be (a) the entire situation described in this sentence; (b) empirical consciousness as described here; (c) self-consciousness under these conditions. Kemp Smith's translation (with a stop after "myself," and continuing "This...") seems to favor (a). I tend to favor (c) because of the next sentence.

[4]Kant to Marcus Herz, May 26, 1789, *GS* 11:52.

[5]The interpretation of Kant's views here is disputed by N. Kemp Smith, *Commentary to Kant's Critique* (London, 1918), pp. xlvii–l, and H. J. Paton, *Kant's Metaphysic of Experience*, 2 vols. (London, 1936), 1, pp. 332–35. I agree with Paton. Their dispute is related to a wider dispute about what exactly is claimed in the Deduction.

[6]In this view of the Deduction I agree with Paul Guyer, "Kant on Apperception and a priori Synthesis," *American Philosophical Quarterly* 17 (1980), 205–212, and Patricia Kitcher (this volume), against, e.g., R.C.S. Walker, *Kant* (London, 1978), pp. 82f.

of rational agency. Here self-consciousness consists in the awareness of reason as having causality when we act on judgments
about what we ought to do (imperatives): "Everything in nature
works according to laws. Only a rational being has the capacity
of acting according to the conception of laws, i.e. according to
principles. This capacity is will. Since reason is required for the
derivation of actions from laws, will is nothing else than practical
reason" (*G* 412g 29e; cf. *A*547f/*B*575f).

Consciousness of laws is a type of self-consciousness insofar
as we are aware of a self that is distinct from particular impulses
and desires and aware of a capacity in the self to modify, inhibit,
and regulate our desires by ought-judgments; we ascribe to ourselves motives and aims beyond the particular feelings and impulses we have at a particular time. Green explains what sort of
self we are aware of here:

> Consciousness of law implies consciousness of a subject to which the
> law relates, and of this self-consciousness is the condition. Conversely,
> self-consciousness, the presentation of the self as an end or as that to
> which all ends are relative, carries with it a distinction between that
> which is good as satisfying a present want, and that which is good for
> me on the whole; in other words that capacity for determination by
> the conception of the desirable, as other than determination by desire,
> which may become determination by the consciousness of law.[7]

Consciousness of myself as an agent is a special case of consciousness of myself as a persisting subject—that unity of consciousness considered in the Deduction. Unity of consciousness,
in Kant's view, requires specific kinds of order and unity in my
experience—I must ascribe to myself continuous or coherent
memories, anticipations, beliefs, and so on. The same is true for
practical self-consciousness. I distinguish my present wants from
myself on the whole; I think of myself as the subject of fairly
stable desires and aims. In forming a conception of my good on
the whole I will want some order in my desires—I will want them

[7]*LK* 117.

to combine so that they promote, rather than frustrate, the fulfillment of other desires.[8]

By developing in this way, with Green's help, Kant's conception of the self that is conscious of laws, we can see why the rational, self-conscious self is the main character in both the theoretical and the practical parts of the critical philosophy. We have now seen how Kant can explain the distinction between the rational and the purely sensuous will. The rational will is not coerced by sensuous impulses; for it distinguishes ought-judgments from simple impulses and is capable of acting on ought-judgments. These ought-judgments need not be moral imperatives. Purely prudential ought-judgments and action on them distinguish the rational from the sensuous will.

FREE WILL AND DETERMINISM

Kant also distinguishes the rational from the sensuous will, however, by claiming that the rational will is free of coercion by sensuous impulses. I have already explained how this is true. But the explanation does not satisfy Kant. He believes that unless the will is free of causal determination by previous phenomenal events, it must be coerced in a way that rules out its freedom: "Obviously, if all causality in the sensible world were mere nature, every event would be determined by another in time, in accordance with necessary laws. Appearances, in determining the will, would have in the actions of the will their natural effects, and would render the same necessary. The denial of transcendental freedom must, therefore, involve the elimination of all practical freedom" ($A534/B562$).[9]

Kant's argument here is this:

1. If phenomenal determinism is true for all events, every event is necessitated by past phenomenal events.

---

[8]See *PE* 85, 127, 152.

[9]It is misleading to call Kant an incompatibilist, since he thinks freedom is compatible with phenomenal determinism of our free actions (assuming that the phenomenal and the noumenal events are the same events differently described,

2. If the will is practically free, some choices are not necessitated by past phenomenal events.
3. Hence if phenomenal determinism is true for all events, the will is not practically free.

This argument is valid. But Kant has not argued for the second step. We will accept it only if we agree that practical freedom is incompatible with universal phenomenal determinism. But that is what Kant is supposed to be proving. Unless we are already incompatibilists about free will and determinism, we have no reason to be convinced by Kant's claim that practical freedom requires transcendental freedom.

Kant could support the second step of the argument with two further premises:

2a. If the will is practically free, some choices are not necessitated by past sensuous impulses.
2b. If choices are phenomenally determined, then they are necessitated by past sensuous impulses.

The distinction between the rational and the sensuous will supports (2a); but further argument is needed, and not provided, to support (2b).

Once Kant accepts the truth of incompatibilism, and also agrees that all desires and actions are phenomenal events, his defense of freedom is hopeless.

'Noumenal events' and 'phenomenal events', or 'things in themselves' and 'appearances', are not descriptions of two disjoint classes of events or things. They are two descriptions that apply to the same thing; everything that appears is also something in itself, apart from the aspects of it that appear. Kant speaks of things "as they appear" as opposed to "what they may be in themselves" (A42/B59) and contrasts "things in themselves" with "the mode in which, owing to our subjective constitution,

---

not different events). But it is his belief in the truth of some form of incompatibilism that convinces him that freedom requires noumena that are not phenomenally determined. Here I have benefited from Allen Wood's more favorable view of Kant (this volume). In the discussion of Green I omit his arguments to show that the self-conscious self cannot be part of nature or determined by natural causes; see *PE* 88f.

they appear" (*A*251). He makes it clear that he is speaking of the same things as appearances and as things in themselves.

Now if an event is determined, it is true of it under all true descriptions that it is determined, even though only some true descriptions, those referring to the relevant laws, show why it is determined. Hence if an event is phenomenally determined under its phenomenal description, it is also phenomenally determined under its noumenal description.[10] Now Kant believes free choices are noumenal events, that these are also phenomenal events, and that as phenomenal events they are phenomenally determined and hence not free. He must then admit that the noumenal events are also phenomenally determined, even if it is not the noumenal description that shows why they are phenomenally determined. But if phenomenal determination is incompatible with freedom, these noumenal events cannot be free. Kant is wrong when he thinks he can defend freedom, concede phenomenal determination of phenomena, and concede that phenomenal determination excludes freedom. If he is right to claim that practical freedom requires transcendental freedom, and right to allow the truth of phenomenal determinism, then practical freedom is impossible. To maintain the possibility of practical freedom we must reject at least one of Kant's premises. It is best to give up the incompatibilist assumption, for which Kant has no good argument.

Kant's incompatibilism needs to be noticed because it affects his account of freedom. We have seen that he has a plausible account of the difference between the free rational will and the coerced animal will, when he speaks of self-consciousness and the awareness of imperatives. But this account will not satisfy Kant when he attends to his belief in incompatibilism. For self-conscious rational action may be no less causally determined by past events, and hence no more free, than any other events. Kant offers a good account of freedom but then makes it hard for himself to use it. We will see that this happens elsewhere in his moral theory.

[10]Contrast, e.g., the solution, sympathetic to Kant, offered by Donald Davidson, "Mental Events," in *Essays on Actions and Events* (Oxford, 1980).

MORAL AND NONMORAL MOTIVES

I have discussed Kant's incompatibilist account of freedom because it influences his moral theory in important and disastrous ways. He wants to distinguish the nonmoral motives and choices from the moral motive. Only actions on the moral motive are free. The type of freedom considered here ought not to be the freedom of the rational, as opposed to the sensuous, will. Someone could surely act on rational rather than animal desires and still not act on a moral motive; we suppose there are people who act freely and responsibly, but still immorally, and Kant supposes so, too (for example, $A554/B582$; KpV 98fg 102e). He creates some difficulties for himself, however.

The main difficulty is Kant's tendency to regard all motives other than the moral motive as simply expressions of the desire for pleasure. He supposes that when we act on any nonmoral motive we are moved by the desire for pleasure and not acting freely. This is "heteronomy of choice, or dependence on natural laws in following some impulse or inclination" (KpV 33g 33e). Hence every choice that does not rest on the moral motive rests on a desire for pleasure; every such choice is subject to natural laws; hence every such choice is phenomenally determined; hence no such choice is free. Hence the moral motive, and it alone, must be noumenal. Here is an argument from psychological hedonism plus incompatibilism to the noumenal status of the moral will alone.

Kant might also argue from psychological hedonism to incompatibilism. If all phenomenal choices are desires for pleasure, then to that extent we are coerced by the desire for pleasure, hence not practically free; hence the moral choice must be noumenal, since it is free. This argument is weak. How do we know that all phenomenal choices are desires for pleasure unless we first assume that moral choices are not phenomenal?

If Kant agrees that only the moral motive is noumenal, he forces a grave difficulty on himself. For he takes transcendental freedom, requiring noumenal indeterminism, to be necessary for responsibility. If he claims that only actions on the moral motive are noumenally caused, he must infer that these are the only free actions, and hence that if I act on a nonmoral motive, I am not responsible for my action; hence immoral people turn out not to be responsible.

This is plainly not the result that Kant intends, and in some works he tries to avoid it by distinguishing negative from positive freedom. In the *Foundations* (G 446g 64e) he seems to think of negative and positive freedom as simply two inseparable sides of the same freedom. Elsewhere, however, he presents them as two different types of freedom and allows that someone could have negative freedom without positive (*KpV* 33g 33e; cf. *KpV* 30g 30e; *TL* 212fg 8fe). In this view, the immoral person acts on phenomenal motives and is determined by them but is not coerced by them; he is capable of acting on the moral motive but does not. Though he could have been noumenally motivated, he is phenomenally motivated.

This solution, however, is hardly satisfactory. We cannot act on a phenomenal motive without acting on a noumenal motive too. Hence we cannot say that the negatively free person acts *only* on a phenomenal motive. Conversely, we cannot act on a noumenal motive without acting on a phenomenal motive, too; hence we cannot say that the positively free person acts *only* on a noumenal motive.

Suppose, then, that both negatively free and positively free people make noumenal choices about the kinds of phenomenal choices they will act on. Let us allow that the immoral person chooses to act on a sensuous motive. Unfortunately, the moral person cannot effectively choose anything else, since all phenomenal choices rest on sensuous motives. He can effectively choose only to act on sensuous motives, which is the immoral person's choice, too. Kant can hardly claim that the moral person acts on sensuous motives all the time, against his will; that would apparently make him *less* free than the immoral person.

Here Kant is the victim of incompatibilism combined with psychological hedonism. He needs to allow that some phenomenal choices are not simply expressions of the desire for pleasure; once he allows this he can show how the moral person makes different phenomenal choices from the immoral person's. But once Kant says that, he loses one argument for his claim that the moral will must be noumenal; he must rely entirely on his incompatibilism, which will not distinguish the freedom of the moral will from the responsibility of the immoral will.

We have seen, however, that this need not be Kant's account of the free and rational will. His references to practical self-consciousness showed us the sort of account he needs. The free rational will is the will of a subject who is conscious of himself as a continuing subject with a conception of a good distinct from the satisfaction of this or that present desire. The moral will should differ, in this view, from the nonmoral and the immoral will in the way it conceives the good that is distinct from the satisfaction of a particular desire. To use Green's terms, both the good and the bad will seek self-satisfaction, but they seek it from different sources.

How might the difference in conceptions of self-satisfaction indicate a difference in freedom, or how could we show that one person is determined by practical reason more than another? A rational agent is guided in fulfilling his particular desires by some conception of his more permanent good. But he may or may not be guided by practical reason in deciding on his permanent goals; he may not even realize that practical reason is competent to decide them. If a free will is a will guided by practical reason, then a will more fully guided by practical reason is freer than a will less fully guided by it, and the freer will realizes a capacity of the less free will. Here we can understand Kant's claims about negative and positive freedom. I have not yet explained why acceptance of the moral law should be a uniquely full expression of positive freedom, but I will return to that question later.

This appeal to self-satisfaction is reasonable if we want to explain how a rational self is capable of choosing to act on the moral law or on sensuous impulses. But does Kant need or want to explain this? When he says I am capable of acting, or have the power to act, on the moral law, what does he mean? If he just means that it is possible that I act on the moral law, then he need not appeal to choice; for possibility does not imply a rational power. It is possible that I be struck by lightning, since it is possible for lightning to strike where I am; it does not follow that I have the rational power, that I can choose, to be struck by lightning, since my choice may be altogether ineffective.

If my 'power' to act on the moral law is a mere possibility, then it need not be a power to choose to act on it; hence Kant need not explain how such a choice is possible for a rational agent. But Kant wants to persuade us that we are responsible for not acting on the moral law, and a mere proof of the possibility of acting on it is not sufficient for responsibility for not acting on it, since I am not responsible for not being struck by lightning. Responsibility requires a power of rational choice; hence Kant must after all explain how a rational self can choose to act on the moral law.

Indeed, he seems to intend us to have a rational power:

> But ask him whether he thinks it would be possible for him to overcome his love of life, however great it may be, if his sovereign threatened him with the same sudden death unless he made a false deposition against an honourable man whom the ruler wished to destroy under a plausible pretext. Whether he will or not perhaps he will not venture to say; but that it would be possible for him he would certainly admit without hesitation. He judges therefore that he can do something because he knows that he ought, and he recognizes that he is free—a fact which, without the moral law, would have remained unknown to him. [*KpV* 30g 30e]

Here Kant will have proved far less than he needs if he refers only to possibility. The awareness of the moral law must be supposed to make us aware of a power of rational choice.[11]

We are right, then, to ask Kant how a rational self chooses to act on the moral law. The answer that Kant needs must refer to a self that is much more like Green's self than like Kant's divided self. The self that chooses cannot already choose on moral grounds. Nor can it choose on purely hedonistic grounds, since they would make the choice to be moral a fundamentally heteronomous one. The choice must be a rational choice for a ra-

---

[11]These questions about possibility and rational power seem to arise for Wood's account of Kant's views (this volume). They suggest that Sidgwick's problem may be less illusory than Wood thinks.

tional self; and Green's conception of self-satisfaction shows us what Kant needs.

TYPES OF IMPERATIVES

If we urge Kant to rely this far on his own account of practical self-consciousness, we apparently force a further difficulty on him. The account I have just outlined assumes that moral and immoral wills share a goal—self-satisfaction—and differ only in their conceptions of that goal and of ways to achieve it. This account may seem alien to Kant's views. For he sharply distinguishes types of imperatives and therefore sharply separates the moral will from others. Only the moral will acts on a categorical imperative; other wills are motivated entirely by a hypothetical imperative. If both the moral and the immoral will were seeking self-satisfaction, then both would be acting on a hypothetical imperative about how to achieve self-satisfaction. Hence even if our account of the free will is Kantian, Kant himself cannot accept it when he describes the moral motive.

This objection rests on an important and controversial Kantian assumption. When Kant divides imperatives, he assumes that all nonmoral motives are desires for pleasure. Green protests, quite reasonably, against the assumption. He agrees that *if* all nonmoral motives are simply desires for pleasure, they must be entirely distinct from, and discontinuous with, the moral will. But he rejects the antecedent of this conditional: "Kant's error lies in supposing that there is no alternative between the determination of desire by the anticipation of pleasure and its determination by the conception of a moral law."[12]

Kant assumes that an imperative referring to one of a human being's ends must ultimately depend on his desire for happiness and will just prescribe means to happiness (*G* 414g 31e; *KpV* 22–

---

[12]*LK* 119; cf. *PE* 160.

25g 20–24e).[13] Hence the imperative will lack the force of a moral imperative. It will depend on how much I care about my pleasure on one occasion or another and on what I happen to find pleasant. At this stage, practical reason has no role in determining the end to be pursued; it is confined to the purely technical task of discovering means to ends adopted on nonrational grounds.

Sometimes Kant sees that a desire for happiness does not by itself present us with a definite end that leaves us with only simple technical tasks. To aim at happiness is not yet to have a definite specification of an end to aim at (*G* 418g 35e; *KpV* 25g 24e). However, the only specification we need is instruction about how to achieve a feeling of pleasure. It is hard to find the elements of happiness because they are all empirical, and we can only make guesses about what will cause us most pleasure (*G* 418g 35e). Hence principles of self-love "can indeed contain universal rules of skill (how to find means to some end), but these are only theoretical principles," not practical laws (*KpV* 25–26g 25–26e).

We can see why Kant thinks no imperative prescribing means of achieving pleasure could be universal and independent of inclination in the way a moral principle has to be. But he is mistaken in supposing that only an imperative that meets all his conditions for being a categorical imperative can be universal and independent of inclination in the proper way. The desire for self-satisfaction is not a mere empirical inclination but a necessary feature of a rational will as Kant's own account of practical self-consciousness shows us. A principle that prescribes what to do to achieve self-satisfaction need not be a purely technical maxim. It may present a *conception* of self-satisfaction, instructing someone to live for the pleasures of power, or wealth, or playing bridge, or for the fulfillment of moral requirements.

In his division of imperatives Kant has no obvious place for

---

[13]"It is astonishing how otherwise acute men believe they can found a difference between the lower and the higher faculty of desire by noting whether the conceptions which are associated with pleasure have their origin in the senses or in the understanding. When one inquires into the determining grounds of desire and finds in them an expected agreeableness resulting from something or other, it is not a question of where the conception of this enjoyable object comes from, but merely of how much it can be enjoyed" (*KpV* 225fg 21e; see *KpV* 22–25g 20–24e; *G* 414g 31e, 417g 35e).

principles specifying self-satisfaction. They will be hypothetical insofar as they prescribe actions by reference to some end. But they do not prescribe actions by reference to an end external to themselves, and so do not prescribe them as instrumental means; here they differ from the hypothetical imperative that Kant describes.

Moreover, if we were right earlier in wanting Kant to explain how a rational will can choose to be moral, he needs principles that present conceptions of self-satisfaction. For these principles explain a rational will's choice for or against morality. We saw before that Kant cannot both describe this choice plausibly and maintain that all nonmoral motives are merely desires for pleasure. For similar reasons he cannot maintain that all imperatives meet his conditions for being either categorical or hypothetical.

Kant has given no reason, then, to convince us that moral imperatives could not be principles that correctly prescribe ways to achieve self-satisfaction.[14] Such principles need not depend on psychological peculiarities of different people; and they need not simply prescribe means to happiness. They depend not on merely empirical features of actual human beings but on necessary features of a rational will.

RESPECT FOR MORALITY

So far I have suggested that Kant's account of practical self-consciousness might lead him to a conception of the moral and the nonmoral self that is different from the conception that underlies his division of imperatives. I have suggested that he

[14]Kant has two other objections to imperatives relying on happiness: (a) they involve empirical prediction and uncertainty; (b) they prescribe conflicting actions for different people. Here it is not clear that (a) clearly distinguishes prudential from moral imperatives. Kant does not explain why (b) is a legitimate condition for a categorical imperative; but if it is, Green's argument about the common good (see the section "The Common Good") is a possible answer. See *KpV* 27fg 27e; and L. W. Beck, *Commentary on Kant's Critique of Practical Reason* (Chicago, 1960), p. 98.

could reasonably regard moral principles as imperatives prescribing ways to achieve self-satisfaction. I now want to strengthen the previous suggestion that perhaps Kant actually needs such a conception of moral imperatives.

Kant distinguishes the rational self, moved by awareness of the moral law, from the sensuous self, moved by pleasure and pain. How do these two selves appear to one another? It is fairly easy to imagine that the rational self will not find much to admire in the sensuous self; and we might expect that the sensuous self will not find much to please it in the rational self. The two selves seem to have no methods or aims in common. They interfere with each other; the sensuous self forces the rational self to struggle to execute its choices, and the rational self frustrates the desires of the sensuous self.

Some less antagonistic relations seem to be demanded. For Kant expects awareness of the moral law to produce respect in the sensuous self. Respect is not an ordinary pathological feeling that explains why I act on the moral law; it is the effect, not the cause, of acting on the consciousness of the law (*KpV* 72–73g 75e; *KU* 222g 57e). Nor is it a wholly pleasant or favorable feeling, since the sensuous self is aware of the frustration and restraint it suffers.[15] Respect includes a feeling of humiliation. Nonetheless, it is eventually favorable to the moral law; it is a feeling that encourages us to follow the moral law more steadily; hence it is an incentive of practical reason.[16]

Why is the sensuous self favorably disposed to the moral law? Respect is not just amazement, fear, awe, or admiration, which might apply just as well to mountains, volcanoes or hurricanes (*KpV* 76g 79e). Nor can it be simply a feeling of humiliation. I may have this feeling if my feeble efforts at building a wall are

[15]"Freedom, the causality of which is determinable merely through the law, consists, however, only in the fact that it limits all inclination, including self-esteem, to the condition of obedience to its pure law. This limitation exerts an effect on feeling and produces the sensation of displeasure, which can be known a priori from the moral law" (*KpV* 78g 81e).

[16]"Hence this humiliation occurs proportionately to the purity of the law; for that reason the lowering of the pretensions of moral self-esteem (humiliation) on the sensuous side is an elevation of the moral, i.e. practical, esteem for the law on the intellectual side" (*KpV* 79g 82e).

swept away by a single wave, or if my feeble efforts at argument are swept away by a single devastating objection. But no respect necessarily results; I do not necessarily even respect the objector, if it was a simple objection that any fool could see but I had overlooked. But if all the sensuous self sees in the moral law is a powerful force capable of frustrating sensuous impulses, why is respect appropriate? So far the moral law looks more like a powerful tyrant; even if its power excites awe, why should it not excite fear, loathing, and caution, rather than respect?

The respect that concerns Kant is intended to include the sensuous self's consciousness of its own unworthiness (*KpV* 77g 80e). To be aware of my unworthiness is not to be aware simply of some inability. I must think of myself as failing to meet some standard that I recognize and accept. As Kant says, respect is "the feeling of our incapacity to attain to an idea that is a law for us" (*KU* 257g 96e). If Kant ascribes a sense of unworthiness to the sensuous self, what standard is he ascribing to it? If it is purely hedonistic and self-seeking, why should the moral law make it feel unworthy?

Kant raises a further puzzle when he claims that the self feels itself not only humiliated but also elevated by awareness of the moral law: "The soul believes itself to be elevated [*erheben*] in proportion as it sees the holy law as elevated over it and its frail nature" (*KpV* 77g 79e). In the moral law we discover "the sublimity [*Erhabenheit*] of our own nature (in its vocation)" (*KpV* 87g 90e). This discovery produces a feeling of pleasure: "The feeling of the sublime is therefore a feeling of pain arising from the want of accordance between the aesthetical estimate of magnitude formed by the imagination and the estimation of the same formed by reason. There is at the same time a pleasure thus excited, arising from the correspondence with rational ideas of this very judgment of the inadequacy of our greatest faculty of sense, in so far as it is a law for us to strive after these ideas" (*KU* 257–58g 96–97e). This is why there is so little displeasure in respect that "once we renounce our self-conceit and respect has established its practical influence, we cannot ever satisfy ourselves in contemplating the majesty of this law" (*KpV* 77g 79e).

This favorable attitude of the sensuous self to the moral law is an attitude that Kant seems unable to explain. If the sensuous self is the hedonistic self that Kant describes, it has no reason to be favorable to the moral law. Hence if the sensuous self is favorable to the moral law, it must include more than Kant tells us. In particular it must be favorably impressed by the domination of reason over sensuous impulses:

> The object of a pure and unconditioned intellectual delight is the moral law in the might which it exerts in us over all antecedent motives of the mind. Now, since it is only through sacrifices that this might makes itself known to us aesthetically (and this involves a deprivation of something—though in the interests of inner freedom—whilst in turn it reveals in us an unfathomable depth of this supersensible faculty, the consequences of which extend beyond reach of the eye of sense), it follows that the delight, looked at from the aesthetic side (in reference to sensibility) is negative, i.e. opposed to this interest, but from the intellectual side, positive and bound up with an interest. Hence it follows that the intellectual and intrinsically final (moral) good, estimated aesthetically, instead of being represented as beautiful, must rather be represented as sublime, with the result that it arouses more a feeling of respect (which disdains charm) than of love or of the heart being drawn towards it—for human nature does not of its own proper motion accord with the good, but only by virtue of the dominion which reason exercises over sensibility. [*KU* 271g 111–12e]

If the awareness of the domination of reason over sensibility is to be a source of delight, what sort of self could delight in it? In supposing that we are capable of being moved by awareness of the moral law alone, Kant ascribes to us the capacity to act on pure practical reason; but this is not enough to explain our capacity to be delighted by our capacity to act on pure practical reason. The capacity to be delighted by action on reason belongs to a self that already cares about being moved by reason. Fortunately, Kant is entitled to assume a self with this concern. The sort of self he needs is the rational, self-conscious self that we have found to be required for part of his account of free will. The self-conscious self is aware of itself as a continuing system of rational desires. It is concerned with itself as a rational agent and with the fulfillment of its rational desires. This sort of self could indeed be expected to take an interest in its capacity to be moved by reason independently of sensuous motives; and so this is the sort of self that can be imagined to take pleasure in being moved by the moral law. So far we can defend Kant. The price of this defense is the rejection of Kant's claim that every act not caused by awareness of the moral law is caused by a sensuous motive, a mere desire for my own pleasure.

What, then, must the sensuous self be like if it is favorable to the moral law? We should return to our previous account of practical self-consciousness. Kant not only accepts this account but needs it to justify his claims about respect for the law. The rational self is aware of itself and of possibilities for its self-satisfaction. If the moral law presents a conception of the self and of its satisfaction, then it may indeed appear to the nonmoral self in a way that Kant's claims require.

We can now appreciate one serious difficulty in a Kantian claim that has rightly been found both appealing and dubious. Kant claims that the moral law reveals personality to us and, by revealing to us the personality of ourselves and others, shows why no one with personality should ever be treated merely as a means to the end of another (*KpV* 87g 90e). The imperative that prescribes treatment of rational beings as ends in themselves is supposed to rest on the claims about personality.

What is the personality that matters here? It seems to be confined to the acceptance, or capacity for acceptance, of the moral law. The moral person seems to be sharply distinguished from the empirical person:

A person is a subject whose actions can be imputed to him. Moral personality is thus the freedom of a rational being under moral laws. (Psychological personality is merely the power to become conscious of one's self-identity at different times and under the different conditions of one's existence.) From this it follows that a person is subject to no other laws than those which he (either alone or at least along with others) gives himself. [*TL* 222g 21e; cf. *TL* 417g 75e; *Rel* 26–28g, 21–23e.]

49

With the moral self Kant contrasts the sensuous self with "reason subservient to other incentives" (*Rel* 28g, 23e).

This moral personality is supposed to appeal to human beings: "Man, as belonging to two worlds, must regard his own being in relation to his second and higher vocation with reverence and the laws of this vocation with the deepest respect" (*KpV* 87g 90e). The pure moral law itself "lets us perceive the sublimity of our own supersensuous existence and subjectively effects respect for their higher vocation in men who are conscious of their sensuous existence and of the accompanying dependence on their pathologically affected nature" (*KpV* 88g 91e).

The moral personality presents to us a will that does not rely on sensuous motives in forming its aims but is thoroughly guided by practical reason; the moral law reveals to us the possibility of this sort of person. But who will actually be interested in these promises of the moral law? The moral self needs no convincing, since it is already free of sensuous motives. But Kant claims that the human being, including his nonmoral aspects, will respect the law and moral personality. This is the respect that is unintelligible if it is ascribed to the nonmoral self as Kant describes it.

The remedy for Kant's mistake is his account of psychological personality. We should not dismiss it with Kant's "merely." Someone who is aware of himself as a self-conscious agent with a capacity for self-satisfaction may indeed find something to interest him in the moral law. The moral law reveals a way of treating oneself and other rational agents that promotes their full satisfaction as rational agents. The status of another as a rational agent with the same conception of himself may explain why he should be treated as an end in himself. The agent who can take claims about the moral law seriously is not the nonmoral self that Kant often describes but the rational, self-conscious self that is unduly slighted in Kant's facile contrasts between the sensuous and the moral self.

Sometimes Kant avoids his oversimple contrast. A human being who is capable of acting on the moral law becomes evil when he subordinates the moral law to the law of self-love that prescribes means to his own happiness, narrowly construed: "Hence the distinction between a good man and one who is evil cannot lie in the difference between the incentives which they adopt into their maxim (not in the content of the maxim), but rather must depend on *subordination* (the form of the maxim), *i.e. which of the two incentives he makes the condition of the other*" (*Rel* 36g, 31e). Why does he adopt one policy over the other? It cannot be because one will be a more efficient means to his happiness, since he has not yet chosen the exclusive aim of promoting his happiness; if that were his fixed aim, he could not consider making the moral law supreme. The rational free self must mistakenly choose to pursue its own happiness or else choose to follow the moral law. This is the same self that must also be capable of respecting the moral law. If Kant is right here, then he can hardly be right to claim that we are moved either by desire for pleasure or by awareness of the moral law. One choice must rest on neither motive; this is the choice about whether to be moved by the moral law or by pleasure. If Kant tries to understand that choice, he must consider what considerations will seem relevant to a rational, self-conscious will that is committed in advance neither to pleasure nor to the moral law. This will is the sort of will that Green describes.

Hence Kant's claims about respect for, and rejection of, the moral law show that Green was right to reject the Kantian antithesis between the purely sensuous and the purely moral self. We must also reject it, on Kant's behalf, because it undermines some crucial Kantian claims. Kant presents a conception of a free self as rational self-consciousness; because of his other metaphysical views he does not use this conception of the self as often as he needs it. Green's criticism of Kant is not purely external, resting on premises that Kant has no reason to accept. It is an important internal criticism that Kant would be well advised to accept.

THE COMMON GOOD

We may be convinced by the criticisms developed from Green but still see no positive support for Kant here. We may concede that Kant needs to appeal to rational self-consciousness to defend some of his claims about the self and morality. He needs to appeal to it because his other conception of the self makes his claims evidently hopeless. But does a better conception of the rational self make Kant's claims eventually any less hopeless?

To answer this question we need a clearer account of how a rational self might come to respect Kantian moral principles. Green offers an account that seeks to answer this question. Kantian morality demands impartial respect for other rational agents as ends in themselves. Green's account of the self requires us to connect this impartial respect with the rational agent's concern for his self-satisfaction. Characteristically, Green replaces Kant's sharp antithesis with a gradual development:

> Moral experience thus constituted, there arises through reflection on it in a certain stage of development the practical idea of an absolute moral law.... This idea may then rightly be called a priori in the sense that it only arises in moral experience because that experience implies the presence of a "non-sensuous" agent, a self-consciousness not reducible to, or produced by, any number or kind of desires, but which renders desires into elements in a moral character. It is a mistake to call it so in the sense that in this abstract and recognized form it is given in the moral experience of men to begin with; still more in the sense that it is separable from that experience and antecedent to it; nor is this what Kant really meant to convey.[17]

Three stages in this development should especially concern us:

1. Self-consciousness and the desire for self-satisfaction require a desire for self-realization.
2. Self-realization requires the awareness of a common good.
3. Awareness of a common good requires impartial concern for the good of rational agents.

Here "requires" does not mean that you cannot be at the earlier stages without going on to the later stages. Green believes that

[17] *LK* 105; cf. *LK* 124, *PE* 202.

each stage rationally requires progress to the next stage, but someone may fail to see this. I will comment on each stage, to see what the rational requirements are supposed to be.

In speaking of self-realization Green refers to the realization of a person's capacities, "some best state of being for man—best in the sense that in it lies the full realisation of his capabilities, and that in it therefore alone he can satisfy himself."[18] Self-realization includes more than I have included so far in self-satisfaction. As I have conceived self-satisfaction, it consists in the orderly satisfaction of the desires of a continuing self. Why should such a self desire the realization of its capacities? Green believes that the satisfaction of a *self* demands more than the satisfaction of desires. The self includes more than desires; it also includes capacities, and the satisfaction of the whole self will require the realization of my capacities.

Green claims that the idea of a common good "equally underlies the conception both of moral duty and of legal right." If we see some reason, apart from fear of superior force or calculation of future advantage, to obey a positive law or a moral law prescribing action for the good of others, then the reason "can only spring from a conviction, on the part of those recognizing the authority, that a good which is really their good, though in constant conflict with their inclinations, is really served by the power in which they recognize authority."[19]

A rational agent is assumed to see reason to do all and only the actions promoting his self-satisfaction. He sees reason to do what a law requires him to do for the good of others. If he believed that his good consists only in states of himself without regard to the states of others, he would see no reason to promote the good of others. Since, however, he sees reason to promote the good of others, he must believe that doing this promotes his self-satisfaction. Hence he must take his own self-satisfaction to include the good of others. There must be a good that is good both for himself and for the others, hence a common good.

We can see why a common good is necessary if we accept

[18]*PE* 173.
[19]*PE* 202.

Green's conception of a rational agent and of reasons for obeying a law. But how is a common good possible or reasonable? Green sees a gradual development here, too. Most people are closely associated with others—members of their family or close friends—so that they come to conceive the good of another as part of their own good.[20] Green argues that this extension of my concern is reasonable and justifies its further extension. My concern for the good of others as my own good makes my own good more secure and permanent, since others will outlive me,[21] and allows me to find my own good in more states and activities than I would find it in otherwise. I can find my own good widely extended, however, only if I take to others the attitude I take to myself and want to promote their good for their own sake, treating them as ends in the same way I treat myself. Here the furthest development of my concern for my own self-satisfaction is impartial concern for others as equal to myself.

This progress in conceptions of self-satisfaction and the common good provides Green's answer to the problem that Kantian morality sets for him: How can he show that a rational self's concern for its own satisfaction justifies the impartial concern for rational beings that is required by morality? Kant thinks this cannot be shown. He thinks any argument like Green's is ruled out because of the impartiality required by moral principles. Green, however, replies that Kant is misled by his crude, hedonist conception of the nonmoral self. Once we avoid Kant's errors, and prefer Kant's own better account of the rational will, we can see how morality is a reasonable concern of the nonmoral self.

GREEN'S DEFENSE OF KANT

Some of the steps in Green's argument certainly need further discussion and criticism. But we perhaps tend to dismiss this sort

[20]See *PE* 199–201.
[21]*PE* 230–32.

of argument too quickly in a discussion of Kant; we may think its failure is inevitable because it seems to miss the point of Kantian insights into morality. We may think that Kant's major contribution to moral theory is the sharp division he marks between the moral and the prudential, and more generally between the unconditional imperatives of morality and the hypothetical imperatives that must result from any teleological conception of the grounds of moral principles. We may accept Kant's account of morality and so decide to reject morality; or we may accept morality and reject Kant's account of it; or we may accept or reject both Kant's account and morality. It may seem utterly misguided, however, to accept morality as Kant conceives it, and then to try to derive it from an agent's concern with his own self-satisfaction.

I have been defending Green's view that this attempt to link morality with self-satisfaction is not necessarily misguided and that Kant cannot afford to dismiss it as misguided either. We have seen that Kant has a plausible account of the rational self; that insofar as he abandons it he ruins his account of the free will and of the moral self; and that his own views on respect for morality force him back to his better account of the self. Kant's better account of the self makes the prospect of deriving morality from self-satisfaction no longer a hopeless prospect.

On one important point, then, Green is right. An account of morality that is teleological to the extent of relating morality to self-satisfaction is not, or not only, a rival to a Kantian view. It is actually a defense of a Kantian view, and we can see from Kant's own point of view why he needs this defense.

If our criticism has been right, then part of Kant's moral theory is the missing of an opportunity. We saw earlier how the rational, self-conscious self should be the center of Kant's account of practical reason as it is the center of his account of pure reason and empirical knowledge. The principles of empirical knowledge are taken to reflect requirements of rational self-consciousness. The principles of morality might be taken in an analogous way to reflect the requirements of rational self-consciousness, and sometimes Kant has the analogy in mind. He misses an opportunity, however, because of his views on free will and his crude conception of the nonmoral self. But though his theory as a whole does not fulfill the promise Kant sometimes makes, it suggests at least how we might try to fulfill Kant's promise. To this extent Green's criticism and development of Kant deserves attention as a possible fulfillment of Kant's promise.

It is not unusual for some of a philosopher's views to suggest further developments in a direction that the philosopher himself does not take. Sometimes the philosopher may be wise to avoid the developments. In this case, however, Kant is unwise. Some of the gravest difficulties in his metaphysical and moral theories are related to his conception of the self and of its relation to the moral motive. If we take the hint from his claims about respect, we can see ways to revise his view of the self. The revisions will not leave Kantian moral theory untouched; and inevitably they will raise new difficulties while they remove old ones. But these revisions to Kant inspired by Green's account of him will not remove all that is distinctive and valuable in Kant.

COMMENTARY

Kant on Freedom and the Rational and Morally Good Will

Ralf Meerbote

Kant has often been criticized for purportedly untenable dualisms, such as those between form and content, categorical and hypothetical imperatives, moral and nonmoral motives, noumenal and phenomenal causes, and rational and pathologically necessitated agents. Among the consequences of his dualisms are said to be the following: Kant's notion of moral motives is empty in that such motives prescribe no actions or cannot move an agent to act; he has a "two-selves" view of persons and with it no unified theory of agency; and he is an incompatibilist, jeopardizing either his account of freedom or his analysis of causation in the Second Analogy.

It cannot be disputed that on occasion Kant expresses the aforementioned distinctions in untenable ways and defends views not consonant with what he elsewhere, albeit in piecemeal fashion, develops in a more acceptable manner. It is one of the ironies of many an exegesis that all too often critics propose to improve upon Kant's theses, only to succeed either in espousing views already quite recognizably Kant's own or in arguing for conclusions quite recognizably not Kant's own and even argued against by him. T. H. Green's defense of Kant, ably elaborated and seconded in the preceding essay by Terence Irwin, is an example of a less-than-warranted rescue effort.

In addressing the last four of the above-mentioned dualisms,

I shall concentrate on three basic points: (a) What is Kant's considered view on the nature of rational human action—and is the freedom of such actions incompatible with the universal causality of the Second Analogy? (b) What roles does Kant assign to pleasure in rational action and how does acting nonmorally differ from acting morally? (c) What sorts of teleological constraints on acting morally can and does Kant allow?

FREE AND RATIONAL WILL

The issue of possible incompatibilism between universal causal determination of events and descriptions of rational human action as free arises for Kant explicitly in his Third Antinomy; the place to look for his solution is naturally enough, his resolution to that antinomy (*A*532/*B*560 to *A*558/*B*586). Prominent in his description of rational human actions is their characterization as springing from a causality of reason. Such a causality is described by Kant as the power of a rational being to determine oneself to act. This description gives rise to the question whether to say that a rational being determines oneself to act is to introduce conditions sufficient for the production of some events, to wit, those events which are actions determined by a rational being and incompatible with the conditions of determination of events laid down in the Second Analogy. Actions are mental events for Kant (to be distinguished in some respects from bodily or material changes) and all events are temporal. Hence actions are temporal, as Kant's discussion of the empirical determinability of inner states in his Refutation of Material Idealism assumes. Temporality of actions immediately creates problems for Kant when he (at *A*551/*B*579) holds that causality of reason "does not begin to be at a particular time."[1] He means that such causality does not "work" in time at all. Many commentators have professed to find the following view in Kant: that there are nou-

[1]All translations are my own.

menal, nontemporal conditions which 'underlie' sequences of phenomenal, temporal events. 'Noumenal' is sometimes paraphrased as "merely or wholly intellectual, not empirically real" and the meaning of 'underlie' is at least partly explained by saying that noumenal conditions determine sequences of phenomenal, temporal events, using 'determine' in a different sense from that used in the Second Analogy. This reading of 'underlie' is important for such a 'noumenality-interpretation' because this reading is supposed to be able to embrace Kant's claim that causality of reason *determines* action. The issue of incompatibilism arises here because it may seem that the purported two species of determination are in conflict with one another.

A noumenality-interpretation is sometimes put forward in which Kant is believed to mean that noumenal conditions do not determine but 'underlie' phenomenal sequences in some other way. Such an interpretation cannot provide positive evidence for ascribing incompatibilism to Kant because that issue concerns purported conflicts between different (types of) determinations of (some) events. It is this issue, and only this issue, that constitutes Kant's problem in the Third Antinomy. To say in this context, therefore, that conditions of action are compatible with conditions of determination of phenomenal sequences but that they include noumenal conditions which are not determining is not to raise any incompatibility issue. On the contrary, such a statement provides part of the resolution of that issue, as we shall see. At the same time, any noumenality-thesis has to be dealt with gingerly, because if noumenal conditions 'underlie' actions, the same or different noumenal conditions 'underlie' phenomenal events as well.

The reason Kant's claim of nontemporality of causality of reason is a problem for him is that nothing nontemporal can determine or be determined in any sense of 'determine' that Kant ever defends and makes intelligible. Despite the fact that he on occasion uses the terms "causality of reason" and "determination through reason," it is Kant's considered position that the only intelligible conception amounts to this: determination is of events (in time) and determination of events is their predictability and retrodictability in accordance with causal, lawlike principles.[2] (This conception must be understood to include determinations of times and places at which events take place.) All determination of events is phenomenal determination. The best indication that this is Kant's considered opinion lies in his distinction between determining and nondetermining (such as teleological) judgments, since ascriptions of purposive actions to agents turn out to be expressed by judgments of the latter sort. To say that such ascriptions are expressed nondeterminingly is to say, negatively, that in them there occurs no use of concepts entering into lawlike connections. This (*negative*) characterization must not be confused with saying that in such ascriptions it is denied that the described actions also fall under concepts which do enter such connections. For tokenings of propositional attitudes in persons, and for tokened actions requiring such attitudes, the view that can plausibly be ascribed to Kant is Davidsonian anomalous monism. According to this interpretation, rational actions under an action-description are token–token (but not type–type) identical with some phenomenal events under determining descriptions. Anomalousness (under a description) of such actions is a necessary condition of their freedom, and whatever the sufficient conditions for freedom are, they could not under this view be given as determining conditions under free-action descriptions.

Such a reading of Kant rejects incompatibilism between rational action and events under determining description because it declares the former to be a set of events (token–token identical with a subset of events under determining descriptions). But does Kant reject incompatibilism in this or any other fashion? Relevant texts are somewhat ambiguous, although it clearly is the intent of the resolution of the Third Antinomy to reject

---

[2] I am disregarding one other, very special, use Kant puts the notion of determination to, namely, pure and a priori mathematical determination. (There are reasons to believe that Kant's views on such determination are less than fully intelligible.) The determination at stake here is empirical, causal determination. A priori legislated conditions of empirical determination determine a priori in the sense that they are necessary conditions of empirical determination. I may also point out that "determination through reason" does not mean "empirical determination requiring the use of the faculty of reason" but "determination of a sort requiring reason as the effective ground for the occurrence of an action-event."

incompatibilism. At $A534/B562$ Kant says that an agent's power of choice (of actions) is capable of "bring[ing] about something" (an action) even "against the power and influence of...natural causes." Earlier in the same passage we are told that if all causation were "[of] nature" (that is, phenomenal), every event would be determined in time through another event, and in this fashion freedom of action would be denied. This so far is incompatibilist. But notice that at the end of $A534/B562$, actions are nonetheless said to be (or to have consequences that are) "in respect to the temporal order determined in accordance with empirical laws." Hence the conditions *effective* in bringing them about need themselves to stand under determining descriptions. Kant concludes $A534/B562$ by saying that causality of reason is or has the power to initiate a sequence "all on its own." It is difficult to see what this last conclusion is to mean if we assume Kant realizes that purported noumenal nondetermining conditions are irrelevent to the issue of incompatibilism and that no noumenal determining conditions can be forthcoming, given his official analysis of 'determination'.

Now consider $A537/B565$. Here Kant tells us that an action considered from the point of view of its intelligible cause can also "at the same time" be considered as an event determined in accordance with the (causal) necessity of nature. Surely "can be considered" here has the force of "can be correctly considered." Hence Kant is claiming numerical identity of actions with determinable events. $A536/B564$ already claims the same identification.

In both $A536/B564$ and $A537/B565$, noumenalism is introduced, since Kant speaks of an intelligible cause *not* part of a phenomenal sequence (and hence apparently not token–token identical with any member or members of such a sequence). And yet it is Kant's intent here to give a compatibilist analysis of the effective conditions of actions. Because he wants to deny that there is determination of or by his intelligible cause,[3] he has to

---

[3]Kant's "official" views on determination have the consequence that intelligible causes do not determine. In the spirit of anomalous monism, what Kant says means that in an "intelligible-cause" description no concepts entering into lawlike connections occur. From the point of view of a dualism, Kant would mean that

opt either for an anomalous dualism or an anomalous monism.[4] The former view does not introduce conditions *effective* in producing actions. The incompatibilism issue concerns effective conditions. This leaves only the latter view and this view is compatibilist. Any action worthy of the title of determining or determined action is token–token identical with an event under a determining description.

I shall clarify this by suggesting that Kant has in mind the following *positive* characterization of what is nondeterminingly ascribed as intelligible cause. To describe an action as having an intelligible cause is to describe it as falling under a rationalization requirement, and tokenings in an agent of representations constituting such requirements are effective in producing actions only because they (and the actions) are token–token identical with events under determining descriptions. I am not claiming that Kant fully sees or accepts this. The ambiguities in the text and his persistent (even if often pointless) flirting with noumenalism are sufficient disproof of such a strong claim. I am claiming that Kant says enough about determination to commit him to a compatibilist conception of rational human action, along the lines of anomalous monism, even though he on occasion evades a compatibilist resolution. Hence Kant is committed to rejecting the claim that determination excludes rational action. Any critic of Kant's can only wish in this regard that Kant had been clearer in his arguments and in assessing their consequences.

Furthermore, as far as rationalization requirements are concerned, it can be argued that Kant understands such requirements readily enough and that his understanding is of fundamental importance for this theory of rational and of moral human action. Rationalization requirements express the reasonableness of actions for an agent. They are noumenal conditions, if 'noumenal' expresses the fact that their nondetermining de-

---

an intelligible cause is not identical with a determined or determining condition. Kant could allow determination of or by an intelligible cause, in a dualist fashion, only if he held the position that in an "intelligible-cause" description concepts occur that enter into lawlike connections.

[4]Nonanomalous views are ruled out because of Kant's considered views on determination. See note 3.

scriptions are not schematizable and are not phenomenal descriptions. The agent's self-conscious representing of himself under rationalization requirements is a representing of himself as a rational agent. Moreover, it is in this fact concerning self-conscious agents, and not in any purported incompatibilism between actions and determined events, that Kant finds the freedom of the agent.

According to $A534/B562$, human choice of action is not pathologically necessitated. There is excellent reason to believe that Kant understands pathological necessitation to be causal sufficiency of sensations (impulses of the senses) in the production of events constituting some types of behavior. For him to say that *such* causal determination is absent in human agency is to say (negatively) that sensations are not causally sufficient for the production of human actions. (They will still be necessary for some actions, since human agents are pathologically affected.) This is not to say that human agency is not causally determined, since pathological necessitation is not the only type of causal determination possible.[5]

Kant's positive account of human agency, developed in *KU*, section 10 and elsewhere, is as follows. Human agents take interest in actions and act from propositional representations of what they desire and from beliefs about means sufficient, or likely to be sufficient, in bringing about what is desired. The conjunction of desires and beliefs concerning means constitutes the agent's reason for performing the action, which constitutes the means. This composition of the agent's reason and the propositional nature of relevant representations Kant also characterizes by saying that human agents act from conceptions or from representations or maxims. Kant's well-known distinction between acting in accordance with categorical imperatives and acting in accordance with hypothetical ones must be understood in

---

[5]Hence anomalous monism as an interpretation of human agency is not blocked by $A534/B562$. Nonetheless, the trouble with Kant's exposition here is that because of his struggles with noumenalism he does not squarely face the issue of what types of event, distinct from sensation-events, can determine such agency. At any rate, Irwin's premises (2) and (2b) in the preceding essay are not accepted by Kant.

terms of what he considers to be important differences in the two cases concerning the content of desires and relevant beliefs possessed by the agent as well as the conditions under which the desires and beliefs arise.

As far as their logical form as prescriptions is concerned, we can think of imperatives of both types as conditionals in the following sense. They are of the form, "Given my desire to bring about B, if I want to bring about B, I need to do A, since A is sufficient for (or will contribute towards) bringing about B." The difference between the two types lies in the fact that in a case of acting from a categorical moral imperative, my desire to bring about B (an act or state of affairs represented by the agent as having moral value) is an a priori desire, not due to empirical conditions on desires (or not due to heteronomous conditions, as we might call them). At the same time, the particular character of the content of the desire in a case of acting from a moral imperative has obvious consequences for what the agent will represent when he represents the connection between A and B, since the suitability of performing A in achieving a moral B needs to be represented.

In contrast, acting prudentially or in accordance with hypothetical or technical-practical imperatives requires empiricality (or heteronomy) of relevant desires and of representations of means–end connections which have their conditions of application in theoretical, that is, phenomenally determinable events and states of affairs. The believed means–end connection is in this sense also heteronomous. Kant would have been better off had he described his distinction as one between nonheteronomous and heteronomous imperatives.

This latter way of expressing the distinction is still not an entirely happy one, because even actions based on a heteronomous imperative are in at least one of their components autonomous. The reason for this is as follows. Kant typically thinks of autonomy as positive freedom, and although there are passages in which he reserves both notions exclusively for acting on moral imperatives, he also often thinks of positive freedom as the sort of freedom he invokes in his discussion of human agency at $A534/B562$. That means autonomy of some required representations is a necessary condition for an agent's acting under rationalization requirements because reasoning and deliberating require epistemic autonomy (autonomy in epistemic contexts). Hence any rational action is free in that it has at least one autonomous component.[6]

In view of the foregoing, it is mistaken to say that according to Kant there is a sensuous will and a different rational will. Instead, Kant holds a unified theory of acting under rationalization requirements. The theory at the same time affords him a distinction between nonheteronomous and heteronomous desires and beliefs (provided such a distinction can be drawn on independent grounds). Hence (if all is well with the distinction) Kant is afforded a way of saying that actions on a categorical imperative are free in yet another regard; namely, in regard to the desire that is part of their rationalization requirements. In all cases of rational action, Kant is describing the agent as having capacities (and interests) that allow (and induce) the agent to distinguish between the long-term self with its long-term interests, inclinations, and beliefs on the one hand and momentary interests and beliefs on the other. A Kantian rational agent can distinguish between what is likely and true and good on the whole and what only appears true and what is pleasant at the moment.[7]

The best textual evidence in support of ascribing this unified theory to Kant is given, first, by his various discussions of empirical practical reason,[8] according to which such reason is reason in its empirical employment rather than a capacity less than reason, and, second, by his intermittent attempts at distinguishing between what is good (or of value) and what is of the nature of the pleasant (pleasure), in a manner that does not identify the good with the moral good.[9] The best systematic reason for

[6]A full statement of the freedom of all rational actions, including those from technical-practical imperatives, can be found in Kant's lectures on metaphysics, *VM*, 253–71.

[7]I shall return to goodness and pleasure in the next section.

[8]See, for example, *KpV* 19–21g, 17–19e; *L*, section 32; *KU*, Introduction, and also First Introduction; *GS* 20: 196ff.

[9]Not only the pleasant need be what is good with qualifications. See, for example, *KpV* 57ffg 57ffe; *G* 393fg 9–10e.

ascribing the unified theory to Kant lies in the preceding characterization of the rationalization requirement together with the observation that lack of pathological necessitation of reasoned action (according to $A534/B562$) makes for freedom of action.

MORAL AND NONMORAL MOTIVES

I have argued that Kant's conception of rational human agency is wider and more unified than has sometimes been believed. I have also maintained that actions on a categorical imperative are more free than other actions, so that freedom allows of degrees. It has turned out to be false that there are two different kinds of human agency (one "sensuous" and the other "rational") and that only actions on a categorical imperative are free. But Kant's distinction between heteronomous desires and beliefs and non-heteronomous ones still needs to be accounted for, all the more so because Green and others have charged Kant with being a hedonist (in nonmoral contexts) and have argued that because of hedonism Kant distinguishes moral from nonmoral reasons in a manner that is too formal and fails to accord an agent's rational interests their proper role in moral reasons. Two preliminary matters need to be considered.

1. What does Kant mean when he says that an agent's pleasure and displeasure (in or due to impulses of the senses) make an action heteronomous?
2. Does Kant believe that only the pleasure and displeasure of an agent make an action heteronomous?

Heteronomy on the side of initially given desires means an agent on at least some contingent occasions finds himself with the desire in question. In an overwhelming number of passages, Kant says that such desires take the form of anticipations of future pleasures by the agent (or self-awareness of the agent's present pleasures). At the same time, other heteronomous desires will be generated on the strength of rationalization connections between actions. Kant believes that in the end such extended heteronomous desires can be traced back to initially given desires. Heteronomy on the side of believed means–end connections entails the empirical, contingent nature of the connection under empirical laws of nature. Empirical, contingent factuality provides the common denominator for both initial desires and heteronomous means–end connections. If Kant believes that in the end all heteronomous desires concern the present or future pleasure of the agent, then apparently all heteronomous imperatives are in the end instructions concerning how to achieve such pleasure.

Yet even here Kant distinguishes between an agent's momentary pleasure (present or future) and the agent's estimation of his or her happiness.[10] More importantly, in some passages Kant introduces a conception of goodness wide enough to *allow* for assignments of values to action-objects (or their nonaction consequences) not identical either to moral value ("the only unqualified good") or to what is pleasant for the agent.[11] For example, capacities and talents could qualify for such assignments. They would be of qualified goodness but therefore of goodness. Hence Kant *can* allow for a third case of an agent's acting on a stable conception of what is qualifiedly good, not identical with his or her pleasures. Nonetheless, it must be admitted that when Kant squarely faces the question of such goodness, he declares it to be of instrumental goodness for the production of the agent's pleasure. It also should be pointed out that he on occasion allows for sympathy and altruistic feelings, but he does so only intermittently and in these cases may be inconsistent in his psychological theory. I am only claiming that Kant can allow for the third case in that he has the means for describing the agent as acting in a manner overriding his or her own present or anticipated pleasure. With Irwin I would describe such an agent as acting from rational self-consciousness as a continuing self.

---

[10]Kant defines happiness as the agent's awareness of the pleasantness of life without interruptions (still along hedonist lines). See *KpV* 22–26g 20–26e.

[11]See note 9.

For the most part, Kant slips into some form of hedonism.[12] Now question (2) becomes crucial. Even if Kant were to agree that there are goods of human actions not identical with the agent's pleasure, and not only instrumentally good for pleasure—such as the agent's natural capacity and talents, their realization and development, and the good of other agents, understood broadly as values of objectives of actions, performed by them or by the agent regarding them in pursuit of self-satisfactions, and capacities of others—he would still treat all such goodness as qualified and heteronomous. The question, Is Kant a hedonist? is irrelevant to the question, How does Kant propose to distinguish between nonmoral and moral actions? The sorts of conditions Green appeals to in his argument toward the common good as a rational objective of rational agents would be considered by Kant to be themselves heteronomous and hence inappropriate as moral justifications of actions.

Consider the case of my altruistically helping an acquaintance of mine. On the side of whatever nonhedonistic initial desire there may be it would still be true that I contingently find myself with the desire, and the conditions under which this desire arises in me can in principle be accounted for in terms of an empirical account of my life's circumstances. On the side of believed means–end connections (in this or other nonmoral and nonhedonist actions), what I believe concerns contingent states of affairs under empirical laws of nature. Reasons for action licensed by Green's argument fare no better than altruistic reasons. It is true that to speak of laws of nature here is to stretch a point, but it is far more reasonable to ascribe to Kant a willingness (and an insistence) to stretch the point than a willingness to count Green's cases as cases of morally autonomous action. What I mean is this: hedonistic explanations of action already assume that laws of nature determine pleasure. This is no trivial assumption, since pleasure presumably is a sensation quale and, as far as I can tell, irreducibly mental according to Kant. Moreover, the goodness

---

[12]It is worth pointing out that he holds the view that pleasure is the mark of successful execution of an intention. This does not mean that pleasure is the sole motive of action, although Kant may have been confused about this distinction.

of the pleasant (or that the pleasant is sought) must also somehow be considered to be a matter of empirical laws. The stretching of the point concerns the fact that the seeking of the above-mentioned goods must now also be considered subject to explanations by empirical laws. On the assumption that we can do so, I claim that according to Kant acting so as to bring about the goods to which Green refers is to be acting in accordance with high-level conceptions still of the nature of empirical, contingent means–end connections and hence still heteronomous. Green's rational self-satisfaction is heteronomous.

My account invites the response that if it correctly describes Kant's position, then Kant simply has no way of characterizing moral action. According to my account rational self-satisfaction and acting so as to bring about self-satisfaction in others are still heteronomous. What is there left to play the role of nonheteronomous interest? On the side of initial desires in moral action, Kant tells us that none are contingently given, since he holds moral feelings and desires to arise in an agent subsequent to the agent's conception of the moral law. Moral feelings are in this respect 'intellectual' and to the extent that contemplating action from the moral law is pleasurable, the pleasure is not due to pathological affection (but neither would such feelings be those of rational satisfaction in pursuit of heteronomous goods). In a moral action, the agent does not find himself contingently in a state of moral desire or feeling. Rather, Kant holds that the agent in a moral action acts from what he has legislated in an a priori fashion as a necessary condition on the permissibility of heteronomous goodness-producing actions.

On the side of believed means–end connection, the agent represents, not any empirical contingent connection, no matter of how high a level, but the very a priori legislated necessary condition the conception of which produces moral feelings. Because this is the content of the agent's belief, the objective of the moral action is not heteronomously connected to the reason for the action. That is, moral justifications are internal to the conception of the action as moral. Autonomy of moral action lies in this fact of internal connection and in the origin of the connection as a priori legislated. Kant describes this state of affairs as consisting of actions based on pure, not empirical, interest. It is for this reason that Green and others charge Kant with having an empty conception of moral action. From Kant's point of view acting so as to bring about rational self-satisfaction either in oneself or in others (or so as to help bring about rational self-satisfaction in others) is heteronomous. That agents act so as to bring about self-satisfactions in any agent or agents is still described by some (undoubtedly quite abstract and high-level) empirical principle and constitutes an objective of rational action not properly internal to the actions in question. It constitutes a state of affairs not a priori legislated and does not lay down conditions that are synthetic and a priori—that is, conditions necessary for the permissibility of actions. Acting from any sort of rational self-satisfaction is a contingency (and undoubtedly a truth) not supplied by the legislative will and hence is heteronomous. Green's emendation of Kant is so radical a departure as to constitute a rejection of Kant's conception of moral action rather than a friendly amendment or an elaboration of what is already implicitly contained in Kant.

Kant agrees with Green that the common good is to be rationally sought after by an agent, but he disagrees that this fact constitutes moral action. Green's argument is a good argument for grounding other-regarding concerns in one's own nonmoral interests and in every agent's interest in rational self-satisfaction. Neither altruism nor Green's account furnishes a Kantian foundation for morality. If it were true in the actual world that agents do not act so as to bring about some agent's rational self-satisfaction (if this can be imagined), Kant's moral imperative is still supposed to hold.[13] Hence Green's argument does not justify the moral law. And if it is true in the actual world that agents act out of rational self-satisfaction (as it at least sometimes is) but somehow it could be, and were, true that the moral imperative as a matter of fact forbids any action that can bring about rational self-satisfaction, then the imperative is still supposed to bind agents. Hence agents in this case would

[13]Perhaps one may imagine a world in which every agent is just playing and finds himself with no interest that needs satisfying. In such a world agents would still be required to treat each other with respect.

be morally bound not to achieve any sort of satisfactions. Such radical consequences of Kant's position are of course the reasons (or among the reasons) Kant is charged with being entirely too formal. Worse, such consequences would seem to make the moral law an arbitrarily legislated artifact and participation in Kant's moral institution arbitrary and irrational. Artifactuality seems to be a characterization on which Kant insists, but arbitrariness and irrationality of the moral law constitute serious criticism. As I conclude my discussion with an analysis of this criticism in the next section, it becomes obvious that although Kant and Green again agree up to a point, Green urges a resolution that Kant does not accept.

TELEOLOGICAL CONSTRAINTS ON THE MORAL LAW

In light of the just-mentioned consequences and criticisms, can Kant provide a nonmoral account of the reasonableness of being moral, without allowing moral justifications to lapse into heteronomy? I believe he can do so by giving nonmoral descriptions of the broadly based empirical context of the a priori legislation and of the likely success of agents' achieving self-satisfactions of agents through actions in accordance with the moral law. There is perfectly good and obvious nonmoral reason for believing that agents act to achieve self-satisfaction of agents and that conflicts will arise in the course of such pursuits. Agents certainly do not know that they live in a world in which this is not so. Furthermore, there is good and nonmoral reason for believing that on the whole agents acting in the indicated fashion will achieve considerable self-satisfactions when acting only in ways permitted by the moral law. It may even be true that acting morally maximizes for all agents (as a body) the likelihood of achieving self-satisfactions more persistently and effectively than any other scheme would. These considerations make it reasonable to act morally but do not constitute moral justification of actions.

The issue may be seen in another way. Believing that agents act from motives of self-satisfaction and that on the whole they will achieve their ends in accordance with the moral law is a necessary condition of being moral rationally, given that one wants to achieve self-satisfactions of agents. Such beliefs are justified pragmatically as well as on other grounds. They constitute neither sufficient nor necessary grounds for being moral, since if they did, both having the beliefs in question and their truth would introduce heteronomy into morality. We must appeal to facts of reason, according to Kant, if we want conditions for acceptance of the moral law. Such beliefs or their truth go a long way toward removing the suspicion of pointlessness and irrationality in the concept of acting morally, which seemed to find its way into Kant's account of morality. Nonetheless, to repeat, these considerations do not serve as moral justifications of action.

A distinction between questions internal and those external to the institution of morality is being invoked here. An external account of the rationality of the institution is being given, and the external account is teleological. But none of these teleological considerations find their way into an agent's moral rationalization requirements. In this fashion Kant can attempt to relate autonomously legislated principles to heteronomous conditions without being forced to deny autonomy of the legislation.[14] At the same time, if, contrary to what we have reason to believe, the world we live in were as the radical cases outlined earlier describe it, the world would be an odd and (in the second case) bad place, but Kantian moral justifications would not thereby be weakened.[15] And here is a serious disagreement between Kant and Green, because Green makes the morally good a (complicated) function of what is nonmorally good for rational agents in the actual world.

[14]Principles of epistemic conduct in the first *Critique* provide a useful illustration. The principles can be teleologically grounded by saying that there is good reason to believe that we will maximize reliably our true beliefs by adopting Kant's autonomous, a priori categorial principles as canons of epistemic justification, without thereby saying that such teleological considerations are such canons or that epistemic justification is analyzable in terms of reliability and distribution of true beliefs. True beliefs are the goods in epistemic contexts, and epistemic justification is the analogue to moral justification.

[15]It most likely would be true that if the world were such an odd and bad place, no moral agents would exist to offer any justifications. The world not being such a place is a material condition of the possibility of there existing moral agents offering justifications, but it is no more than that.

III

Kant's Compatibilism

Allen W. Wood

On the issue of free will and determinism, philosophers are usually categorized either as "compatibilists" or as "incompatibilists." Compatibilists hold that our actions may be determined by natural causes and yet also be free in the sense necessary for moral agency and responsibility. Freedom and determinism are compatible. Incompatibilists hold that if our actions are determined to take place by natural causes, then free agency and moral responsibility are illusions. Freedom and determinism are incompatible.

Kant's views on many issues do not fit neatly into the customary pigeonholes, and the free will issue is no exception. He is probably most often regarded as an incompatibilist, and not without justification. Certainly he repudiates Leibniz's compatibilism, which (Kant says) allows us no more than "the freedom of a turnspit" (*KpV* 97g 101e).[1] Yet Kant himself holds that not only are our actions determined by the causal mechanism of nature and but also that they are free. The basic question, he says, is "whether regarding the same effect which is determined by nature, freedom can nevertheless be present or whether freedom is wholly excluded by such an exceptionable rule" (*A*536/*B*564). In answering this question in favor of the former alternative, Kant's avowed purpose is "to unite nature and freedom," to

---

[1] All translations are my own.

"remove the apparent contradiction between the mechanism of nature and freedom," to show that "causality from freedom at least does not contradict nature" (*A*537/*B*565; *KpV* 97g 101e; *A*558/*B*587). But these are precisely the aims of compatibilism. When we consider all Kant's views together, it is tempting to say that he wants to show not only the compatibility of freedom and determinism, but also the compatibility of compatibilism and incompatibilism.

In brief, Kant's theory is that our actions may be simultaneously free and causally determined because we belong to two worlds; this means that our existence can be viewed from two different standpoints. We are, on the one hand, part of nature, of what Kant calls the sensible or phenomenal world. We are objects accessible to empirical observation and natural science. The phenomenal world includes everything as it is subject to our conditions of sense perception and ordered experience. These conditions include space, time, and strict causal connectedness according to necessary laws. From this standpoint, our actions are causally determined. If this were the only standpoint from which we could view ourselves, freedom would be impossible.

Kant, however, holds that nature is only a realm of appearances or things as they fall under the conditions of empirical knowledge. Everything in the phenomenal world, including ourselves, also has an existence in itself, not subject to those conditions. This other realm, that of things in themselves, cannot be known by us, but it can be thought, through our pure understanding, as a noumenal or intelligible world. Because we cannot know our noumenal selves, we cannot know whether they possess the freedom our phenomenal selves lack. Yet because space, time, and causal order are on Kant's theory necessary attributes only of the phenomenal world, there is no way to rule out the possibility that the noumenal self is free. This leaves it open to us to postulate or presuppose noumenal freedom as the metaphysical condition of our moral agency, with which our consciousness of moral obligation acquaints us. Thus when we view ourselves as objects of empirical science, we regard our actions as causally determined and not free. On the other hand, when we assume the role of moral agents, we "transpose ourselves into members of intelligible world," regard our existence as not subject to the empirical conditions of space, time, or natural causality, and think of ourselves as free (*G* 453g 72e).

Kant's compatibilism is of a most unusual sort. The usual intention behind compatibilism is to deny that there really is any deep metaphysical problem about free will, to suppress the free will problem at the least possible metaphysical cost. Most compatibilists try to show how free choices may be comfortably accommodated in the chain of natural causes, so as to present a unified picture of ourselves as both moral agents and objects of scientific observation. Kant's compatibilism, however, is based on the aggressively metaphysical distinction between phenomena and noumena; far from unifying our view of ourselves, it says that freedom and determinism are compatible only because the self as free moral agent belongs to a different world from that of the self as natural object. (Norman Kretzmann has commented to me that this may be likened to saying that a married couple is compatible, but only as long as they live in separate houses.)

I venture to say that Kant's solution to the free will problem strikes nearly everyone who has ever studied it as thoroughly unsuccessful, a metaphysical monstrosity that gives us a far-fetched if not downright incoherent account of our moral agency. At any rate, that is what I used to think. I am still in partial agreement with those critics who find problems in reconciling Kant's account of our free agency with some of the more commonsense features of his own ethical theory. And I share with more orthodox compatibilists the hope that there may exist a simpler and less counterintuitive solution to the free will problem. Still, I am more impressed with the successes of Kant's theory in solving the problem it sets for itself than I am appalled by its shortcomings. As we shall see, the free will problem arises for Kant in a form in some respects idiosyncratic to Kant, and the problem for him is unusually acute. The causal determinism in which Kant believes is very strict, and the conditions for moral responsibility set by Kantian ethics are very strong. Further, Kant's moral psychology blocks the only simple and natural sort of compatibilist solution. What I find quite surprising is that

Kant does succeed in reconciling freedom and determinism in the context of his philosophy, and that Kant's compatibilism involves no greater revision of our commonsense view of our agency than it does.

KANT'S CONCEPT OF FREEDOM

Kant distinguishes between 'transcendental' (or 'cosmological') freedom and 'practical' freedom. Transcendental freedom is a purely metaphysical concept, the concept of a certain sort of causality. Transcendental freedom is "the faculty of beginning a state spontaneously or from oneself [*von selbst*] (A533/B561). A transcendentally free being is one that causes a state of the world without being subject in its causality to any further causes; that is, a "first cause," or an unconditioned beginner of a causal chain. Practical freedom, on the other hand, is free agency; it is what we ascribe to ourselves when we think of ourselves as morally responsible for what we do.

Regarding practical freedom, Kant distinguishes two concepts: a "negative" concept and a "positive" one. Practical freedom in the negative sense is "the independence of our will [*Willkür*] from necessitation through impulses of sensibility" (A534/B562). We are free in this sense if we are capable of resisting our sensuous desires, of acting contrary to their dictates or at least without having them as motives of our action. Kant apparently believes that nonhuman animals altogether lack the capacity to resist sensuous impulses, that the action of an animal is always the direct result of some sensuous impulse. When such an impulse occurs in an animal, it cannot fail to act as the impulse dictates. It has no faculty of countermanding the impulse or suspending action on it in order to deliberate and weigh different desires against each other. Kant calls the animal's will an *arbitrium brutum*, in contrast to the human *arbitrium sensitivum sed liberum*, which is affected by sensuous impulses but not necessitated by them (A534/B562).

This concept of practical freedom is "negative" because it describes the free will in terms of the way it does *not* operate. Kant's positive conception of practical freedom, on the other hand, describes the free will in terms of what it *can* do. Kant believes that unlike the brutes, human beings have the power to resist particular sensuous impulses and the power to deliberate about which ones to satisfy and how best to satisfy them. In addition, Kant ascribes to us the power to act from a wholly nonsensuous or a priori motive, to conform our will to a moral law self-given by our own reason. Freedom in the positive sense is thus the capacity to act from this nonsensuous motive, "the capacity to will a priori" (*VpR* 129g 104e). This positive sense of freedom is derived, of course, from Kant's moral theory. In general, we may be held responsible for our actions only to the extent that we have the capacity to do what morality commands of us. Kantian morality commands that we act according to a law we give ourselves a priori. Consequently, practical freedom consists in the capacity to be motivated by such a law; it is "the authentic legislation of pure and as such practical reason" (*KpV* 33g 33e).

The free will problem arises for Kant because he believes that practical freedom requires transcendental freedom and that there is no room in the causal mechanism of nature for a transcententally free being (*A534/B562*). All causes in the natural world are sensible or empirical and all necessitate their effects. Consequently, if our actions were determined by them, then they would be necessitated by something sensuous (so that we would lack practical freedom in the negative sense) and there would be no room for a nonsensuous motive for our actions (so that we would lack practical freedom in the positive sense). Practical freedom requires that we be able to determine our actions entirely from within ourselves, through our own legislative reason. Natural causes, however, belong to an endless regressive chain in which there is no spontaneous or first cause. We can think of ourselves as practically free, therefore, only by thinking of our actions as subject to a transcendentally free cause lying outside nature.

Because practical freedom, the freedom required for moral responsibility, must involve the capacity to do what morality demands of us, it is obvious that any account of practical freedom must depend on some account of the demands of morality. In Kant's philosophy morality has an especially close association with practical freedom. For Kant, morality is autonomy, it is the conformity of the will to a self-given law of reason. Acting morally, then, is not merely one thing among others that a practically free being can do, but it is the peculiar function of morality to actualize practical freedom.

It has seemed to some of Kant's critics, such as Henry Sidgwick, that an insoluble problem is involved in Kant's doctrine in that only autonomous or moral action actualizes practical freedom.[2] For in that case, apparently only moral or autonomous action is free action, while immoral or heteronomous actions are all unfree. If only actions motivated by pure reason are free, then actions motivated by sensuous desires must be necessitated by the mechanism of nature. Thus it seems that Kant is committed to saying that we are morally responsible only for moral or autonomous actions and that no one can be held responsible for immoral or heteronomous actions.

This problem is illusory, however. If Kant did hold that our immoral or heteronomous actions were determined by natural causes, then he would have to hold that these actions are unfree; that the will that performs them is an *arbitrium brutum*. But Kant's actual view is that since our will is free, our heteronomous actions are performed from sensuous motives without being necessitated by them. Even when we act from sensuous motives, we do so as having the capacity to be moved by the a priori law of reason; we act as practically free beings, and hence are responsible for what we do. If our actions were sensuously necessitated, as by natural determinism, then it would follow that they are all performed from sensuous motives. The converse of this does not hold, however. Not every action performed from sensuous motives must be naturally necessitated. The human will, according to Kant, is sensuously "affected" (*affiziert*) but not sensuously "necessitated" (*nötigt, necessitirt*). Sensuous motives, when we act on them, have for us a *vim impellentem* but not a *vim necessitantem* (*A534/B562*; *VM* 182).

---

[2]Henry Sidgwick, *Methods of Ethics* (New York, 1966), pp. 511–16.

It is true that when Kant describes practical freedom in the positive sense as "the legislation of pure practical reason," he seems to imply that only autonomous or moral actions are truly free actions. Careful attention to his language shows that for him practical freedom consists in the *capacity* for autonomous action and can exist even when this capacity is not exercised. Thus Kant describes practical freedom in the negative sense as "that property of [the will's] causality by which it *can* be effective independently of foreign causes" (*G* 446g 64e, italics added). Again, he says it is "not being *necessitated* to act by any sensuous determining ground," implying that a free being may be motivated by sensuous grounds without being necessitated by them (*TL* 226g 26e, italics added). Freedom in the positive sense, he says, is "the *power* [*Vermögen*] of pure reason to be of itself practical" (*TL* 213–14g 10e, italics added). And he defines the free will (*Willkür*) as "the will that *can* be determined by pure reason" (*TL* 213g 10e, italics altered). Further, "freedom of the will is the *capacity* to determine oneself to actions independently of a *causis subjectis* or sensuous impulses" (*VpR* 129g 104e, italics added). We are practically free and morally responsible for our actions whenever we act as having the power or capacity for autonomous action, whether or not that power is exercised or actualized in what we do. Kant's view is that except "in tenderest childhood, or insanity, or in great sadness which is only a species of insanity," we always do possess the power to act autonomously, even if we seldom exercise it (*VM* 182). Autonomous actions are "freer" than heteronomous ones in the sense that autonomous actions are an exercise of freedom—that is, they actualize the capacity in which practical freedom consists. In heteronomous actions, we fail to exercise our freedom (our power to act autonomously) insofar as we submit ourselves to the motivation of natural impulses. This is wholly different from action of an *arbitrium brutum*, which altogether lacks the power to determine itself independently of the sensuous impulses on which it acts.

Philosophers distinguish two senses of freedom that may be relevant to moral responsibility: the 'liberty of spontaneity' and the 'liberty of indifference'. Loosely speaking, we are free in the sense of spontaneity if we are the cause of our own actions, and free in the sense of indifference if we could have done otherwise than we in fact do. Kant's theory of practical freedom appears to involve both spontaneity and indifference, at least in certain specific or qualified ways. Autonomous action is spontaneous in a very strong sense, because our acts have their determining grounds entirely a priori in our reason, and are wholly independent of all external causes. But even heteronomous action is spontaneous in quite a strong sense. Although heteronomous acts are motivated by sensuous desires, which Kant regards as 'foreign' to our rational will, they are not causally necessitated by such desires. As free agents, we act from sensuous motives only by incorporating them into our maxim, the principle adopted freely by our will. Practical freedom is always spontaneity because it requires transcendental freedom, the capacity to produce an effect without being determined by any prior or external cause.

Kant also ascribes a form of indifference to the human will. He even defines will (*Willkür*) generally as "a power to do or refrain at one's discretion" (*TL* 213g 9e). Clearly every one of our heteronomous actions could have been other than what it is, since it is performed by a being who has the capacity to act autonomously. Further, because our will is sensuously affected, the possibility always exists that we will fail to exercise our freedom. Hence every one of our autonomous actions also could have been other than what it is.

Kant, however, flatly refuses to define freedom in terms of this indifference. Freedom is the power to choose according to legislative reason. According to Kant, "freedom cannot be located in the fact that the rational subject can make a choice which conflicts with his legislating reason, even if experience proves often enough that this happens (*TL* 226g 26e). For Kant, freedom consists in a one-way difference, so to speak. That is, freedom consists in the ability to act autonomously even when we do not, but it does not consist in the possibility of acting heteronomously, even if this possibility always does exist for us. If an action is performed from sensuous motives, then it is a free action only if the agent could have acted instead on a priori motives. If a being acts on a priori motives, however, it may be free even if there is no possibility that it could have failed to act as it does. A free will that altogether lacks this indifference is what Kant calls a "holy will," for example, the divine will:

> [The capacity always to act according to reason must certainly be in God, since sensuous impulses are impossible to him.] One might raise the objection that God cannot decide otherwise than he does, and so he does not act freely but out of the necessity of his nature. . . . But in God it is not due to the necessity of his nature that he can decide only as he does. Rather it is true freedom in God that he decides only what is suitable to his highest understanding. [*VpR* 132g 105–106e]

According to Kant's theory, practical freedom is the power to act from a priori principles. A being may have this power even if there is no possibility of failing to exercise it and hence no possibility of acting other than it does. Such a being is free, and therefore responsible for its inevitably rational acts.

Kant even goes so far as to say that "only freedom with regard to the inner legislation of reason is really a power; the possibility of deviating from legislative reason is a lack of power" (*TL* 227g 26e). Here again we must avoid the mistake of thinking that for Kant the failure to exercise our power to will autonomously is the same as the failure to have that power, hence the same as the failure to be free. What Kant means is that the possibility of deviating from legislative reason is not a power of any sort but is due instead to a certain sort of weakness or lack of power. This view is quite defensible. Not every possibility is a power. Some possibilities, in fact, are due to a lack of power. The human will has the power to act autonomously and this power is its freedom. If it acts heteronomously, it still has this power, but it has failed to exercise it. Such a failure is not due to a lack of freedom but rather is a failure of execution, a failure to exercise the freedom we have. And this failure is due in turn to a certain weakness or lack of power, leading to a lapse in exercising our freedom. Moral weakness, which makes it possible for our action to deviate from legislative reason, is a lack of power, but it is not a lack of that power in which freedom consists.

Consider a parallel case. An indifferent swimmer may have

the power to save himself if he falls into deep water. But he has no power, only a possibility, of drowning in the same eventuality. Although he has the power to swim, he may drown if he does not exercise that power effectively, due (say) to confusion or panic. In the latter case, his possibility of drowning is due to a kind of weakness or lack of power, though not to a lack of the power to swim. The indifference of the human will, on Kant's theory, is rather like the indifference of this swimmer. The swimmer has the power to swim, which he may exercise and save himself, or he may fail to exercise that power and drown, due to a weakness or lack of power leading to a failure of execution. The moral agent has freedom, the power to act autonomously, and may exercise that freedom by conforming one's will to the moral law, or one may fail to exercise it and follow sensuous desires, due to a weakness or lack of power in one's moral character leading to a failure of execution. The possibility of deviating from legislative reason is thus due to a lack of power and not to a lack of freedom.

We may now understand how the free will problem for Kant is different from the free will problem faced by most incompatibilists. Kant does *not* hold in general that freedom is incompatible with causal determination or even necessitation of the free being's actions. As we have just seen, Kant holds that a holy will is free even though its acts are necessitated, because they are necessitated from within by reason rather than by the sensuous impulses that are foreign to our rational nature. In this respect Kant's view is much closer to that of some compatibilists (such as Spinoza and Leibniz) than it is to that of standard, hardline incompatibilists, who see freedom as incompatible with any sort of causation or necessitation.

Kant does not believe, then, that freedom is incompatible with causation generally, but only that it is incompatible with *natural* causation, with the sort of causation found to act on the will within the realm of appearance. He believes this for two overlapping reasons, one of them derived from his moral philosophy and the other from his moral psychology. First, Kant believes that the moral motive, action on which is alone an exercise of freedom, is an a priori motive, and therefore one that cannot be given to us through nature or the causes acting in nature. Second, he holds the complementary belief that the only natural causes that do act on the will are sensuous impulses, motivation by which precludes motivation by reason. In short, the free will problem arises for Kant because he is a thoroughgoing psychological hedonist about all the natural causes that might act on our will. He holds that empirical psychology is excluded in principle from understanding all rational deliberation and all action on the motive of reason. This means that the free will problem would not arise in the same form for someone who is less of a crude Benthamite about the empirical psychology of motivating and allows for the possibility of accounting for rational deliberation and action through natural causes. A standard compatibilist response to the free will problem in its Kantian form seems open to any such person.

FREEDOM AND NATURE

Let us now turn to Kant's attempt to solve his problem, to reconcile freedom with the mechanism of nature given the strictures of his moral philosophy and moral psychology. First we must clarify what Kant does and does not intend to establish. Kant does not pretend to prove that we are free or to provide arguments in favor of any speculative doctrine he believes must be true if freedom and determinism are to be compatible. No such doctrines, he holds, could be either provable or disprovable. What Kant means to show is only that, as far as we can prove, freedom and determinism may be compatible. Kant is fond of forensic analogies. Let us use one here. Kant's role regarding freedom is somewhat like a defense attorney's role regarding his client. Because practical freedom is presupposed by morality, we may assume that freedom is innocent until proven guilty, that the burden of proof lies on those who would undermine our moral consciousness by claiming that we are not free. In confronting the prosecution's evidence against his client, a defense attorney may exploit this fact about the burden of proof by concocting a plausible theory explaining the allegedly incriminating evidence. The attorney need not show that his theory is the correct one, only that it has enough plausibility to introduce a reasonable doubt concerning the prosecution's theory. Likewise, in defending our freedom, Kant concocts a metaphysical theory which, if true, saves our practical freedom despite the fact that our actions are determined by natural causes. Kant does not need to show that this metaphysical theory is correct; indeed, he frankly admits that he cannot. But neither, he claims, can the opponent of freedom refute the theory. Kant rests his defense of freedom on his claim.

The problem Kant faces is formidable. As we have just seen, Kant holds that the human will has freedom, which is the power to resist sensuous impulses and to act from nonsensuous motives. At the same time, Kant also holds that human actions fall under the unexceptionable law of natural causality:

> All the actions of man in appearance are so determined . . . according to the order of nature that if we could investigate all the appearances of his will as to their grounds, then there would not be a single human action we could not predict with certainty and be able to know as necessary from its preceding conditions. [A550/B578]

Kant hopes to save himself from an open contradiction here by distinguishing two standpoints for viewing our actions, each involving a different sort of cause to which the action may be attributed. It is possible, he says, "to regard an event on the one side as a merely natural effect, yet on the other side as an effect of freedom" (A543/B571). As an appearance or phenomenon, the human self plays a natural causal role in the production of its actions, which are events in nature and appearances as well.

> Every efficient cause, however, must have a *character*, i.e. a law of its causality, without which it would not be a cause. And then we as subjects in the world of sense have first an *empirical* character, through which our actions as appearances stand in thoroughgoing

connection with other appearances according to constant laws of nature. [*A539/B567*]

We also have an existence in itself as noumenon or intelligible subject, outside the conditions of sensible nature, unknowable but still thinkable through pure understanding. In this subject we "must make room for an *intelligible character* through which it is the cause of those same actions as appearances, but which is not itself an appearance and stands under no conditions of sensibility" (*A539/B567*). As effects of our empirical character, our actions are necessitated by natural causes and hence unfree. But as effects of our intelligible character, it is possible that the same actions are produced by a transcendentally free cause, which is not necessitated by anything sensuous and is capable of autonomous or a priori volition.

It is not immediately clear how this theory is supposed to reconcile freedom and determinism, or even how it can be self-consistent. If our actions are indeed causally determined by natural events, then they are apparently necessitated by sensuous impulses acting on our empirical character. From this alone it seems to follow that our actions are unfree. How can anything that might be true about our actions from another standpoint render these same actions free? How can it remove the necessitation of our actions by sensuous causes or restore to us the capacity of acting from a priori motives, which this necessitation appears once and for all to preclude?

Two problems arise here; one concerns the liberty of spontaneity and the other the liberty of indifference. First, practical freedom is the capacity to will autonomously, to act from a priori motives. How is it possible for us to have this capacity if a natural or empirical cause can always be cited for what we do? Second, moral responsibility requires that for any heteronomous action we perform, we must have the capacity to act other than we in fact do. How is this possible if every one of our actions is in principle predictable and knowable as "necessary from its preceding conditions"?

I believe Kant is aware of both problems and attempts to solve them. Let us consider each attempt in turn.

EMPIRICAL CAUSALITY AND INTELLIGIBLE CAUSALITY

Regarding the problem of spontaneity, I believe that a careful consideration of Kant's texts reveals that according to the theory he is proposing, our free actions are *never* produced by natural causality in the way they would have to be if only natural causality pertained to them. Kant holds that the two sorts of causality do not merely exist side by side but that, at least in the case of human actions, phenomenal causality is grounded in noumenal causality. He asks:

> Is it not possible that although for every effect in appearance a connection with its cause according to natural laws is indeed required, this empirical causality itself, without in the least interrupting its connection with natural causes, can be an effect of a causality which is not empirical but intelligible? [*A*544/*B*572]

More specifically, Kant holds that although our actions are causally determined in time by our empirical character and other natural events, this empirical character itself is the effect—or, as he also says, the "sensible schema" (*A*553/*B*581)—of the intelligible character, which is freely determined by us outside empirical conditions. Kant says that "reason has causality in regard to appearance; its action can be called free, since it is exactly determined and necessary in its empirical causality (the mode of sense). For the latter is once again determined in the intelligible character (the mode of thought)" (*A*551/*B*579).

Empirical causality regarding human actions is an effect of intelligible causality, which (on the theory Kant is proposing) is transcendentally free. Hence empirical causality, on this theory, does not involve the sensuous necessitation of actions, as it appears to do when we ignore its intelligible ground. Practical freedom, says Kant, presupposes that ... an action's cause in appearance is not *so* determining as to preclude a causality lying in our will, a causality which, independently of these natural causes and even contrary to their force and influence, can bring about something determined in the temporal order according to empirical laws, and thus can begin a series of events wholly of itself. [*A*534/*B*562]

Again, "If appearances were things in themselves, then freedom could not be saved. For then nature would be the complete and self-sufficient determining cause of every event" (*A*537/*B*565). Kant's theory apparently holds that because appearances are not things in themselves, nature is *not* the complete and self-sufficient cause of events, at least not of human actions. Rather, the complete and self-sufficient cause of actions is our free will, located in the intelligible world. Nature, in the form of sensuous impulses, enters into the production of our actions only insofar as we freely permit sensuous motives to be substituted for a priori rational principles in determining our choices. The free causality of the noumenal self, Kant says, "is not merely a concurrence, but complete in itself, even when sensuous incentives are not for it but wholly against it" (*A*555/*B*583).

It is tempting to describe Kant's theory by saying that for this theory the natural or empirical causes of actions, their causes in the world of appearance, are not real causes but only apparent causes; furthermore, that on this theory everything in the phenomenal world goes on, by a sort of preestablished harmony, just as if our actions were caused by antecedent natural events, but in reality their causes lie outside nature altogether, in a free will hovering above nature in the intelligible world. I believe, however, that Kant would reject this description as a distortion or caricature of his theory. Kant's principle of empirical causality says that every event in time is determined by antecedent events according to necessary laws. For Kant every human action does conform to this principle. This conformity to natural laws entitles the empirical events upon which our actions necessarily follow to be called the empirical causes of those actions: nothing more is, or could possibly be, required for them to deserve that title. They are not, therefore, merely apparent causes, but the real causes of our actions insofar as they fall under the mechanism of nature. The antecedent events are not "complete" and "self-sufficient" causes, however, because the causality of human actions can be viewed from another standpoint, that is, as the effects of freedom.

Although Kant's position here is thoroughly self-consistent, it reveals something noteworthy and possibly suspicious about his conception of causality. The concept of cause is bound up with that of causal efficacy, a notion David Hume variously, and aptly, called a cause's "power," "energy," "force," or "that very circumstance in the cause, by which it is enabled to produce the effect."[3] Regarding this notion philosophers have exhibited two general tendencies. One tendency, which we may call the Aristotelian, is to treat causal efficacy as a property of substances or agents and to regard it as a primitive notion, unanalyzable but built into our basic understanding of how things work. The other, which we may call the Humean tendency, is to treat causal efficacy as a property of events or states of the world and to try to analyze it in terms of some relation between these events allegedly simpler or more accessible to our knowledge than that of causal efficacy itself. The two leading candidates for such an analysis have been the relation of constant conjunction between similar events and the conformity of events to natural laws governing their temporal order.

Kant does not opt unambiguously for either tendency. He wants to treat causality in the sensible world as the conformity of events to laws determining their order in time. Kant's disagreement with Hume about whether these laws are knowably necessary is a disagreement between two philosophers who both follow the Humean tendency regarding natural causality. Kant, however, wants to reserve for himself a more Aristotelian notion of causal efficacy, to be ascribed to free agents as members of the intelligible world. If we agree that Kant's theory at this point is coherent, then it seems to provide a counterexample to the extreme Humean view that we can conceive of causal efficacy

[3]David Hume, *Enquiry Concerning Human Understanding* (Oxford, 1979) section 7.

only as some feature of the temporal order of events. For the theory says that our actions are determined in the temporal order by natural laws, but the causal efficacy responsible for them does not lie in the temporal series at all, but outside it in the intelligible world. If we can imagine this at all, then it suffices to show both that we can conceive of events as lawfully ordered in time without attributing causal efficacy to those events upon which others lawfully follow, and that we have a notion of causal efficacy which has nothing whatever to do with the temporal order of events and the laws governing it. For this reason, stubborn Humeans may reject Kant's theory as unintelligible and his solution to the free will problem along with it. I will not pursue this issue here. But we have seen that if we assume Kant's views about causality are coherent, we must agree that his theory succeeds in showing how natural causality could be compatible with the spontaneity of the human will in its intelligible character.[4]

Timeless Agency

There remains the problem of indifference, of showing how we can have the capacity to act autonomously even when we do not so act, and even when our heteronomous actions are causally determined to take place. Kant admits that insofar as we conceive ourselves as empirical agents, who cause our actions through the

[4]I am inclined to say that Kant's refusal to opt exclusively for the Humean concept of cause sheds light on another of the vexed questions of Kantian metaphysics: the causal relation between noumena and phenomena generally. Kant holds that things in themselves cause appearances, or that they appear to us by exercising a causal influence on our sensibility. For two centuries critics have charged Kant with inconsistency or incoherence for holding this doctrine. The critics charge that on Kant's own showing causal relations can obtain only between temporal events, so that it is inconsistent for Kant to regard things in themselves (which are timeless) as causes. It is certainly true that for Kant all empirically knowable causes hold between events in time, since such causes are all Humean. Kant means to allow us through pure understanding to *think* of Aristotelian causes as the noumenal ground of phenomenal objects. The pure category of cause and effect (or ground and consequence) seems to be for him neither exclusively Aristotelian nor exclusively Humean. Here again, Kant is thoroughly self-consistent, although it is easy to see why his critics say he is not and hard to blame them for perceiving something fishy about Kant's doctrine at this point.

temporal flow of events, we cannot conceive of ourselves as able to do other than we do. Every one of our actions is strictly determined by the temporal series that precedes it, and this series reaches far into the past, before our birth. "Since the past is no longer in my power, every action which I perform is necessary because of determining grounds which are not in my power. This means that *at the point in time when I act* I am never free" (*KpV* 94g 98e, italics added). Time, however, is for Kant only a form of sensibility; only as phenomena or appearances are we necessarily in time. As noumena or things in themselves we are subject neither to time nor to the law of causality which goes along with it. As free agents, according to the theory Kant proposes, we are timeless beings.

Kant here presupposes another controversial metaphysical doctrine, that of timeless eternity. The attribute of timelessness, which some theologians ascribe to God alone, Kant's theory must ascribe to every one of us insofar as we are transcendentally free. Some philosophers doubt that we can make sense of the notion of timeless eternity. Some object especially to the idea that a timeless being might be the cause of temporal events, and in particular they object to the idea that it can be thought of as causing events that occur at different times. Clearly, if we cannot form a coherent notion of timeless eternity or a coherent account of a timeless being causing events occurring at different times, then Kant's solution to the problem of freedom is untenable. Once again, however, I will not try to settle this difficult metaphysical issue here. The point I want to investigate is whether, granted that such an account can be coherently formulated, Kant is capable of reconciling natural determinism with the indifference necessary for moral agency.

How is the timelessness of the noumenal self supposed to safeguard our ability to do otherwise than we in fact do? In order to answer this question, we must look more closely at Kant's metaphysical theory of the case, and in particular at the way in which our timeless existence as noumena is supposed to produce our actions, which unfold in the course of time. In the moral subject's noumenal existence, Kant says,

Nothing precedes the determination of his will; every action and, in general, every changing determination of his existence, according to the inner sense, even the entire history of his existence as a sensuous being, is seen in the consciousness of his intelligible existence as only a consequence, not as a determining ground of his causality as a noumenon. From this point of view, a rational being can rightly say of any unlawful action which he has done that he could have left it undone, even if as an appearance it was sufficiently determined in the past and thus far was inescapably necessary. For this action and everything in the past which determined it belong to a single phenomenon of his character, which he himself creates. [*KpV* 97–98g 101e]

Kant's theory seems to be the following. Events in time follow a necessary order, as determined by their natural causes. A particular timeless choice of my intelligible character affects the natural world by selecting a certain subset of possible worlds, namely, those including a certain moral history for my empirical character, and determining that the actual world will be drawn from that subset of possibilities. For each such choice there is an almost endless variety of ways in which I might have chosen differently, and endless variety of possible empirical selves and personal moral histories I might have actualized. Of every one of my misdeeds it is true that I would have left it undone had I made a different timeless choice. Hence it is in my power to leave any misdeed undone, despite the fact that in the actual world it follows inescapably from what preceded it in time.

When Kant says of my unlawful action that it and its causal determinants belong to my character, he may intend to claim that my timeless choice affects the course of the phenomenal world merely by affecting the constitution of my empirical character, which is of course an important causal factor in what I do. This would bring Kant's theory into line with the common-sense idea that we are responsible for our actions because we are responsible for our characters. An obstacle to this way of squaring Kant's theory with common sense is that on his theory the phenomenal effects of my timeless choice appear to extend far beyond the constitution of my empirical character. Indeed, my empirical character is itself causally determined by preceding events, and ultimately by events very remote in time from my life and actions. If I am responsible for my character, then my timeless choice must affect the whole course of the world's history, insofar as history includes the actions I in fact perform. Ralph Walker even maintains Kant's theory has the monstrous consequence that I am morally responsible for everything that happens in the course of the actual world, since this world as a whole results from my timeless noumenal choice: "I can be blamed for the First World War, and for the Lisbon earthquake that so appalled Voltaire. Gandhi is no less guilty than Amin of the atrocities of the Ugandan dictator."[5]

In rescuing Kant from these supposed consequences of his theory, it may help to keep in mind that on Kant's theory my intelligible choice is supposed to impinge on the course of the world not by directly selecting a certain history of actions for me. Rather, what my intelligible choice fundamentally decides is my empirical character, the kind of person I will be, or as Kant puts it in the *Religion*, the "fundamental maxim" on which I will act (*Rel* 31g 26e). Even if my choice somehow issues in a world containing the First World War, the Lisbon earthquake, and the deeds of Idi Amin, it seems reasonable to hold me morally responsible only for those events which must belong to the actual course of things because I have the empirical character or fundamental maxim that I do. Kant must admit that on his theory this may include events that happen at places and even times remote from my life history in the temporal world. Yet Kant can reply that because in principle we know nothing about how our timeless choices operate on the temporal world, it must be impossible for us to say with confidence which events these may be. It seems open to Kant to suppose that they correspond to those events for which we normally regard ourselves as morally responsible. We must keep in mind that the purpose of Kant's theory is not positively to establish that we are free or morally responsible for our actions and their consequences, but only to suggest one possible way in which the moral responsibility

[5]Ralph Walker, *Kant* (London, 1979), p. 149.

we ascribe to ourselves may be reconciled with the mechanism of nature. We altogether misconstrue the status and function of this theory for Kant if we try to use it to justify or preempt moral common sense concerning such matters as the empirical scope of our moral responsibility.

FATALISM

But here we must face another objection to Kant's theory not too different from the preceding one. Although Kant does permit us to say of our unlawful actions that we could have left them undone, it may appear that his theory forces on us a certain fatalism about our character and actions at odds both with common sense and with the spirit of Kant's own moral philosophy. As we have already seen, Kant allows that if we had enough knowledge of someone's character and circumstances, "his future conduct could be calculated with as much certainty as a solar or lunar eclipse" (*KpV* 99g 103e). Suppose, then, that I have enough knowledge about myself to calculate that I will perform a certain unlawful action, for instance, that I will tell a certain malicious lie about an acquaintance against whom I bear an envious grudge. On Kant's theory it is true that I can avoid telling this lie, in the sense that I could have timelessly chosen a different intelligible character from my actual one, resulting in a different empirical character and a different moral history for myself. Yet it appears I already know enough about myself to be certain of my timeless choice regarding this particular action. For I know I will tell the lie and I know this lie is inescapably determined by past events which have already occurred. Hence I know to that extent which possible world I have timelessly chosen to actualize. My future action of telling the lie must therefore seem to me like a past action, or rather like the inevitable future result of a past action, which I can see coming but can no longer prevent. My malicious lie is an action I could have avoided (by choosing a world with a past different from the actual one) but it seems to be an action from which I am now powerless to refrain. As I now view myself, it seems that both my character (as a malicious liar) and my future act of lying are something fated for me. Perhaps I am in some sense to blame for them, but I cannot view myself as now able to alter or to avoid them.

This fatalism is obviously incompatible with the spirit of Kant's moral theory. But one measure of its appeal as an interpretation of Kant's theory of freedom is the fact that it was adopted, not only as an interpretation of Kant, but even as the profound truth of the matter, by Arthur Schopenhauer. Citing Kant's theory of the intelligible and empirical characters, Schopenhauer alleges that it supports his own thesis that everyone's conduct is inescapably determined for good or ill by an innate and unalterable moral nature. According to Schopenhauer, the merit of Kant's theory is that it shows that I am wholly responsible for what I do, despite the fact that it is false to say that I could have done otherwise, except in the sense that in the same circumstances, a different person, with a character different from mine, would have acted differently.[6]

I believe that Schopenhauer's interpretation of Kant is based on some clearly fallacious reasoning from Kant's theory. Insofar as a person's intelligible character is timeless, it apparently must also be immutable. Certainly, however, Kant intends his theory to be compatible with every conceivable state of affairs concerning the constancy or alterability of our empirical character through the course of a lifetime. Presumably this theory is that for every imaginable course of conduct in the phenomenal world, there is a timeless choice of an intelligible character that would yield that course of conduct. Hence there are some such choices whose results in the world of appearance involve changes in empirical character, drastic conversions from evil to good, or sudden degenerations from good to evil. For Kant, whether there are such changes in fact cannot be settled a priori on metaphysical grounds.

Kant also has a reply to the charge that his theory implies we

---

[6]Arthur Schopenhauer, *The World as Will and Representation*, tr. E. J. F. Payne (New York, 1958), 1:286–307; *On the Freedom of the Will*, tr. K. Kolenda (New York, 1960), pp. 26–64, 81–83; *On the Basis of Morality*, tr. E. J. F. Payne (Indianapolis, 1965), pp. 109–115.

no longer have the power to alter our future conduct. Kant does hold that by knowing enough about our character and situation we can predict with certainty what we will do. Yet it does not follow from this alone that we lack the power to do otherwise. Consider once again my malicious lie. I know how strong my grudge against the victim is, and I know myself well enough to be quite certain that I will persist in my resolve to slander him, that no sense of shame, no pity for my victim, still less any moral scruples, will dissuade me from carrying out my sinister intention. I can predict with absolute certainty that I will tell the malicious lie. But however certain I may be, I am not in the least inclined to think that it is not in my power to refrain from lying when the time comes. On the contrary, although I am certain that I will tell the lie, I am no less convinced that I still can refrain from telling it. It is misleading to express my conviction, as shallower compatibilists sometimes do, by saying that I could refrain from lying *if* I wanted to refrain. For that might suggest that, given my actual wants, I do *not* have the power to refrain. This, however, is exactly what I do *not* believe. Rather, what I believe is that although I know beyond a shadow of a doubt that I *will* tell the lie because I know I want to tell it, nevertheless I still *can* refrain from telling the lie.

Why do I have this belief, despite my certainty about how and why I will act? The belief, I suggest, rests on two other beliefs I have about myself and my future action. First, I believe it depends on me whether I will tell the lie or not. Second, I believe my influence on the situation will become effective regarding the lie only at the time the lie is actually told and not before. These are the reasons I believe that it is now still in my power whether I will lie or not. If Kant's theory can accommodate these two beliefs about myself, it can also accommodate my belief that it is still in my power to refrain from telling the malicious lie I know I am going to tell.

Kant's theory *can* accommodate both beliefs. As we have seen, this theory does show how my actions all depend on me alone, despite the fact that they follow causal laws and are predictable according to them. Kant also holds that my free choice itself becomes effective regarding a given action only at the time the action is performed. "Every action," says Kant, "irrespective of the time relation in which it stands to other appearances, is the immediate effect of the intelligible character" (*A553/B581*). It is an illusion to suppose that my timeless choice of an intelligible character is located so to speak at the beginning of time, so that it operates *through* the series of natural causes. Rather, we must treat our timeless choice as spontaneously determining each individual act as that act occurs in time, so that in judging it "we presuppose that we can wholly set aside how [the agent's previous course of life] may have been constituted, and regard the past series of conditions as not having happened, but regard this act as wholly unconditioned with respect to the previous state, as if with this act the agent instigated a series of consequences wholly of itself" (*A555/B583*).

Kant's theory at this point resembles Boethius's resolution of the problem of human freedom and divine foreknowledge. Boethius argues that because God is timeless, God's knowledge of what we will do in the future is not literally foreknowledge. Focusing on the certainty and immediacy of this knowledge, we do best to say that God knows perfectly what we do *simultaneously* with our future action, much as I might know an event that is transpiring before my very eyes. Just as my present knowledge does not predetermine or constrain what is happening, so God's perfect and immediate knowledge of what we will do does not compromise our freedom.[7] In a similar manner, Kant's theory says that our timeless choice does not predetermine our actions but has its influence immediately on each of them and should be considered simultaneous with each act as it occurs in the temporal order. Once again, some philosophers maintain that it is incoherent to claim that a single timeless choice can be simultaneous with each of a number of different events occurring at different times. This problem (which I do not believe is insoluble) is built into the very notion of a timeless being exerting influence

[7]Boethius, *Consolatio philosophiae*, *Corpus Christianorum* (Turnholti, 1957), Lib. 5, Prose 4–Prose 6.

on temporal events.[8] Kant's idea that our timeless choice is si-multaneous with each of our acts raises no *new* problems not already involved in the notion of timeless agency, and it follows closely one main line of traditional thinking about how timeless agency might operate. Kant's theory, therefore, does not commit him to fatalism about our future actions.

Of course, it is still obvious that this theory does not leave intact our commonsense conception of our free agency. As countless critics of Kant have observed, we surely do think of our moral agency as situated in time. We suppose that our free choices are made in the temporal flow, reacting to the course of events as it unfolds. We believe that we are free "at the point in time when we act," and not timelessly, as Kant's theory requires.

Timeless agency also forces other revisions in our self-con-ception as moral agents not easily harmonized with Kantian eth-ics. For example, it makes nonsense of the goal of moral improvement or moral progress, literally understood, a goal to which Kant often attaches considerable importance. On Kant's theory, only our external actions occur in time; our freedom, to which alone true moral worthiness or unworthiness pertains, is timeless, and hence incapable of literally changing for better or worse.

Further, although Kant's theory may allow us to conceive of ourselves as acting on the world at different times, it does not seem that it can consistently allow us to conceive of ourselves as acting *in* time, or producing events *within* and *through* intervals of time. Thus Kant's theory cannot permit us to conceive of ourselves as *trying* or *striving* to produce a certain result over a period of time. Kant's theory need not deprive us of every con-ception of ourselves as trying or striving, since there may be a notion of trying or striving that is instantaneous and simulta-neous with the result striven for. (The old notion of a mental 'volition' simultaneous with every voluntary action might be one

---

[8]The problem is well stated by Anthony Kenny, "Divine Foreknowledge and Human Freedom" in Kenny, ed., *Aquinas* (Garden City, N.Y., 1969). It is equally well resolved, in my opinion, by Norman Kretzmann and Eleonore Stump, "Eternity," *Journal of Philosophy* 78 (1981), 429–58.

such conception of 'trying'.) But Kant's theory does deprive us of the idea that we may produce a future result by continuously striving to produce it throughout the interval of time which now separates us from it. For instance, there is no place in Kant's theory for the idea that I may resist some passion or inclination of mine tomorrow by struggling with it today, and by striving throughout the day to purify my motives and fortify myself for the crucial hour of decision. The problem is not that I cannot imagine myself having all the thoughts and performing all the actions that I think of as part of this process, for certainly I can. The problem is that I cannot think of them as connected parts of an exercise of agency through time. I can only think of them as results or products of (timeless) agency, and not as the actual exercise of it. In time, there are only *facta*; yet trying or striving is not a *factum* but a *facere*. It is this exercise of agency Kant's theory will not allow me to conceive as a temporal process.

The absence of trying or striving is of course no problem for a timeless God, whose omnipotence and moral perfection presumably obviate the need for trying or striving of any sort. The absence surely is a problem for dedicated Kantian moral agents, however, who must think of themselves as struggling constantly with their unruly inclinations and striving throughout their lives to make the idea of duty the sufficient motive of every action. In some writings after 1793, Kant seems to recognize that his theory cannot accommodate moral striving or moral progress, literally speaking. And he seems to want to employ the notion of our noumenal "disposition" or "attitude" (*Gesinnung*) as a sort of timeless analogue or substitute both for moral striving and moral progress. In these passages, Kant seems to be saying that we think of ourselves as striving and morally progressing in time only because we as temporal beings can form no positive notion of timeless eternity: "For then nothing remains for us but to think of an endlessly progressing change in the constant progress toward our final end, through which our *attitude* remains always the same. (But our attitude is not, like this progress, a phenomenon; rather it is something supersensible, and so does not alter in time)" (*EaD* 334g 98e). In the moral life, then, as in Goethe's heaven, *alles Vergängliche ist nur ein Gleichnis*—"Everything transitory is only a parable." Temporal striving and moral progress are the moving images of our eternal moral attitude, which we cannot conceive directly but to which we can relate only through such temporal images or parables. Kant thus hopes to preserve our ordinary experience of moral struggles in time and moral progress through time not as literal truth, but only as the best way we have of representing to ourselves a truth we cannot directly experience or literally comprehend. Nevertheless, Kant must not pretend to deny that his theory requires staggering revisions in our commonsense conception of our agency, even in those features of his theory very dear to Kant himself.

In assessing Kant's compatibilism, it may help to remind ourselves that his theory of timeless agency is put forward only as a means of exploiting the burden of proof in the free will problem, which falls to those who would show that freedom is incompatible with determinism. Kant is not positively committed to his theory of the case as an account of the way our free agency actually works. Indeed, Kant maintains that no such positive account can ever be obtained. Kant does not pretend to know how our free agency is possible, but claims only to show that the impossibility of freedom is forever indemonstrable. If what bothers us about Kant's theory is that it seems too farfetched and metaphysical, then it may help at least a little to realize that once the theory has served Kant as a device for showing that freedom and determinism cannot be proven incompatible, he is just as content to dissociate himself from it and adopt a largely agnostic position on the question how our freedom is possible.[9]

---

[9]It may be argued that the implausibility of Kant's theory makes it unsuitable to his purpose, in the following way. According to the analogy drawn earlier, Kant may be likened to a defense attorney offering a theory of the evidence with a view to creating a reasonable doubt concerning the prosecution's theory. In a courtroom not just any logically possible theory of the evidence will do: the defense attorney's theory must be plausible enough to create a reasonable doubt. Some may believe Kant's theory of noumenal causality and timeless agency is too farfetched to pass this test. Kant's reply to this sort of objection is quite clear, however. In matters of transcendent metaphysics, questions of conjecture or probable opinion never arise: "In this species of investigation, it is in no way allowed to hold *opinions*. Everything which looks like a hypothesis is a forbidden commodity; it should not be put up for sale even for the lowest price, but should be confiscated as soon as it is discovered" (Axiv). This case is unlike the typical

On the other hand, we are justified in expressing some discontent over the fact that the best theory Kant can come up with is one that involves such radical revisions in our conception of free agency. At any rate, this shortcoming makes it difficult to credit the advertisement frequently given for Kantian morality, that it is a moral philosophy faithfully representing the moral life as the ordinary agent experiences and lives it. As with many advertisements, this one calls our attention only to the more palatable and wholesome ingredients in the product, and carefully avoids listing the artificial ingredients with ugly names which, though necessary to keep the product from spoiling, may render it much less appealing.

Before we dismiss Kant's solution, we must take a long, sober look at his problem. The fact is that the free will problem is an old and intractable one. It is bound to be especially so for a strict determinist whose moral philosophy and moral psychology require as a condition of responsibility that I be capable of actions whose motivation lies altogether outside my natural, sensuous being.

Even those who do not face the free will problem in its Kantian form must confront the difficulties raised by more standard incompatibilists. We may doubt that any solution to these difficulties exists that does not force us to abandon common sense in some way, either to alter the moral judgments we make or to revise our commonsense conception of our agency. In the end, solving the free will problem may not be a matter of "saving common sense" (for that may be quite hopeless). Rather the solution may be a matter of saving as much of it as we can, and especially of saving those parts of it which matter most to us. I believe Kant saw the situation in this way, and I suggest we may assume that he decided that the temporality of our agency is the

---

court case in that there is no question here of deciding whose theory is the more probable. In matters of metaphysics, any theory which can be neither proven nor disproven with apodictic certainty must count as equally probable. If Kant's theory of the case cannot be strictly disproven, then the contentions of the opponent of freedom cannot be proven. Because the burden of proof is on the opponent of freedom in this case, it follows that the only verdict we can render is to acquit freedom of the charges brought against it.

necessary ransom that must be paid to the free will problem if our high vocation as moral agents is to be preserved.

Others, of course, may have different worries and priorities and may wish to negotiate a different settlement. Nonetheless, they should not suppose they can get something for nothing. Moreover, they should evaluate Kant's solution in terms of his own problem. From this standpoint, we may conclude that unless we are prepared to argue for the positive incoherence of certain doctrines which constitute Kant's theory of the case—doctrines about phenomena and noumena, about Humean causality in nature and Aristotelian causality outside it, or about timeless agency and its temporal effects—then we must judge Kant's compatibilism a success in solving the problem it sets itself.

Kant's Theory of Freedom

Jonathan Bennett

Great knowledge, skill, and judgment have gone into Allen Wood's extraction from Kant's texts, and partial defense, of a certain theory of freedom (see preceding essay). I shall later mention one respect in which I am not sure he has got Kant right, but otherwise the interpretation is flawless. I shall argue, however, that although it is worthwhile to identify Kant's theory of freedom as Wood has helped us to do, the theory itself is worthless. I shall not list the reasons that Wood anticipates being brought against the theory. I do have those too, being unconvinced that the concepts of noumenon and of timeless agency are really intelligible. When Kant says of a noumenon that "nothing happens in it" and yet that it "of itself begins its effects in the sensible world" (*B*569), he implies that there is a making-to-begin which is not a happening; and I cannot understand that as anything but a contradiction. Kant himself has trouble relating timeless choices to the temporal world. On the one hand, "at the point in time when I act, I am never free" (*KpV* 94g 98e); on the other, "In the moment when he utters the lie, the guilt is entirely his" (*B*583). Never mind. For present purpose I concede noumena, timeless agency, non-Humean causation—*the lot*. With all of that granted, the theory is still worthless.

According to the theory, a free choice by my intelligible character causes me to have empirical character E. How can this be so, if there is also a deterministic causal explanation for my possession of E? How can a free choice cause this part of the natural causal chain without breaking the chain? Wood answers on Kant's behalf that my intelligible choice causes not only my possession of E but also a complete natural causal history for my possession of E. Kant didn't ever actually say this but Wood thinks that Kant's theory "must" be construed in this way. I'm not sure that it must, but in the meantime I shall assume that it is.

One significant fact about my character E is that I have beliefs about the Holocaust. These beliefs were partly caused by the Holocaust. Does Kant's theory make me responsible for what was done to the Jews of Europe when I was a child? Not necessarily, says Wood. In his version of Kant's theory, what I am morally responsible for is not the actual causes of my having character E but rather "those events which *must* belong to the actual course of things because I have the empirical character...that I do" (italics added). The actual Holocaust does not satisfy that condition if I *could* have had those beliefs in a world in which they were false and there was no Holocaust. And similarly for every event that has helped to shape me and over which we would ordinarily say I had no control: perhaps each and every one of them is inessential to my having character E.

I shall not discuss that as it stands. Kant is not out of trouble here unless Wood's defense works not merely for events but also for states of affairs. We have to consider the set of possible worlds where I have character E, and ask whether there are any remotely past states of affairs which obtain—that is, propositions that are true—at all of them but not at all deterministic worlds whatsoever. One might think, for example, that in 1929 oxygen exists not in all deterministic worlds but in all the ones where I am born in 1930 with character E; and so by Kant's theory I am morally responsible for the presence of oxygen in the universe in 1929. Wood's defense must be to suppose that neither that nor any other prenatal state of affairs is causally required for my having character E: it was causally possible for me to burst onto the scene in 1930 *whatever* the scene was like before I arrived.

That makes the supposed choice of a causal history safe by

making it vacuous; and Wood seems to intend it to do so. But it makes other things vacuous as well, draining all the content out of the notion of causal order. The thesis that every possible prenatal state of affairs is causally compatible with my having character E would be merely silly unless it was based on the general thesis that every possible sequence of states of affairs falls under some set of causal laws. But that thesis is not available to Kant: it would make nonsense of, at least, his Second Analogy and of his inference from determinedness to predictability.

Wood appeals to our ignorance of "how our timeless choices operate on the temporal world," but that does not help. The theory is that our free choices result in some present states of affairs, and also that choosing a certain state of affairs involves choosing a complete deterministic causal history for it. From those two bits of the theory, and a proper understanding of determinism, it follows that we freely choose states of affairs that antedate our births. This is a *proof* that these so-called timeless free choices are nothing like exercises of moral responsibility, and thus that Kant's theory about them is worthless.

The foregoing tells against a version of Kant's theory for which there is no direct textual evidence. Perhaps Kant himself would try in some less fatal way to reconcile my empirical character's being naturally caused with my freely choosing to have it. That may be what he is doing when he describes as "an effect of intelligible causality" not *this causal chain* but "*this empirical causality*" ($B572$, italics added), suggesting that what I freely choose are not the causally interrelated items but rather the causal relation that links them. Wood quotes this passage, but I am not sure what he makes of it. He certainly does not remark that it might offer an alternative to his fatal solution to Kant's problem. I must admit that if it is an alternative solution I don't really understand it; still, it reminds us that Kant may have other things up his sleeve, so that we ought not to condemn his theory merely on the strength of Wood's rather creative version of it.

Here is a fresh proof that the theory is worthless. Never mind the natural causes of my having character E; let us simply consider what the theory says about my responsibility for my having E itself. Suppose that one fact about the kind of person I am is that I am insane. Wood quotes Kant as implying that in that case I cannot act autonomously, which must mean that my insanity is not a consequence of noumenal choice on my part (see preceding essay and *VM* 182). But Kant could not conceivably have grounds for saying that or, more generally, for supposing that the results of noumenal freedom come anywhere near to coinciding with the matters for which we regard ourselves as morally responsible. Even if we do not—as apparently Wood does not—hold Kant to his statement that "reason is present in all the actions of men at all times and under all circumstances" (*B*584), Kant still has no basis for distributing reason through the actions of men in a manner acceptable to us, for example, for denying that noumenal freedom shines brightest in the daily doings of small babies and schizophrenics. It is essential to his theory that nobody could possibly have grounds for any claim about what range of empirical facts is attributable to noumenal freedom— apart of course from claims based on the requirements of consistency.

From the fact that Kant associates noumenal freedom with "reason", one might infer that someone who manifestly cannot reason lacks noumenal freedom, but that inference would be mistaken. Kant does tie his theory to a contrast between "sensuous impulses" (*B*562) and "understanding and reason" (*B*574–75), but the former include every motivating episode that has natural causes, and the latter—understanding and reason—are described by Kant as faculties that "we distinguish ... from all empirically conditioned powers." The line he is drawing, then, does not cut through the empirically given facts; rather, it has all the given facts (including empirical-world reasoning) on one side and the dark noumenal theory (including otherworldly reasoning) on the other.

Wood doesn't dispute any of this. In face of it, he offers us the possibility that noumenal freedom has a scope that corresponds to what we ordinarily take to be the scope of moral responsibility. "It seems open to Kant," he says, "to suppose that [freely chosen events] correspond to those events for which we normally regard ourselves as morally responsible." This is backed by the observation that all Kant aims to establish is a possibility.

Wood is right to point out that sometimes Kant accepts the complete divorce of his theory from the world of human conduct as we experience it, and says that he wants to establish not even a real possibility but merely a lack of self-contradiction in our beliefs about freedom (*B*xxix, *B*586). But Kant is not candid about how many other beliefs about freedom are equally vindicated by his theory. For example, in the famous discussion of the malicious lie (*B*582–83), it is significant that he takes a *malicious* lie whose natural causes include "the viciousness of a natural disposition insensitive to shame," thus inclining us to agree that the lie's causes do not excuse the agent—"the guilt is entirely his." But Kant's theory allows us to pass that judgment not only in this case but also in one where the natural causes of the lie involve a profound psychopathology in someone who is not vicious and is greatly given to shame; and Kant's choice of example seems designed to help us to overlook that fact.

Even more striking are the places, not mentioned by Wood, where in the very act of declaring his theory's empirical emptiness Kant sneaks some content into it. For example, he says that because we don't know how much to attribute to noumenal freedom "the real morality of actions . . . remains entirely hidden from us" (*B*579n); but Kant doesn't mean this as radically as he ought to, for he adds that therefore "no perfectly just judgments can be passed" on anyone's empirical character. The suggestion that we can at least approximate to justice is something to which Kant is not entitled. A second example: Kant says that someone's "intelligible character can never be immediately known" and that it must "be *thought*" (*B*574). So far, so good, but there is more— the intelligible character must "be thought in accordance with [*gemäss*, in agreement with, by the measure of] the empirical character," which implies that we know something about how the empirical relates in detail to the noumenal. A third example of Kant's giving in one phrase what he takes away in the next is his saying that a person's intelligible character "is completely unknown" and then adding "save in so far as the empirical [character] serves for its sensible sign" (*B*574).

I do not dispute that insofar as Kant had a single doctrine about noumenal freedom it was the one Wood attributes to him, namely, that our beliefs about freedom do not logically conflict with determinism; that determinism should obtain and yet those beliefs be true is logically possible. But I protest that this kind of possibility is not worth establishing, as may be seen from the fact that endless other sets of opinions are also shown by Kant's theory of freedom to be possible—for example, that only madmen and babies are morally responsible—and the theory provides no means for adjudicating amongst the sets.

Lewis White Beck even questions whether this is a theory about "freedom" in our ordinary sense of the word. What the theory provides, he says, is "not what is meant by freedom in any interesting sense, because it is indiscriminately universal," his point being that it "seems to justify the concept of freedom, if anywhere, then everywhere."[1] Wood responds to this objection by setting aside Kant's "reason is always present" remark and offering a version of the theory which says nothing about the scope of noumenal freedom, thus allowing that freedom *could* be present in exactly the cases in which we intuitively think it is. That undercuts Beck's premise, but his conclusion still stands. As well as being silent about the scope of freedom, Kant's theory implies that we cannot have grounds for any specific opinion about what that scope is; and that fact debars it from being about 'freedom' in the ordinary sense just as would the theory's implying that most of our opinions about the scope of freedom are false.

Anyway, let us keep sight of the fact that although the Kantian theory says that our untutored opinions on freedom might be right, it offers no way in which that could be other than sheerly fortuitious—no suggestion about how the truth of those opinions might help to explain why we have them. In the absence of that, the possibility that they are true is of no interest.

So much for Kant's official central theory. Most of us have long thought it to be dead, and after Wood's restorative measures the corpse still refuses to stir. What remains to be considered is the thick detail of Kant's live thinking about freedom, and in conclusion I want to say a little about that. This is a matter on

---

[1]Lewis White Beck, *A Commentary on Kant's Critique of Practical Reason* (Chicago, 1960), p. 188.

which Wood and I disagree sharply. I see myself as turning from what is dead in Kant's writings to what is alive; as setting aside Kant's map and getting out into the countryside with him; but when I did that in *Kant's Dialectic* it convinced Wood—as he reported in his review of the book—that "Bennett is not really much interested in Kant's philosophy itself."[2] Wood's use of the phrase "Kant's philosophy itself" expresses a view about what we should be looking to Kant for, a view I believe is wrong. His own opinion notwithstanding, Kant was bad at grand theory construction. Where he was superb was in the informal discussions surrounding the theories: his sensitivity and subtlety of response to conceptual pressures and tensions make those discussions wonderfully instructive, though these same qualities lead him into intricacies and inconsistencies. In ignoring the latter, Wood ignores Kant's greatest strengths as a philosopher. Turning his back on what doesn't fit the large theoretical structure, which he calls "Kant's philosophy itself," he is turning away from the life in Kant's text in order to preside over a corpse.

In *Kant's Dialectic* I attended not only to Kant's official theory but also, more fully, to various hints and indications in his informal discussions. The following sketch outlines my strategy and contrasts it with Wood's approach in the preceding essay.

I agree with Kant: there *is* an apparent clash between a freedom thought and a determinism thought, and the two *are* reconcilable because of some difference in angle or level or standpoint. But I hold that there are two distinct clashes, and two reconciliations; and although Kant did not consciously notice this, the two show up very differently in his text, a fact that indicates his sensitivity to the difference between them.

One of the two conflicts concerns moral accountability, which surfaces in Kant's discussion when he speaks of blame and guilt and of what didn't happen but "ought to have" (*B*562, *B*578, *B*582–83). Most of us find that our propensity to blame can be made to look unfair by its being brought up hard against the hypothesis of determinism—and yet somehow most of us think

---

[2]Jonathan Bennett, *Kant's Dialectic* (Cambridge, Eng., 1974); Allen W. Wood, "Kant's Dialectic," *Canadian Journal of Philosophy* 5 (1976), 595–614, at 596.

that we would sometimes blame people even if we believed determinism were true. I find Kant valuable as a pointer to the acuteness of this problem and to the unacceptability of the standard shallow kind of compatibilism. In *Kant's Dialectic* I sketched a possible solution to this, based on P. F. Strawson's great essay, "Freedom and Resentment."[3] Here is the core of it. Start with the idea of my resentment of something you have done to me. Then consider a case in which you have done something I dislike, though not essentially because of how it affects me, and I hold it against you, adopting an attitude like resentment except that it lacks the essential reference to myself. This 'vicarious resentment', as it might be called, is blame. Strawson holds that all our praise- and blame-related responses to human conduct should be understood as developments from the more personal attitudes and feelings of gratitude and resentment. The nature of these personal 'reactive attitudes' and their role in our lives explain why they are inappropriate under some conditions, for example, why it is unsuitable to resent a baby's disturbance of one's sleep by its crying. That then lets us explain the various conditions under which praise and blame are inappropriate: if the conditions are not satisfied, what follows is not that *judgments* involved in praise and blame are false but rather that *feelings and attitudes* involved in praise and blame are inappropriate. These explanations have not the slightest tendency to imply that if determinism is true then all praise and blame is wrong, but Strawson puts us in a position to explain why determinism is often thought to be a threat to praise and blame. Here is how.[4] The personal reactive attitudes which are the home ground of praise and blame are, in large measure and for most people, in some sort of conflict with the objective attitude in which one seeks to gather the facts, to understand the situation, to discover the etiology of the behavior so as to alter its chances of recurring.

[3]Bennett, *Kant's Dialectic*, sections 66–67; P. F. Strawson, "Freedom and Resentment," in his *Freedom and Resentment and Other Essays* (London, 1974), pp. 1–25.
[4]I am relying partly on a development of Strawson's ideas in my "Accountability," in Z. van Straaten, ed., *Philosophical Subjects* (Oxford, 1980), pp. 18–47, especially pp. 25–28.

Gratitude for a gift, for instance, does not sit easily in the mind alongside an attitude of active inquiry into the gift's causal origins. Thus reactive attitudes are in conflict or tension with the frame of mind in which one so much as raises the question of an action's causal nature: it is not that determinism logically conflicts with blameworthiness, but rather that the raising of the question of determinism conflicts with the feelings and attitudes that go into blame and make it what it is. That also explains, less damagingly than is otherwise possible, why many people who think that if determinism is true then no one is blameworthy are also apt to think that if determinism is false then still no one is blameworthy.

This shares certain abstract features with Kant's theory of freedom: it is deep and systematic and does not accuse the incompatibilist of mere conceptual muddle; and it denies that a full treatment of blameworthiness can be given purely in terms of our perception of the given facts. The big difference between Strawson and Kant is that whereas Kant's theory ties blameworthiness to a thought of ungiven facts, Strawson's says that we must go outside all the facts and introduce a dimension of feeling.

It was Kant who taught me that there is a second prima facie conflict between freedom and determinism. Rather than blame for an action already performed by oneself or someone else, this conflict concerns practical deliberation by an agent wondering what to do. In a nutshell, deliberation involves viewing some questions about the future as radically open, while determinism seems to imply that they are all really closed. Kant presents this matter in a wonderful paragraph which says that "reason does not here follow the order of things as they present themselves in appearance, but frames for itself...an order of its own [and] presupposes that it can have causality in regard to all these actions" (*B*575–76).

Because this is an essentially first-person problem, it is in the context of it that Kant links the concept of noumenon to how "man knows himself" (*B*575). Also, because the problem is about future actions rather than past ones, it is here that Kant speaks of "imperatives" and of what "ought to be" (*B*575–76) rather than of what "ought to have happened."

In *Kant's Dialectic* I defended a treatment of this matter stemming from an insight of Ryle's.[5] Kant invites us to contrast (a) following the order of things as they present themselves with (b) framing for oneself an order of one's own and, as he sometimes says, acting under the idea of freedom. What *is* this contrast? What would it be to behave in that manner (a) from which Kant's theory of freedom is supposed to rescue us? The only clear, literal sense I can make of it is to suppose that (a) involves looking at one's future not as a deliberating and deciding agent but rather as a predicting self-observer who tries to work out what he will do by applying causal laws to his known present condition. Determinism threatens us with this by implying that there always is a sufficient basis for such a prediction, that is, that each of our actions was in principle susceptible of being soundly predicted in advance of its happening. We do not know enough actually to do this, of course, but we cannot be comfortable with the thought that our practical deliberations are a *pis aller*, that our status as deliberating agents is a pure product of ignorance. That is what Kant offers to rescue us from. He is saying that our deliberating stance is securely and deeply grounded, that it is not in danger—even in principle—of being swept aside by an inrush of knowledge of our structure and the laws that govern us.

If that is not what is involved in Kant's contrast between (a) and (b), then I do not know what is. I can find no clear alternative to it in his text or in the secondary literature.

If my interpretation is right, then Kant is right—or may very well be. As Ryle pointed out decades ago, the existence of facts about me that would warrant confident predictions about how I will act does not imply that it is possible, even in principle, that I should make such predictions. The facts on which a given prediction would have to be based might not be facts if I were thinking the prediction; and so there may be narrow limits on how much self-prediction it is *in principle* possible for me to do, whether or not determinism is true and however much knowledge I acquire.

[5]Bennett, *Kant's Dialectic*, sections 68–69; Gilbert Ryle, *The Concept of Mind* (London, 1949), p. 197.

Thus, we can unapologetically regard ourselves as *fully* entitled to approach our futures in a deliberating rather than a predicting manner. The thought "I can do this only because I am ignorant" can be dismissed as a scare story that is very likely false even if determinism is true. So a certain peculiarity in the notion of self-prediction serves as a barrier which—without invoking noumenalist metaphysics—prevents the determinist thought from conflicting with the deliberating agent's belief that some options are still 'open' in the sense that the decision amongst them must be approached in the deliberator's and not the predictor's way.

This again has significant points in common with Kant's theory. In particular, it performs a reconciliation by bringing in not only the viewpoint of the observer of the given facts but also another viewpoint; with the difference that I make it the viewpoint of the agent, not that of the thinker of the ungiven facts.

In my handling of these two problems—accountability and agency—Kant's contrast between the observer's point of view and the noumenal point of view is replaced by a pair of contrasts: one between the observer and the emotional responder, the other between the observer and the agent.[6] You may protest that this is mere word-play, and irrelevant to what is really going on in Kant's pages. I think otherwise: I think that by reading Kant dispassionately and thinking hard about what he says—including many of the little twists and turns of phrase—I have learned some philosophy that is not contained in the frozen object Wood calls "Kant's philosophy itself." I submit that this approach is better: it contributes more to learning the truth, avails itself more fully of the Kantian texts, and does more honor to the genius of their author.

[6]In an unpublished paper entitled "Freedom and Objectivity," which is to be part of a forthcoming book, Thomas Nagel also treats freedom as generating two problems, one about accountability and one about agency, and he treats Strawson as crucial to the former, and Ryle's self-prediction point as crucial to the latter. Nagel's insightful treatment of self-prediction finds in it a moral significance which I did not see there.

IV

Kant's Real Self

Patricia Kitcher

The theory of the self officially presented in the *Critique of Pure Reason* is profoundly unsatisfactory.[1] Kant claims that there are two selves. One, the "phenomenal self," is "passive," subject to natural laws and hence unfit to be the object of moral criticism. The real or "noumenal," self is completely unknown and unknowable. Kant seems to believe that the "two-selves" theory can solve, in a single stroke, both the problem of determinism and moral responsibility, and the problem of how knowledge of general truths is possible. In fact, this theory can resolve neither quandary. A noumenal, unknown self is an impossible target for moral criticism and it is at best unclear how we can know that an unknown self creates the formal characteristics of the phenomenal world.

Many commentators have noted that the two selves of the official theory are joined by a third self. This self enters Kant's system with the doctrine of the "transcendental unity of apperception." Because the primary attribute of the I of apperception is to think—it is "[the] I or he or it (the thing) which thinks" (*A346/B404*)—I will refer to this self as the thinking self. Given that the *Critique* is primarily a study in epistemology, it seems

[1]I am grateful to a number of people for probing criticisms and constructive suggestions, including Terence Irwin, Philip Kitcher, Hilary Kornblith, Ralf Meerbote, and especially Sydney Shoemaker.

obvious that the thinking self must be its central character. This interpretation immediately raises a number of difficult questions, however. What exactly is the doctrine of apperception? What is the relation between the thinking self and the two selves of the official theory? How does the introduction of the doctrine of apperception advance the project of defending the legitimacy of the categories? In an earlier paper I offered an interpretation of Kant's theory of the transcendental unity of apperception.[2] Here I shall extend that interpretation by showing how the doctrine of apperception, so understood, relates to the two-selves theory on the one hand, and to the deduction of the categories on the other. I begin with a brief summary of my account of apperception.

An Interpretation of the "Transcendental Unity of Apperception"

In "Kant on Self-Identity," I argued that the legitimate task of the so-called Subjective Deduction (Axvii) was to provide a characterization of the necessary properties of a subject of thought in response to Hume's attack on the idea of personal identity. I interpreted Hume's denial of any real or necessary connection among mental states as a denial of any relation of existential dependence among such states. This interpretation formed the background of my central thesis: Kant successfully meets Hume's challenge by showing that we cannot attribute mental states at all unless we acknowledge a relation of existential dependence among them.[3]

The crucial concept in Kant's reply to Hume is that of 'synthesis.' He introduces this concept with an explicit definition: "By *synthesis*, in its most general sense, I understand the act of putting different representations together, and of grasping what

---

[2]Patricia Kitcher, "Kant on Self-Identity," *Philosphical Review* 91 (January 1982), 41–72.

[3]Kitcher, "Kant on Self-Identity," section 5.

is manifold in them in one cognition" $(A77/B103)$.[4] When Kant speaks of "putting different representations together," he means that the "manifolds" of those representations, that is, the contents of the mental states, are combined in a further mental state. As Kant realized, token mental states occur at different times, so the states themselves are not literally put together. Kant expressed himself in this way to stress that the content of the resultant state is not merely similar to the contents of the earlier states, but is actually produced from the earlier states and their contents.

In light of this passage I offered a definition of 'synthesis' by building on a simpler notion:

Mental state M_1 and mental state M_2 are *synthesized*	$\underset{\text{def}}{=}$	There is some mental state M_3, such that, *ceteris paribus*, the content of M_3, and so M_3 itself, would not exist or would be different had M_1 and M_2 not existed or had different contents

When this situation obtains, we may say that M_3 is the "synthetic product" of M_1, M_2, or both. A general relation of synthesis among representations, or in modern terminology, mental states may then be defined:

M_1 and M_2 stand in the relation of *synthesis*	$\underset{\text{def}}{=}$	M_1 is the synthetic product of M_2, or M_2 is the synthetic product of M_1, or M_1 and M_2 are synthesized

Put more simply, the relation of synthesis among mental states is a relation of contentual dependence.[5]

[4] I have altered Kemp Smith's translation here, rendering "*in einer Erkenntnis*" as "in one cognition," in preference to "in one [act of] knowledge." Except where noted, I use Kemp Smith's translations throughout.
[5] Kitcher, "Kant on Self-Identity," section 4.

Having defined the notion of 'synthesis,' I used that account to clarify the doctrine of apperception. At a superficial level, the thesis of the transcendental unity of apperception claims that representations are impossible unless they can be attributed to a thinking self, an I that thinks (*A*116/*B*131). In the second edition of the *Critique*, Kant is quite explicit about what the relation of belonging to a self involves: "That relation [belonging to an identical subject] comes about, not simply through my accompanying each representation with consciousness, but only in so far as I *conjoin* one representation with another . . . Synthetic unity of the manifold of intuitions, as given *a priori*, is thus the ground of the identity of apperception itself" (*B*133, *B*134 Kant's emphasis). The point is even clearer at *B*135: "[I call all my representations 'mine'.] This amounts to saying that I am conscious to myself *a priori* of a necessary synthesis of representations—to be entitled the original synthetic unity of apperception."

If being attributed to an I that thinks amounts to being recognized as belonging to a contentually interconnected group of representations, why are representations impossible if this attribution cannot be made? A representation that is not part of a contentually interconnected group of representations would not represent anything (*A*116). While Kant offers some explicit argumentation in favor of this claim, the crucial support for it does not come from arguments, but from his improved understanding of mental states. Unlike his predecessors, Kant does not think of the mental states that precede or accompany overt or silent judgments—"judgmental states"—as representing states of affairs through resembling them. Rather, a judgmental state has content, is about a state of affairs, in virtue of "comprehending" other mental states under it, that is, because it is the synthetic product of other states, which are directly produced by the object (*A*68–69/*B*93–94). Those directly produced states, Kant's "intuitions," are mental states, states of a cognitive being qua cognitive being, not because they resemble judgmental states, but because they are synthetic progenitors of judgmental states. Thus, I read Kant as claiming that thoughts without content are not really thoughts; intuitions without concepts are not really intuitions.[6]

To sum up, I interpret Kant's doctrine of apperception as follows: contra Hume's denial of a relation of existential dependence among mental states, Kant argues that all representations, which are possible as representations, must be regarded as belonging to a contentually interconnected system of mental states—an I that thinks. Before considering the status of this thinking I, it is important to note a serious deficiency in Kant's account. Kant equates standing in the relation of synthesis with being states of the same thinking self: the former relation is both a necessary (*A*118) and a sufficient (*B*134) condition for the latter. However, if synthesis is only a general relation of contentual dependence, the contents of the later states being produced as a result of the information contained in earlier states, then it is plainly not a sufficient condition for comentality as pretheoretically understood. If a critic were to claim that my interpretation ignores fifteen crucial passages, then some of my later mental states would be dependent on the observations and ruminations that produced that judgment. Moreover, the relation of synthesis probably is not a necessary condition for comentality either. Seemingly, not all my previous mental states participate in the fashioning of succeeding states, although perhaps it must be possible for them to do so, if they are all states of one mind.[7]

Kant is able to offer only a partial characterization of a thinking self. To complete his task, he would need to specify a more

[6]This interpretation may be controversial. I base it on two points. In a number of places, Kant says that intuitions are nothing to us unless we can be conscious of them (for example, *A*117a, *A*120). I take Kant to hold that we are conscious of a mental state if and only if we can make judgments about it. Hence, any intuition that is anything to us must lead to a judgment. Second, at *A*116 Kant writes: "Intuitions are nothing to us, and do not in the least concern us if they cannot be taken up into consciousness, in which they may participate [*einfliessen*] either directly or indirectly." I read this passage as claiming that an intuition is nothing to us as cognitive beings unless one of two conditions is met: (a) it directly participates in consciousness, that is, it is the subject of a conscious judgment; or (b) it indirectly participates in a judgment, that is, it contributes some input to the judgment. In either case, the intuition is the progenitor of a judgment.

[7]For a very interesting denial of this view, see Jerry A. Fodor, *The Modularity of Mind* (Cambridge, Mass., 1983)

precise relation of informational interdependence which would enable him to demarcate one mental system from another. Kant does not have a more specific relation to offer and, so far as I know, neither do we. When Kant equates the relation of synthesis with the relation of comentality, he intends 'synthesis' to refer to the precise relation of informational interconnection which holds among the states of one mind, or thinking self (see $B$135). There is nothing wrong with using 'synthesis' to refer to a relation that he can characterize only partially. The problem is that this additional usage renders 'synthesis' dangerously ambiguous. Further, on this second usage, Kant is in no position to argue that acknowledging a relation of 'synthesis' among mental states is a necessary condition for the possibility of experience, simply because he cannot even characterize this relation. It is Kant's ambigous usage that enables him to move from his understanding of the nature of mental states to the doctrine that the specific concept of a thinking self is a necessary concept for experience, rather than to a vaguer doctrine about the generic concept of a mental system. Having acknowledged this error, I will usually ignore it, except when explicitly evaluating Kant's contribution to our understanding of the mental.

According to Kant's doctrine of apperception, we must acknowledge the existence of a thinking self in that we recognize that all representations, which are possible as representations, must be regarded as belonging to a contentually interconnected system of mental states. In effect, Kant has offered a transcendental deduction of the concept 'I think'.[8] His reflections on the nature of mental states show that we can acknowlege something to be a mental state only if we acknowledge the existence of, not a mere bundle, but a synthetically connected set of mental states. For Kant, one is having experience only if one is making judgments. For his predecessors and antagonists, we must begin with the assumption that our judgments are about only our own mental states. Hence, Kant has shown that experience is possible only

---

[8]Kant does not explicitly claim that he has established that 'I think' is a necessary concept through a transcendental deduction, but he does say explicitly that the representation 'I think' has categorical status at $A$341/$B$399.

if we have and employ the concept 'I think'. When Kant speaks of "transcendental apperception" or the "transcendental unity of apperception," he is not referring to a mysterious type of self-awareness, a nonoptical look at the self even more rarefied than those allegedly performed by Descartes.[9] Rather, he is indicating that our acknowledgment of this self, the thinking self, has a special epistemological status. It has been shown to be a necessary condition for the possiblity of experience. (For this meaning of 'transcendental,' see, for example, *A*93–94/*B*126.)

Besides synthetic interconnection, Kant tries to carry out the project of the "subjective" aspect of the Deduction by finding other necessary features of a pure understanding (*A*xvii). He claims that an understanding such as ours must classify the contents of intuitions by rules (for example, *A*105); that such an understanding must be accompanied by a "productive" and not merely a "reproductive" imagination (*A*118) and that such an understanding must employ the concept of a "transcendental object" (*A*108–109). Although Kant has been roundly criticized for indulging in armchair psychology, his project is very like that of some contemporary researchers in Artificial Intelligence. Basically, Kant is trying to discover the necessary features of any thinking being relevantly like us (for example, temporal, possessing finite cognitive powers). Similarly, at least some Artificial Intelligence researchers seek to propound general theses about cognitive devices. For example, any cognitive device must have a component that generates hypotheses.[10] It would be interesting

---

[9]Kant does sometimes claim that we do observe particular acts of the self: acts of synthesis. In a passage Dieter Henrich takes as the foundation for his study of the Transcendental Deduction, *A*108, Kant says explicitly that we observe such acts and that it is only because we observe such acts that we know the identity of the self (see Henrich's *Identität und Objectivität: Eine Untersuchung über Kants transzendentale Deduktion* [Heidelberg, 1976], pp. 81ff). Despite the strong textual evidence, I do not regard this as Kant's considered view, because he retreats from this claim almost as often as he makes it. See *A*103/*B*134.

[10]Daniel Dennett points out the similarity between Kant's goals and the goals of some contemporary Artificial Intelligence researchers in "Artificial Intelligence as Philosophy and as Psychology," in *Brainstorms* (Montgomery, Vt., 1978), pp. 109–126, especially pp. 111, 112. Of course, there are salient differences between Kant's project and contemporary work in Artificial Intelligence as well. Most importantly, Kant believed that he had an infallible method for determining

to determine whether Kant is right in recanting most of his specific claims about the properties of thinking beings, but my concern here is with the status that the I of apperception, the thinking self, and its properties are supposed to enjoy.

That status is both complicated and confused. As we have already seen, the doctrine of apperception is a transcendental claim; 'I think' is a "transcendental" concept (for example, $A341/B399$); and the thinking thing is a "transcendental subject of thought" ($A346/B404$). Yet, in the second edition of the *Critique*, Kant describes the thesis of apperception as "empirical," because it imputes existence ($B157a$ and $B422a$). Still, Kant can avoid contradiction because although 'transcendental' and 'empirical' are contrastive terms on two of Kant's uses, where 'transcendental' means 'beyond experience' ($A296/B351$) and 'empirical' means 'within experience,' or where 'empirical' means 'based on experience' and 'transcendental' means 'not based on experience,' there are senses which make the descriptions compatible. 'I think' is an empirical claim, because it imputes existence; it is a transcendental claim, because the acknowledgment of this claim is a necessary condition for the possibility of experience.

On my interpretation of the doctrine of apperception, the thinking I must be phenomenal.[11] For the relation of contentual interconnection holds among mental states, which are themselves phenomenal. Further, in light of that interpretation, 'the transcendental unity of apperception [self-recognition]' would be more perspicuously labeled 'the transcendental recognition of the unity of the self.' This thesis concerns the special epistemological status of the synthetic interconnection of mental states,

---

the necessary properties of thinking beings, namely, the transcendental deduction. By contrast, contemporary researchers are well aware that their hypotheses about the necessary properties of thinking machines are subject to disproof. Still, there is an important methodological bond linking Kant and the artificial intelligentsia: both abjure the attempt to discover how our minds in fact operate in favor of a more abstract description of how any thinking being, within certain parameters, would have to solve certain problems. Further, both operate with a sufficiently impoverished notion of empirical research that they tend to describe their own inquiries as "a priori." (I am grateful to Larry Laudan for leading me to clarify this point.)

[11] I am grateful to Terence Irwin and Ralf Meerbote for making this point clear to me.

so it must fall on the phenomenal side of the phenomenal/nou-menal divide.[12] Just as the arguments of the Principles chapter must be intended to establish the existence of, for example, phenomenal causes and substances, the argumentation I have reviewed from the Subjective Deduction can only be intended to show that a phenomenal thinking self must exist. Assigning the thinking self a phenomenal status is perfectly consistent with the claims that the doctrine of apperception is both 'transcen-dental' and 'empirical,' in the senses just explained. Again, (if Kant is right) the principle of cause and effect is a transcendental claim (*A202/B247*), yet it is also an empirical claim, because, for any event, it posits the existence of some cause (*A178ff/B221ff*), yet causes and effects are phenomenal.

Nevertheless, my interpretation of the doctrine of appercep-tion must overcome a severe obstacle. The problem is that when Kant squarely faces the issue of the status of the I of appercep-tion, his considered opinion is that the thinking self is not phe-nomenal. Early in the B version of the Paralogisms chapter, Kant clearly implies that thinking beings are noumenal (*B409–410*). Later in the same chapter, he claims that the 'I think' is neither appearance, nor thing in itself (*B423a*; see also *B157*). Although these passages are individually perplexing and mutually incon-sistent, they agree in denying a phenomenal status for thinking selves. To defend my interpretation of the central message of the Subjective Deduction, I will argue for two theses: first, even though Kant had reasons for rejecting a merely phenomenal thinking I, they were not good reasons; second, Kant's reasons for denying a phenomenal status to the thinker were completely independent of the theory of apperception itself. If both these claims can be established, then it is legitimate for an interpre-tation of the doctrine of apperception to dismiss the factors that led Kant to claim noumenal status for thinkers; we may pursue instead the clear implication of the Subjective Deduction that the thinking self is phenomenal.

---

[12]I provide further reasons for assigning a phenomenal status to this thesis in a later section.

Patricia Kitcher

The Thinking Self and the
Phenomenal/Noumenal Distinction

Three different aspects of Kant's philosophy commit him to regarding the I of apperception as noumenal, or at least as non-phenomenal: his views about morality and the possibility of salvation, his claim that the constitution of a thinking thing is unknowable in principle, and his construal of phenomenal properties as unreal. I list these factors in order of the increasing difficulty of separating what I will claim is an extraneous doctrine from the doctrine of apperception. I will tackle the issues in order.

Among its other roles, the first *Critique* is supposed to serve as a prolegomenon to the later *Critiques*. Its most important task is to establish the possibility that we possess the freedom required for morality (for example, *B*xxvii ff). But who is this 'we,' or better, who are these 'I's' whose possible freedom is to be demonstrated? Partly by fiat and partly by trading on his ambiguous usage of 'spontaneity' to refer to both the relative spontaneity manifested by thought (*A*51/*B*75) and the absolute spontaneity required for transcendental freedom (*A*446/*B*474), Kant identifies the real self whose moral status and future life are in question with the thinking self. (For the trade see *A*546–47/*B*574–75 and *B*158a, see also *A*342/*B*400; *B*415; *B*424ff; and especially *A*365.) Given this identification, Kant must deny that the thinking self is phenomenal, because the actions of a phenomenal self would be causally determined (*A*545/*B*573). It is a familiar point that Kant does not really want to distinguish between two separate beings, a phenomenal self and a noumenal self.[13] So, it would be truer to Kant's intentions to say that he must deny that the doctrine of apperception concerns the self under its phenomenal aspect. This maneuver cannot relieve Kant's problem with the status of the unity of apperception, however. We know

[13]This point is made forcefully by, among others, Erich Adickes, *Kants Lehre von der Doppelten Affektion unseres Ich als Schlüssel zu seiner Erkenntnistheorie* (Tübingen, 1929), p. 3, and Karl Ameriks, *Kant's Theory of Mind* (Oxford, 1982), p. 266.

that all possible representations must belong to the unity of apperception; indeed, the principle of apperception is the "first pure knowledge of understanding" (*B*137). If it is a known fact that all representations must be united in one I that thinks, then this fact must be known through the categories and the doctrine of apperception must present a phenomenal aspect of the self (see, for example, *A*248–49). Kant is caught in a contradiction between two tenets of his system that he cannot renounce: our real self is possibly free, and any known fact is known through the categories and hence phenomenal.

Kant appreciated this difficulty and tried to extricate himself from it in a long footnote to the Paralogisms chapter cited earlier (*B*422–23a). The thinking self cannot be phenomenal (because it would be causally determined), and the doctrine of apperception cannot be about a noumenal self, because this doctrine is known, so the I of apperception is ". . . given, given indeed to thought in general, and so not as appearance, nor as thing in itself (*noumenon*), but as something which actually exists, and which in the proposition, 'I think', is denoted as such" (cf. *B*157). But this solution is unavailing: 'existence' is a category. Kant applies another bandaid: "the existence here [referred to] is not a category" (*B*423a). By his own or any other standards, Kant passes beyond the bounds of intelligibility at this point. It is totally unclear what the claim that the thinking I exists is to mean.

I have presented this passage, not to berate Kant for failing to resolve a hopeless contradiction, but to establish that he himself recognizes that his doctrine of apperception clearly implies a phenomenal character for the thinking self. My other point is that the dilemma Kant tries to finesse in this passage does not arise from within his theory of apperception, but from a conflict between the doctrine of apperception and his beliefs about the prerequisites for morality. I think it is unquestionable that Kant would regard this conflict as a compelling reason for denying the I of apperception a phenomenal status. Most contemporary philosophers reject Kant's incompatibilism, however.[14] So without

[14]Of course, there are notable exceptions, including Allen Wood. See his essay in chapter 3, this volume.

paying the exorbitant price of denying our moral status, we may accept Kant's arguments for a phenomenal transcendental empirical (that is, existing) I of apperception.

The direct conflict between Kant's moral goals in the *Critique* and the view that thinking I's are phenomenal probably supplied most of the actual motivation for this denial of the latter claim. Still, Kant draws on a number of diverse elements in his philosophy to marshal the case against a phenomenal thinker. In the more cautious negative sense of the term, 'noumenon' indicates "a thing so far as it is *not an object of our sensible intuition*" (*B*307, Kant's emphasis). Kant claims repeatedly that the thinking self is not and cannot be an object of sensible intuition; thus, it cannot be known (see *B*158; *A*350; *A*400; *B*422); thus, it must be noumenal (*B*409). The conclusion that the I that thinks cannot be known is supported by four considerations of different degrees of reasonableness. First, like Hume, Kant believes that we do not introspect a thinking self through our power of inner sense (*A*107). Second, Kant believes that outer sense is incapable of divulging a thinking being (*A*357). Because we possess only two types of intuition, inner and outer, it would seem to follow that the thinking self cannot be intuited by us at all. This argument is terribly weak, however. Kant's assertion that the properties that outer sense can capture—extension, impenetrability, cohesion, and motion—"neither are nor contain thoughts, feeling, desire, or resolution" (*A*358) seems to be based on nothing more than a revulsion to materialism.[15] In any event, because a thinking self can be realized in matter—a central nervous system, for example—Kant is simply wrong that we cannot perceive a thinking thing through outer sense.

Further, Kant misrepresents the epistemological access to the thinker provided by inner sense. Even though we do not introspect a continuing subject of thoughts, we might infer the existence of a continuing thinker from the mental states with which we are presented. In fact, the doctrine of the transcendental unity of apperception declares that we must make this

[15]Karl Ameriks details Kant's antimaterialism in *Kant's Theory of Mind*, chapter 2.

inference if we are to recognize mental states as such. Kant states that "whatever is connected with perception in accordance with empirical laws is actual, even although it is not immediately perceived" (*A*231/*B*284, cf. *A*226/*B*273). If this position is combined with the view that empirical laws are "special determinations of still higher laws" (*A*126), namely transcendental principles, then Kant should be committed to maintaining "*a fortiori,* whatever is connected with perception in accordance with transcendental principles is actual."[16] And, of course, Kant does maintain that we must acknowledge the existence of the I of apperception. The simple argument presented earlier is based on the assumption that we cannot infer the existence of things beyond our observations, a position Kant himself explicitly rejects. He is able to reach the conclusion he wants, that we have no knowledge of the thinker either "through awareness or through reasoning" (*A*355, my translation), only by failing to apply his general epistemological principles to this case. I conclude that Kant's observations about inner and outer sense should not have led him to believe that thinking I's are unknowable.

The third consideration Kant raises in the service of establishing the unknowability thesis is sound, but it does not deliver the conclusion. In a paper on the Paralogisms chapter, I argued that the fundamental insight of Kant's critique of rational psychology is that his own analyses of the necessary properties of any system of mental states cannot tell us the composition of such systems.[17] That is, Kant realized that his highly abstract descriptions of the thinking self were incapable of providing any clues about the constitution of the self. This is an important insight. In contemporary discussions of cognitive psychology and Artificial Intelligence, this notion is often presented as the slogan "function does not determine form." Although Kant's observation is true and important, it shows only that "*from this source,* [namely, an investigation of the necessary properties of thinking

---

[16]Of course, Kant denies that there are any laws of psychology at *MN* 471g 8e. But, given that the principle of apperception is transcendental, this move is futile.

[17]Patricia Kitcher, "Kant's Paralogisms," *Philosophical Review* 91 (October 1982), 515–47.

beings] we learn nothing whatsoever as to what may happen to the soul in changes of the natural world" (*A*401, italics added). It does not follow that we can know nothing at all about our real selves, for abstract properties are still properties. And, it does not follow that we cannot learn anything about the self's constitution from some other source. This essential teaching of the Paralogisms chapter does not entitle Kant to claim, as he does throughout the chapter, that "we do not have, and cannot have, any knowledge whatsoever of any such subject [of thought]" (*A*350).

Finally, Kant sometimes claims that knowledge is somehow irreflexive, that the knower cannot be known. Here are two versions of this line of thought: (a) "the thinking 'I' . . . does *not* know *itself through the categories*, but knows the categories, and through them all objects, in the absolute unity of apperception, and so *through* itself. Now it is, indeed, very evident that I cannot know as an object that which I must presuppose in order to know any object" (*A*401–402, Kant's emphasis); (b) "the subject of the categories cannot by thinking the categories acquire a concept of itself as an object of the categories. For in order to think them, its pure self-consciousness, which is what was to be explained, must itself be presupposed" (*B*422; cf. *A*366, *A*346/*B*404). As far as I can tell, Kant is simply confusing the order of proof with what we might call the order of conceivability. The principle of apperception is the highest principle of Kant's philosophy, so we could not know that principle through the categories, in the sense that we could not derive the principle from the doctrine of the categories. This would be backwards or circular, because the deduction of the categories depends on the principle of apperception. None of this implies that we do not use the categories in thinking about thinking, however. In fact, if Kant is right, then we must use the categories in thinking about thinking, because the only way we can think at all is through the categories. Unless Kant is willing to allow the doctrine of apperception to transgress his own bounds of intelligibility, he should abandon this reason for claiming that the subject of thought is unknowable.

Thus far, I have suggested that Kant has a motive for denying the phenomenality of the thinking self, the conflict between this doctrine and his fundamental beliefs about morality, and that he had a rationale for rejecting a phenomenal thinker, various arguments designed to prove that the thinking self is unknowable. I have also argued that none of these considerations warrant his denial of a phenomenal status for thinkers. It is fairly clear that most of these objections are independent of the theory of apperception; in the one case in which there is a connection, the fundamental teaching of the Paralogisms chapter, Kant's argument does not support the desired conclusion. Let us now turn to a much more difficult issue. On first reflection, the role played by the thinking self in the doctrine of transcendental idealism would seem to require that the thinker not be phenomenal.[18] In P. F. Strawson's classic analysis of the "two sides" of the *Critique*, he presents the darker, psychological side as advocating the view that the thinking self actually produces the phenomenal character of experience.[19] Strawson castigates Kant for indulging in the "imaginary subject of transcendental psychology" (*PFS* 32, 97), wherein he describes how the mind imposes certain features on the world of experience, features that are therefore invariant across all possible experiences. The apparent difficulty for my interpretation of the doctrine of apperception is that if the thinker is the source of the phenomenal character of experience, then seemingly that being cannot itself be phenomenal. Further, if we grant, as I think we must, that the doctrine of apperception is intimately related to the role of the I in transcendental idealism, then this objection to classifying the thinker as phenomenal would come from within the theory of apperception.

Despite its initial plausibility, this line of reasoning is ultimately mistaken, because a phenomenal thinker can carry out the reasonable tasks assigned to the self by transcendental idealism. Setting aside the "good" side of transcendental idealism, which analyzes the concept of a possible experience (*PFS* 117), I will take issue with Strawson's characterization of the "subjective,"

[18]I am grateful to Sydney Shoemaker for goading me into tackling this issue.
[19]P. F. Strawson, *The Bounds of Sense* (London, 1966), pp. 112–13, 22. This book is referred to here as *PFS*, with page numbers.

"questionable," and "incoherent" side, the theory of transcendental psychology. Strawson understands transcendental psychology in terms of the "mind determination" thesis, the claim that synthetic a priori principles are true throughout the world we experience because of the structure of our minds. The textual evidence for the mind determination thesis is decisive (see, for example, A126; A127; B164). Nevertheless, I have presented a very different interpretation of transcendental psychology, as the investigation of the necessary properties of any cognitive being relevantly like us. Because of its affinities with contemporary projects in Artificial Intelligence and cognitive psychology, I will call this the "functional interpretation." This reading is also firmly grounded in the text (see, for example, Axvi–vii; A102; A116; B138). Luckily, we do not have to choose between two well-supported interpretations, because the project I describe as 'transcendental psychology' and (part of) the project Strawson places under that rubric are related.

Strawson regards the central argument for transcendental idealism as proceeding by a "*non sequitur* of numbing grossness," to borrow a phrase he uses elsewhere. The sound argumentative strategy of the *Critique* is to analyze the necessary features of any possible experience, "[But] wherever he [Kant] found limiting or necessary general features of experience, he declared their source to lie in our own cognitive constitution" (*PFS* 15). Again, "[for Kant] whatever is a *necessary* feature of experience is so because of the *subjectivity* of its source" (*PFS* 115). The only explanation Strawson provides for this apparent blunder is that Kant was in the grips of a misleading analogy. It is common knowledge that the way things appear to us depends in part on the constitution of our sense organs. So Kant was led to think of the structure of objective reality itself as partially determined by the nature of our minds. This picture is fundamentally flawed, however, because "the workings of the human perceptual mechanisms . . . are matters for empirical, or scientific, not philosophical investigation" (*PFS* 15). Such an investigation could never establish necessary principles.

Suppose we take Kant at his word, however, and assume that one project of the Transcendental Deduction is to characterize

the features of a *cognitive being* that are necessary for the possibility of experience (*A*xvi–vii). As we have already seen, one
psychological attribute thus necessary is that mental states stand
in the relation of synthesis to other mental states. In particular,
judgmental states must be produced by the combining of information from earlier states. With this outcome of the inquiry I
describe as 'transcendental psychology', we can justify a weak
mind determination thesis. Given Kant's doctrine of the necessary synthesis of mental states, we may think of the contents of
later states as a function of the contents of preceding states. Even
if the function, or one of the functions, were identity, it would
still follow that the content of the resultant state is what it is
because of the content of the earlier state(s) and because of the
nature of the function involved (see *A*68/*B*93; *A*77; *B*107; and
especially *B*150). Further, this inference is no psychological gen-
eralization, but a point of logic. If a functionally interpreted
transcendental psychology is able to generate richer results,
showing that specific ways of synthesizing information are necessary for the possibility of experience, then this method would
support a stronger mind determination thesis. Let us assume,
for example, that any possible experience must include judgmental states produced by A functions, B functions, and C functions.[20] Then certain principles, those described by the functions,
will be true throughout the world of our experience because of
the 'structure of our minds' in the following sense: sensory information which could not be synthesized by the A, B, and C
functions could not be brought to judgment and so could not
be part of our experience (*A*119; *A*122). The world of our experience would reflect the structure of our minds—more precisely, the necessary synthesizing functions—because these
functions would act as a filter, screening out possible collections
of data to which they cannot be applied. Given these results,

[20]There are a number of ways of interpreting the claim that certain syntheses
are necessary to judgmental experience. For example, one could advocate the
claim that these syntheses are all involved in every judgment. In the text, I am
presupposing what seems to me the most reasonable interpretation, namely, that
the categories must find expression not in every judgment, but in any possible
collection of judgments. Cf. Jonathan Bennett's discussion in *Kant's Analytic*
(Cambridge, Eng., 1966), p. 81.

Kant could legitimately claim that the "form" of experience is partially determined by the necessary syntheses of our minds.

Thus, the shocking lacuna Strawson sees at the heart of the argument for transcendental idealism is just not there. Kant sets out to discover the properties of thinking beings that are necessary for the possibility of experience; given his results he may rightly claim that in a certain sense the mind determines the form of our experience. My interpretation of transcendental psychology and Strawson's stand in the following relation: the *project* of transcendental psychology is to discover the necessary properties of thinking beings; the *result* of this study is the mind determination thesis. In other words, transcendental psychology, on my reading, is what supplies the principle argument for the mind determination thesis. (Strawson may mean more by the mind determination thesis than the claims that the contents of the judgmental states inevitably reflect functions of synthesis and that necessary syntheses affect the form of experience in the guise of filters. Specifically, he could reasonably attribute a superaddition thesis to Kant: the mind determines the form of experience by adding material to the raw sensory data. This type of mind determination thesis is not justified by transcendental psychology. I will discuss superaddition at some length later.)

Thus far, transcendental psychology seems to be a reasonable inquiry that yields reasonable results. As this inquiry is carried out in the *A* Deduction and in most of the *B* Deduction, I believe Kant is engaged in a sound and noteworthy philosophical undertaking. The execution is certainly flawed in its details. Kant frequently changes his mind about which syntheses are necessary to the possibility of experience. Further, at points, he seems completely convinced that any thinker must operate with the concept of a 'transcendental object', that is, with the idea that different representations that are to represent a common object must possess a certain unity and coherence (for example, A104). Yet this doctrine seems to be abandoned in the second edition, perhaps because Kant realized that it did not contribute to the deduction of the categories. Particular mistakes aside, however, there is nothing in Kant's practice of transcendental psychology in the Transcendental Deductions to invite Strawson's charge of incoherence. Kant falters only when he tries to characterize his results and when he tries to defend his view of the self in response to criticisms.

We have already encountered the objection. If everything must be thought through the categories, then the thinking self itself must be thought through the categories, and so it must be phenomenal. As noted earlier, when Kant tackles this issue head on, he tries to finesse it. He avers that the self whose states appear to us in inner sense is phenomenal, but the I of apperception is neither appearance, nor noumenon (B156–57). This view is incoherent, because the doctrine of apperception can proclaim the necessity of synthetic interconnection only among the mental states that appear to us in inner sense. Hence, the aspect of the self it discloses must also be phenomenal. It is crucial to realize, however, that nothing we have seen so far in transcendental psychology forces Kant to adopt this impossible position. He could simply admit the consequences of the doctrine of apperception: This theory declares that all of our judgments, from the barest notings of appearances to the most sophisticated scientific judgments, reflect the functions by which we synthesize information, so it implies that the theory of apperception itself reflects the structure of our thought processes. Why is Kant willing to risk incoherence rather than accept this line? We have already seen that he has a very powerful ulterior motive for denying the phenomenality of the thinking self. In this passage, difficulties from within the theory of transcendental idealism provide reasons for resisting the implication that the thinker is phenomenal. Kant's discussion reveals the untoward consequence of the phenomenality thesis that he wants to avoid: "my existence is not indeed appearance (still less mere illusion)" (B157). The problem is that Kant often presents the theory of transcendental idealism as maintaining that the phenomenal world is a sham, phenomenal properties are counterfeit. If the thinker is phenomenal, and if transcendental idealism is given the 'phenomenal equals fake' reading, then transcendental psychology, transcendental idealism, and the doctrine of apperception all collapse into incoherence. Worse still, the thinking selves we all identify as our real selves, whose moral status and potential immortality matters, turn out to be mere illusions.

Kant's reluctance to embrace these implications is hardly a source of wonder. But does he really have to make what can only be a subjective choice between two brands of incoherence? The choice is forced only if he must accept the 'phenomenal equals fake' interpretation of transcendental idealism. In fact, Kant's realist scruples never permit him to endorse this interpretation completely. He does have strong reasons for inclining toward the falsity of the phenomenal, however. Like other natural phenomena, the self appears to us to be governed by causal laws ($A546/B574$). Because the same individual cannot both be determined by causal laws and be free of causal determination, Kant has a choice. He can either opt for the ontological distinctness of phenomenal and real selves, which he does not really want to do (Bxxvii, $A546/B574$), or he can reject our apparent causal determination as illusory. Given the strength of his commitment to his moral enterprise and his unquestioned acceptance of incompatibilism, Kant is condemned to shuttle between these equally unattractive readings of transcendental idealism. However, despite its influence on Kant, this reason for interpreting transcendental idealism as entailing the falseness of the phenomenal is neither compelling, nor intrinsic to the doctrine.

Strawson notes another source of support for this interpretation. It is very easy to read the theory of the Aesthetic as proclaiming the falsity of space and time, as the popularity of the colored spectacles analogy attests. Besides other passages, Kant's opening description of the form and matter of appearance encourages this simple picture ($A20/B34$). The falsity of the categories of the understanding would follow by analogy, and by more than analogy. In a somewhat puzzling footnote to the second edition Deduction ($B160a$), Kant suggests that the spatial and temporal organization of appearance is itself a function of the functions of synthesis. Thus, if space and time are unreal, then the organization produced by the functions of synthesis would be unreal (*PFS* 112–13).

I suspect Strawson may be right in believing that Kant was

occasionally beguiled by the simple colored spectacles picture of the Aesthetic and that this inclined him to adopt an analogous picture of the Analytic. None of this provides a reason for thinking that the functions by which information is synthesized superadd counterfeit properties to the world of appearance, however. It is simply not clear that the doctrine of the Aesthetic requires that space and time are, at bottom, illusions. Even if this were true, however, from a logical point of view it would be irrelevant to Kant's theory of apperception and the necessary functions of synthesis. The claim that our sensory apparatus superadds spatial and temporal properties to the world of appearance either single-handedly, or with the aid of some particular functions of the understanding, neither entails nor is entailed by the transcendental idealism of the Analytic, which asserts only that anything that is thought at all must be the product of function(s) of synthesis. Hence, considerations based on the status of space and time are independent of the role played by the doctrine of apperception in transcendental idealism. So far, we have not found anything in this role that requires the 'phenomenal equals fake' interpretation and so rules out the possibility of a phenomenal thinker.

Let me add a final note about Strawson's use of the unreality of space and time reading. This reading is a crucial element in his portrayal of transcendental psychology as a thoroughly silly enterprise: because the thinker is not phenomenal, the thinker is not temporal, so the syntheses described by transcendental psychology are the "activities" of an atemporal being, and "interactions" between incoming information and the functions of synthesis are not causal (*PFS* 97, 236–39). If my earlier argument is correct, then Strawson's portrait is not only unflattering but unfair. The transcendental psychology of the Subjective Deduction is not committed to denying the reality of spatial and temporal properties.

Kant may have had deeper reasons for believing that he had to accommodate the 'phenomenal equals fake' interpretation, reasons tied to the basic project of the Analytic. Of course, that project is to show how synthetic a priori judgments are possible. Kant states his goal rather precisely in summation:

> Pure understanding is therefore in the categories the law of the
> synthetic unity of all appearances, and thereby originally and as
> prerequisite makes experience possible as regards its form. This is
> all that we were called upon to establish in the transcendental de-
> duction of the categories, namely, to render comprehensible this
> relation of understanding to sensibility, and, by means of sensibility
> to all objects of experience. The objective validity of the pure *a
> priori* concepts is thereby made intelligible, and their origin and
> truth determined. [*A*128, amended translation][21]

For the moment, let us assume that Kant has shown not only
that even the merest judgment of appearance must be the product of synthesis, but that it must be the product of some select
group of synthesizing functions. In that case, he would have
rendered comprehensible how those functions (of understanding) affect the data of sense, and why certain principles might
hold across any range of experiences we can bring to judgment.
The Transcendental Deduction would seem to be a success. Still,
Kant seems to be bothered by residual worries which lead him
to be more sympathetic to the 'phenomenal equals fake' reading
than he should be. The topic of potential difficulties within the
theory of transcendental idealism is enormous; I will only pursue
two obvious lines of objection that would make this reading seem
attractive. It will turn out that neither objection requires the
assumption of the fakery of the phenomenal.

Here is the first objection. Kant's arguments, even if correct,
have not shown that any principles are universally true. He has
shown only that those appearances we are capable of noting must
fall under certain principles. So those principals would cease to
be true if our sensory inputs were such that we were no longer
capable of making judgments. (Kant considers this possibility at
*A*112.) However, nothing in Kant's argument guarantees that
we will be able to continue enjoying judgmental experience.[22]

---

[21]Kemp Smith renders this as: "and thereby first and originally makes experience, as regards its form, possible." This translation seems to import an un-
warranted temporal connotation. Kant's expression is *allererst*, which simply adds
emphasis to the idea that these categories are a prerequisite to experience in its
formal aspect.

[22]Jonathan Bennett makes a related point in *Kant's Analytic*, p. 101.

The *Opus Postumum*'s notorious doctrine of double affection "solves" this problem by explicitly adopting a superaddition thesis: intuitions are actually created by the self, so they will always have those features that enable the self to synthesize them (for example, *GS* 22: 20, 37, 418). This plunge into complete subjectivism is quite unnecessary, however, for Kant has the resources within his system to counter the objection. Kantian necessity was never intended to be logical necessity; alternatively Kant's possible worlds include only those worlds that thinkers relevantly like us are capable of experiencing.[23] So, if his argument for the necessity of particular functions of synthesis is cogent, Kant could reply that various principles have been shown to be valid in any (Kantian) possible world. In particular, these principles would be valid in any world in which a skeptic was capable of objecting to them. Perhaps this objection about the future applicability of the categories to appearances merely reflects a concern about their present applicability, however. The short answer to this worry is that if Kant's argument for particular necessary syntheses is sound (and if he can tie the principles in question to these necessary syntheses), then the fact that we have judgmental experience attests to the applicability of the categories to the actual world of our experience. This skeptical query requires a longer answer if it is construed as asking simply: Granting that we must apply these principles to the world we experience, how do we know that they are really true of our world? I will address this point in the guise of a second objection.

One seemingly clear way to raise the difficulty is to appeal to Hume. As Hume demonstrated, causal judgments inevitably extrapolate beyond their data base. So, even though we must use causal principles, the question remains whether the extra asserted by causal judgments corresponds to anything in reality. Presumably, the same point can be raised about the other categories as well. This line of objection actually begs the question against Kant, however. For on the assumption that the argumentation of the Analytic is sound, then it is incorrect to say

---

[23]See Philip Kitcher, "Kant and the Foundations of Mathematics," *Philosophical Review* 84 (1980), 23–50.

that data statements do not involve a commitment to, for example, the causal principle. Because Kant never shows any inclination to doubt the reasoning of the Second Analogy, for example, I do not believe that his worry could have taken this form. One clue to what might have led him to an excessively subjective version of transcendental idealism is his contrast between his theory and the worthless doctrine of preestablished harmony (*B*167). The problem of how a necessary connection between reality and our representations is possible dominates both the common preamble and the conclusions to both versions of the Transcendental Deduction (*A*92/*B*124–25; *A*128–29; *B*164). Perhaps Kant's worry was that even if he could show that we can only take note of a world which manifests categorical principles, that would not show a necessary connection between the world and our representations, unless he could show that the reality we encounter must yield to categorical syntheses. A superaddition thesis, especially the doctrine of double affection, is an ostensible remedy for this difficulty, since the elements required for synthesis would be conveniently added to the data. Once again, however, this distasteful maneuver is not actually required. Kant could just be more careful about locating the modality. He has not shown, and it cannot be shown, that the world must yield to categorical syntheses and so be thinkable by creatures relevantly like us. What he has shown is that any world we are capable of experiencing must exhibit categorical principles, and that, since we do enjoy judgmental experience, these principles are true of the world we actually encounter.

Finally, Kant might have seen the falsity of the phenomenal as following from his distinction between receptive and intellectual intuition. Good critical principles should reveal the infelicity of this formulation of the correspondence worry: Does the world independently of our interpretive scheme exhibit causal connections? Either this must be read as asking whether the data we receive are capable of being brought to judgment by means of the functions of synthesis, to which the answer is yes; or we are left with the internally inconsistent question of whether the uninterpreted data of experience somehow contain this interpretation within themselves. Suppose, however, that one is enamored of the idea of a nonreceptive, active way of knowing, a way of knowing that does not involve synthesis or interpretation. Then the preceding question can be reformulated: From God's noninterpreting perspective, does the world exhibit causal connections? Given that God does not synthesize data and that the judgments of experience that reflect causal connection are the products of synthesis, the answer to the question would seem to be no. Thus, because phenomenal characteristics are absent from a more adequate world view, the phenomenal is ultimately false. Despite well-founded worries about its intelligibility ($B$307), Kant clung to this notion of an intellectual intuition in contrast to ordinary intuition, ($A$252, $B$159), so this was probably another source of inspiration for a subjective interpretation of transcendental idealism. We may safely dismiss this consideration, however, because the idea of an intellectual intuition is both incoherent and irrelevant to transcendental idealism and the doctrine of apperception.[24]

Let me tie this rather extended chain of argumentation together. The question we have been considering is whether the role of the I of apperception in transcendental idealism requires the assumption of a nonphenomenal I. Strawson's well-known indictment of transcendental psychology implies that a psychologically based transcendental idealism must be incoherent, whether the I of apperception is phenomenal or noumenal. In opposition, I have argued that a transcendental idealism based on a phenomenal doctrine of apperception descends into incoherence only if we assume the falsity of the phenomenal. The obvious reasons for making this assumption, however, turn out to be either unrelated to transcendental idealism or uncompelling or both. Of course, I am not about to claim comprehensiveness. There could be some problem inherent in transcendental idealism that forces rejection of a phenomenal thinker. My real purpose in exploring some apparent difficulties has been to show that the doctrine of apperception, on my reading, is capable of supporting a rather robust version of transcendental idealism:

---

[24]Kant explicitly contrasts intellectual intuition with the "intellectual consciousness" of the thinking I afforded by the doctrine of apperception at Bxla.

we understand how it is possible that certain principles must hold across the entire range of experiences we are capable of having; we understand the possibility that there are other aspects of reality which do not manifest these principles and which we therefore could not think at all, so the useful, negative sense of 'noumenon' is preserved (*B*307). Further, on my interpretation, the supposedly fatal objection to the doctrine of apperception— it must both be known, yet be about noumena—is overcome. The doctrine of apperception is known through the categories; if it could not be known through the categories, then we could not know it at all and we could not make even the barest judgments of appearance. In light of these arguments, I think it is reasonable to believe that a phenomenal self can play the role of the I of apperception in transcendental psychology.

Kant vigorously rejects a phenomenal thinker, yet he cannot consistently advocate a noumenal one. So, in his own hands, his doctrine of apperception is inconsistent with his "distinction of all objects in general into phenomena and noumena" (*A*235/*B*294). On my interpretation, this inconsistency is resolved. To capture the interpretation in an aphorism, Kant should claim that his real self is a real self. That is, he should claim that the self in the *Critique* with which one is meant to identify as one's real self—the thinker—is a real, albeit phenomenal, self. As opposed to the official interpretation, this reading makes the two-selves theory innocuous, because the focus of philosophical interest is a rather interesting character: the transcendental, phenomenal, empirical (that is, existing) thinker.

THE ROLE OF THE DOCTRINE OF APPERCEPTION IN THE DEDUCTION OF THE CATEGORIES

Having used my analysis of the theory of apperception to illuminate how Kant should have understood the relations among the various selves of the *Critique*, I shall provide further support for it by showing how this analysis can clarify the way the doctrine of apperception fits into the deduction of the categories. Specifically, I will consider a question that should be fundamental for analyses of the central argument of the *Critique*, but which has not attracted much serious study, to wit: Why is the transcendental unity of apperception the "highest" principle in Kant's philosophy? I will also consider a related question that has received considerable attention: Why, and in what sense does Kant maintain that consciousness requires self-consciousness?

No one who reads the *Critique* can fail to notice the basic Copernican move, because Kant refers to this step with ritualistic regularity. It must be possible for me to attribute all my representations to the same thinking self, therefore those representations must possess whatever features are necessary to make this attribution possible. Only after this step has been taken can we begin to see why Kant might think that all objects we encounter through our cognitive powers must share some very general properties. As this is a crucial step in Kant's central argument, it is natural to wonder how he is able to take it. How can he maintain that I must be conscious of all representations as belonging to myself?

As Jonathan Bennett, Paul Guyer, and others have noted, it is simply not obviously true that a conscious being must also be self-conscious.[25] Seemingly, cognitive beings could acquire vast stores of information about their environment and never think of themselves. If this doctrine is not obvious, then Kant should argue for it. As these commentators have noted, however, Kant does not seem even to try to argue for this crucial premise.

In light of the preceding analysis of Kant's theory of the thinking self, we can see quite readily both why Kant endorses and employs this thesis and why he provides no (independent) justification for it. As already noted, Kant has a particular view of conscious experience. To be enjoying conscious experience, one must not only be alive and awake and sensorily stimulated, one must be making judgments. Against the background of the epistemological investigations of his predecessors, Kant must as-

---

[25]Cf. Bennett, *Kant's Analytic*, p. 105, and Paul Guyer's "Kant on Apperception and *a priori* Synthesis," *American Philosophical Quarterly* 17 (July 1980), 205–212.

sume that these judgments are about only one's own mental states. Hence, in the *Critique* a conscious creature is a being that makes judgments about its own mental states. Turning to the second half of the doctrine, to be self–conscious, for Kant, is to attribute mental states to one's (thinking) self. As we have seen, Kant does not believe that we are conscious of ourselves in the sense that a self is an object of awareness for us. Thus, Kant would understand the doctrine that consciousness requires self–consciousness as maintaining that any being which makes judgments about its own mental states must be able to attribute those states to its own thinking self.

Kant does not argue for this specific claim, because it is virtually an immediate consequence of the doctrine of transcendental apperception. If, in all cases, I can regard something as a mental state only if I can regard it as belonging to a synthetically connected system, then when I make a judgment about a mental state on the basis of inner sense, I must be able to attribute that mental state to a thinking self. Because I am aware of the state through inner sense, I attribute it to my own I that thinks. The doctrine that consciousness requires self–consciousness is simply the doctrine of transcendental apperception applied to each of our own cases. Presumably, Kant believes that we acquire empirical tests for the self–ascription of mental states as we learn a language. He is not interested in how the average person actually comes to think of himself. What the transcendental deduction of the concept 'I think' establishes is that a philosopher who grants the existence of conscious experience must acknowledge the existence of selves, at least the existence of himself.

Besides resolving the central puzzle about why Kant appears to rest his argument on an unsupported assumption about self–consciousness, my analysis also illuminates another puzzle about Kant's views on consciousness, his estimation of animals. The dilemma is easy to state. Either Kant must deny that animals are conscious, or he must accept a counterexample to the thesis that consciousness requires self–consciousness. The first horn of the dilemma has all the charms of the *bête machine* doctrine, and the second horn is unacceptable, given that the conclusions established by the *Critique* are supposed to be quite general. Norman

Kemp Smith and, in his train, Jonathan Bennett, see Kant as grasping the first horn and so question his knowledgeability about animals.[26] H. J. Paton takes Kant to regard animals as conscious and so to deny that all consciousness requires self–consciousness.[27]

Oddly, both sides to this dispute rely on the same piece of textual evidence, Kant's letter to Marcus Herz dated May 26, 1789.[28] At a superficial level, the letter clearly favors Paton. In describing the possibility that he has the mentality of a subhuman animal (whatever kind of possibility that is), Kant characterizes the situation as his being conscious (*bewusst*) of individual representations. Why, then, are animals not a counterexample to the doctrine of the *Critique*? My analysis provides a straightforward resolution of the problem. The critical doctrine maintains that any being that has conscious experience, in the sense of making judgments about its mental states, must be able to think of those states as belonging to its self. Although animals are conscious, they are clearly not conscious in this sense. Hence, the very factor that supplies the basis for Kant's argument for self–consciousness is missing in the case of animals.[29] Actually the letter makes quite clear the sense in which Kant takes animals to be conscious. The description noted earlier, "I am conscious of individual representations," occurs in a parenthetical remark in apposition to Kant's acount of himself as having representations that influence his faculties of feeling and desire. Obviously, the way out of the animal maze is to say that animals are conscious in a sense that differs from the one employed in the central tenet of the *Critique*.[30] By providing an interpretation of that central tenet, and of Kant's support for it, my analysis allows us to put this attractive strategy to work.

[26]See Norman Kemp Smith, *A Commentary to Kant's 'Critique of Pure Reason'* (New York, 1962), pp. xlvii–l, and Bennett, *Kant's Analytic*, p. 105.
[27]H. J. Paton, *Kant's Metaphysics of Experience*, 2 vols. (London, 1936), vol. 1, pp. 332–35.
[28]Kant to Marcus Herz, *GS* 11:52.
[29]Paton attributes to Kant the view that animals possess outer sense, but not inner sense, see *Kant's Metaphysics of Experience*, vol. 2, p. 383. Thus, for Kant, animals would not have any cognitive access to their mental states, because he takes outer sense to be incapable of representing mentality.
[30]Paton takes this way out in the end, too. See *Kant's Metaphysics of Experience*, vol. 2, p. 383.

Descartes's *cogito* has been the subject of numerous intensive studies concerning its content, its epistemic status, its suitability as a first principle, and a number of other large and small issues. Kant is no less clear, although somewhat less dramatic, in announcing his "*absolutely* first" principle: the transcendental unity of apperception (*A*117a, cf. *B*135). Yet, surprisingly few commentators have raised even the most basic questions about this principle. For example, why and in what sense should this be the "highest" principle of the critical philosophy? W. H. Walsh's handling of this issue is typical. He explains that when Kant says that this principle is "absolutely first," he means that it is "ultimate."[31] Kemp Smith touches on this issue, making the plausible suggestion that when Kant calls the transcendental unity of apperception "original," he means that this principle is the one first established.[32] Kemp Smith's reading raises further questions which are left unanswered, however. Does the principle of apperception just happen to be established first, or must it be established first? If the latter, why is this so? Is Kant right in taking this to be the highest principle in his philosophy?

Kant provides two further clues about the relation of the doctrine of apperception to the deduction of the categories. He characterizes the 'I think' as the "vehicle of all concepts," including the categories (*A*341/*B*399). At *B*132, he claims that it is appropriate to label the principle of apperception "transcendental," because of the possibility of deriving (additional) *a priori* knowledge from it. Using these clues and Kant's crucial claim that this is the "highest" and "absolutely first" principle, we can capture Kant's position in the following two statements:

1. The deduction of the categories will not go through without the principle of apperception.
2. If any other premise or premises are required for the deduction of the categories, that premise or those premises will themselves depend in some way on the principle of apperception. Conversely,

[31]W. H. Walsh, *Kant's Criticism of Metaphysics* (Edinburgh, 1975), p. 51.
[32]Norman Kemp Smith, *A Commentary to 'Kant's Critique of Pure Reason,'* p. 260.

the principle of apperception will not depend on any other premise used in the deduction of the categories.

It is obviously impossible to evaluate these claims without providing at least a very rough sketch of how the deduction is supposed to work. The following reconstruction grows naturally out of my analysis of Kant's views about the thinking self. A representation can be representational, and hence be possible as a representation, only if it belongs to an informationally interconnected system of representations, an I that thinks. But a representation can belong to a synthetically connected system of representations only if it is capable of being synthetically connected to other representations. Allegedly the Metaphysical Deduction has established two claims: all judgments fall under twelve basic forms of judgment; corresponding to these twelve basic forms of judgment are twelve basic types of synthesis ($A79/B105$). In the terminology introduced in section 2, the second claim is that there are exactly twelve basic ways in which a synthetic product may be produced out of preceding representations.[33] Each of these types of synthesizing is associated with a category. Hence, any appearance we are capable of noting is subject to the categories. Perhaps it is helpful to display this argument:

1. Consciousness requires self-consciousness in other words, it must be possible for all my representations to belong to a thinking self (a contentually interconnected system of mental states). (The principle of apperception.)[34]

[33]This view about the relation between the categories and the relation of synthesis is quite close to that presented by Erich Adickes in *Kants Lehre*, p.5.

[34]In "Kant on Self-Identity," I defended a slightly different version of this principle; namely, that it must be possible *for me to attribute* all my representations to a thinking self. These versions are not at all equivalent. The version I used in the earlier paper was required in that case because I was casting Kant's argument as a reply to a skeptic, so the "If you believe X, you must also believe Y" form was necessary. This reconstruction of the Deduction could be similarly cast so that an antiskeptical conclusion is drawn: if you are to attribute judgmental experience, then you must acknowledge that all appearances are subject to the categories. One moves from the antiskeptical form of the argument to the form in the text by granting the antecedent and so detaching the consequent.

2. Therefore, any representation that is possible as a representation must be capable of entering into relations of synthesis with other representations. (From 1.)
3. There are exactly twelve ways to synthesize representations and each is associated with a category. (From the Metaphysical Deduction.)
4. When we speak of appearances, we can only mean something that has been noted as an appearance, that is, as the subject of a judgmental representation. (Kant's definition of experience.)

Therefore all possible appearances are subject to the categories.

The textual support for this basic reconstruction is remarkably straightforward. Kant says, again and again, that all representations must belong to the transcendental unity of apperception and that they must, therefore, possess that synthetic unity which makes it possible for them all to belong to one I that thinks. These excerpts are from $B$131–33, $A$122, and $A$111–12:

> It must be possible for the 'I think' to accompany all my representations. . . As *my* representations . . . they must conform to the condition under which alone they *can* stand together in one universal self-consciousness, because otherwise they would not all without exception belong to me. From this original combination many consequences follow.

> According to this principle (the principle of apperception) all appearances, without exception, must so enter the mind or be apprehended, that they conform to the unity of apperception. Without synthetic unity in their connection, this would be impossible; and such synthetic unity is itself, therefore, objectively necessary.

> In original apperception everything must necessarily conform to the conditions of the thoroughgoing unity of self-consciousness, that is, to the universal functions of synthesis.

Although Kant means more by "synthetic unity," I claim he uses this phrase to indicate at least that representations, or mental states, have whatever coherence or congruence necessary for them to be synthesized. Hence, Kant is saying that the principle of apperception implies that all possible representations must be such that they are connectable by synthesizing. In terms of my reconstruction, he is saying that (1) implies (2).

What is perhaps surprising in my reconstruction is that the categories themselves enter the argument rather bluntly. With no advance warning, material from the Metaphysical Deduction is inserted and the desired conclusion is reached in one step. In the text itself, however, the categories enter the argument in an offhand and undefended manner. For example, at *B*143, Kant is discussing the unity of apperception and the fact that all intuitions are, therefore, *determined* in respect of one of the logical functions of judgment. He continues, "Now the *categories* are just these functions of judgment. . . . Consequently, the manifold in a given intuition is necessarily subject to the categories" (cf. A111). Two pages later, he tries to assuage the reader's sense of shock at the speed at which the conclusion has been reached:

> This peculiarity of our understanding, that it can produce *a priori* unity of apperception solely by means of the categories, and only by such and so many, is as little capable of further explanation as why we have just these and no other functions or judgment, or why space and time are the only forms of our possible intuition. (B145–46)

These texts provide substantial evidence that Kant had in mind an argument quite similar to the one I have presented as a route from the principle of apperception to the necessity of the categories. Why, then, does he regard the principle of apperception as the linchpin of the whole deduction? Why must it be established first? Why is it the independent premise of the deduction, with all other crucial premises depending on it? On my reconstruction, the conclusion announcing the universal applicability of the categories is the direct consequence of one definition and two equally important substantive premises:

2. A representation that is possible as a representation must be capable of entering into relations of synthesis with other representations.
3. There are exactly twelve basic ways to synthesize representations and each type of synthesis is associated with a category.

Kant regards the principle of apperception as the "highest" principle of the deduction because both (2) and (3) depend on it. The second premise's dependence is obvious: it is a straightforward consequence of the principle of apperception. However, (3) also depends on this principle, for if the principle of apperception could not be established, then (3) might be vacuous. The principle of apperception not only extends the province of the categories to all possible representations, it also vindicates the *possibility* of synthesizing representations, which (3) presupposes. As I have presented it, what the argument for apperception establishes is that one cannot acknowledge the existence of mental states and then balk at the idea that mental states are synthetically related. Hence, this part of the Transcendental Deduction offers a retrospective justification for the talk of synthesizing representations in the Metaphysical Deduction. Whereas (3) depends on (1), however, neither (1) nor (2) requires (3), because the principle of apperception does not depend on claims about a privileged set of concepts. As already noted, Kant produces a transcendental deduction of the concept 'I think' out of the minimal assumption that we make judgments about at least our own mental states.

I have tried to vindicate my analysis of the principle of apperception and Kant's claims about the importance of this principle by showing how, on my analysis, this principle can be understood as providing the basis for the crucial premises in a plausible reconstruction of the deduction. My reconstruction contains an obvious difficulty, however. The Metaphysical Deduction makes a large contribution to the overall deduction and that is not at all satisfactory. The question arises whether, on my interpretation, the principle of the transcendental unity of apperception is too weak to serve as the first premise in the deduction of the categories. Unless this principle of apperception can be used to launch at least an apparently sound deduction of something like the categories, then my characterization of the real hero of the *Critique*—Kant's thinker—will have to be rejected. Obviously, a full and genuine exploration of the question is work for another occasion, but I will conclude with some summary observations.

I view the principle of apperception as making the following contribution to the deduction of the categories. It proclaims that all mental states, insofar as they are to be representational, have content, must have whatever properties are necessary for belonging to a system of representational states. In particular, they must have whatever properties are necessary to permit the integration of information from different states in a resultant state. I do not know whether this starting place can lead to a proof of the universal applicability of anything like Kant's categories. However, it is extremely likely that there are some general constraints on the kinds of information that can be handled in this type of system. Further, if we then add specific facts about our perceptual system, it might well turn out that our minds can operate only in certain quite definite ways and only on particular kinds of information. Thus, even if this premise cannot serve in a successful deduction of any of the categories, it could well play a crucial role in arguments showing, among other results, why Kant was right in principle about the categories.

Self-Consciousness and Synthesis

Sydney Shoemaker

In the first part of her essay "Kant's Real Self," Patricia Kitcher offers an attractive account of how Kant's notion of synthesis, and his principle of the transcendental unity of apperception, might be understood. It is attractive because it attributes to Kant a plausible philosophical doctrine and makes good philosophical sense out of some obscure and puzzling pronouncements. Synthesis, she suggests, consists in the existence of a relation of "contentual dependence" between different mental states. A state is the "synthetic product" of other states if its content would not exist, or would be different, if those other states had not existed or had had different contents. States stand in the relation of synthesis if one is the synthetic product of the other or if some other state is the synthetic product of both. Kant's official view is usually taken to be that synthesis is an "act" that produces such relations of contentual dependence; but Kitcher thinks that it is better to dispense with the act and take "synthesis" to refer to the relations between the mental states. Now the relation of synthesis as just defined can obtain between mental states of different persons; to adapt Kitcher's example, if I raise an objection to her paper, she will have a mental state that is the synthetic product of the mental states I had in raising the objection. But Kitcher takes Kant to hold that there is a particular sort of synthetic relation that can hold only between mental states of one and the same person, or one and the same mind or self, and she maintains that although Kant never gives a satisfactory characterization of this more specific relation, it is this relation that he usually means by "synthesis." Apparently she takes him to hold that it is the existence of relations of synthesis (in this narrower sense) between mental states that constitutes their being states of a single mind or self. More important, she takes him to hold that it is essential to the very existence of a mental state, and to its having the content it does, that it belongs to a system of states related by this relation of synthesis. And this, according to Kitcher, is what the principle of the transcendental unity of apperception (for short, the principle of apperception) asserts.

Kitcher compares this view with a view underlying recent work on Artificial Intelligence (AI), and in another paper she compares it with recent "functionalist" views about mental states—I take it that the two comparisons come to the same thing.[1] The view she attributes to Kant might be characterized as what results when a functionalist account of mental states is combined with a view about personal identity that has been around for some time. Beginning with John Locke, many philosophers have suggested that the identity of a person or mind over time should be analyzed, not in terms of a relation of successive mental states to some soul-substance or mental substratum, but in terms of relations the successive mental states have to one another. To employ a useful term of John Perry's, different mental states belong to the same person because they are related by the "unity relation" for persons, and the job of analyzing personal identity is taken to be that of specifying what this unity relation is.[2] Recent accounts of personal identity along these lines have stressed that the unity relation will involve causality, partly because the unity relation is held (following Locke) to involve memory, and because memory arguably involves a causal relation between a memory and what the memory is of. But Kant's relation of synthesis will itself be a causal relationship, or something close to

---

[1] See Patricia Kitcher, "Kant on Self-Identity," *Philosophical Review* 91 (1982), 41–72.

[2] John Perry, "The Problem of Personal Identity," in Perry, ed., *Personal Identity* (Berkeley, Los Angeles, and London, 1975).

it—for it is a relation of counterfactual dependence. So one might say that Kant's view, as interpreted by Kitcher, is a version of the causal theory of personal identity, with the relation of synthesis playing the role of the unity relationship. But whereas on some versions of this view the mental states that are bundled into a single self by the unity relation are what they are quite independently of their being so related, this is not true on the Kantian version. And here is where Kant's view can be seen as a kind of functionalism. Functionalism says that what constitutes a mental state as being the particular mental state it is, and so as having the representational content that it does, are its causal relations to other mental states and to sensory inputs and behavioral outputs. What constitutes a particular state as being a belief having a certain content is that it is such as to be caused by certain sense experiences and that in combination with certain mental states it will influence the person's other menal states, and ultimately his behavior, in certain ways. And what makes other mental states count as sense experiences having such and such contents is that they are caused in certain ways and are such as to play a certain sort of role in the production of beliefs. On such a view, a mental state must belong to what Kitcher calls a "contentually interconnected group of representations," and the contents of the different representations in the group will be determined holistically; given the causal relations that hold (or can hold) between them, what content any one of them has is partly determined by, and partly determines, what the contents of the others are.

Because I believe that something along these lines is true, I am intrigued by the claim that this view can be found in Kant, and that it can play the role of the doctrine of apperception in the Transcendental Deduction.[3] It can do this if it can be shown that the "functions" involved in synthesis, those whereby the contents of the mental states are determined by their relations to other mental states (and inputs and outputs), correspond to

---

[3]There is a brief sketch of such a view in Sydney Shoemaker, "Identity Properties and Causality," *Midwest Studies in Philosophy* no. 4 (1979); a more extended presentation appears in Shoemaker, "Personal Identity, a Materialist's View," in Sydney Shoemaker and Richard Swinburne, *Personal Identity* (Oxford, 1984).

the Kantian categories in such a way that only sensory information that conforms to the categories can be brought to judgment and so can be part of experience. Kitcher does not attempt
in her essay to show that this is the case; but I take it that she
thinks that it is at least possible that it both is the case and can
be shown to be so by Kantian arguments. If this could be shown,
it would be an important achievement indeed.

One attractive feature of Kitcher's interpretation is that it construes the doctrine of synthesis so as not to be committed to what
she calls the 'phenomenal equals fake' interpretation of transcendental idealism. Also attractive is her view that, despite Kant's
own pronouncements, there is no good reason why he should
not hold that the 'thinking self' is phenomenal. Kitcher says that
her reading "makes the two-selves theory innocuous." I do not
see why it does not lead to the outright rejection of the two-
selves theory; there seems, according to Kant-as-revised-by-
Kitcher, to be just one self (for each of us), namely, a phenomenal
one.

Attractive though I find Kitcher's interpretation, there is one
thing that puzzles me about it. It is customary to interpret Kant's
principle of apperception as in some crucial way involving the
idea that consciousness requires self-consciousness. And Kitcher
writes as if this were so. Indeed, in her sketch of the Transcendental Deduction she formulates the principle of apperception
as follows: "Consciousness requires self-consciousness, in other
words, it must be possible for all my representations to belong
to a thinking self (that is, a contentually interconnected system
of mental states)." This is puzzling, for what follows the "in other
words" does not seem at all equivalent to what precedes it. Although the second part of the statement happens to contain the
word "my," what it states is simply the general thesis about mental
states and synthesis sketched in the first part of Kitcher's essay.
One would think that if this thesis is true at all, it is true even
in the case of creatures, for example, subhuman animals that
are totally lacking in self-consciousness—creatures that have beliefs about their environments, but never have beliefs (or other
propositional attitudes) about their own mental states. Certainly
a functionalist account of mental states, and of what determines

the contents of mental states, is as plausible for such creatures as it is for us. This means that synthesis, as interpreted by Kitcher, is as much a feature of the mental life of such creatures as it is of ours. So synthesis (as so interpreted) does not as such involve self-consciousness; moreover, if the principle of apperception is the principle that mental states must be such as to be capable of entering into contentually connected systems of mental states, then it does not, by itself, imply the principle that consciousness requires self-consciousness. And this hardly squares with the way Kant formulates it.

Kitcher does try to make room in her account for the Kantian doctrine that consciousness involves self-consciousness. She claims that "in the *Critique*, a conscious being is a being that makes judgments about its own mental states." This is because "against the background of the epistemological investigations of his pred-ecessors, Kant must assume that . . . judgments are only about one's own mental states." (I find the historical claim here puz-zling; although many philosphers have had careless moments in which they have written as if all of one's judgments are about one's own mental states—for example, about one's own "ideas"— I do not know of any who have held this as a considered opinion.) At any rate, supposing that Kant had reasons for assuming that our judgments are about our own mental states, then, says Kitcher, for him the doctrine that consciousness requires self-conscious-ness comes down to the doctrine that "any being that makes judgments about its own mental states must be able to attribute those states to its own thinking self." This, Kitcher claims, is "virtually an immediate consequence of the doctrine of tran-scendental apperception." She spells this out as follows:

If, in all cases, I can regard something as a mental state only if I can regard it as belonging to a synthetically connected system, then when I make a judgment about a mental state on the basis of inner sense, I must be able to attribute that mental state to a thinking self. Because I am aware of the state through inner sense, I attribute it to my own I that thinks. The doctrine that consciousness requires self-consciousness is simply the doctrine of transcendental apper-ception applied to each of our own cases.

I do not see how the reasoning here is supposed to go. It does follow from the principle of apperception that in judging something to be a mental state of any sort, I am committed to regarding it as belonging to a synthetically connected system, and so to a self—for according to the principle of apperception (as interpreted by Kitcher) this is entailed by being a mental state. But it is one thing to judge that a state belongs to some self or other, and quite another to judge that it belongs *to me*—I am not, after all, the only self in the world. So how do I get to the judgment that *I* have the state in question—that it belongs to my own "I that thinks"? Kitcher's answer is: "Because I am aware of the state by inner sense, I attribute it to my own I that thinks." But this had better not mean that I get to this self-attribution by a deduction having as a premise that *I* am aware of the state by inner sense—for that would assume that I have the very sort of self-knowledge we are trying to explain. Some, of course, would claim that my thoughts are simply given to me in inner sense *as* my thoughts, that is, that they somehow come stamped as *mine*. If this is so, then of course we do not need the principle of apperception to explain how I get to the judgment that these thoughts belong to me—for that my thoughts belong to me is a sheer tautology. But if the thoughts are given to me only as thoughts having certain contents, then all the principle of apperception will do for me is to tell me that they must belong to some self or other, and that is far from explaining how I get to the judgment that they belong to me. I do not deny, of course, that it is fishy in the extreme to suppose that I might be conscious "by inner sense" of what is in fact my thought and not know that it is mine; but I cannot see that the principle of apperception (as interpreted by Kitcher) helps to explain *why* it is fishy.

I have been stressing the difference between the weak claim that in judging on the basis of inner sense that something is a mental state of some sort I am committed to regarding it as belonging to a synthetically connected system, and the stronger claim that in so judging I am committed to regarding the mental state as belonging to me, that is, to that particular synthetically connected system that is myself. But there is another claim that is intermediate in strength between these, namely that in judging on the basis of inner sense that something A is a mental state of some sort, and in so judging at the same time that B is a mental state of some sort, I am committed to judging that A and B belong to the *same* synthetically connected system. This claim seems plausible, and it seems, if anything, more directly suited to the needs of Kant's Transcendental Deduction than the principle that consciousness requires self-consciousness. But is this claim an immediate consequence of the principle of apperception as Kitcher interprets it? That is, whether or not this principle has the consequence that consciousness implies self-consciousness, does it at least have the consequence that consciousness implies awareness of what Bertrand Russell called the "copersonality," or what we can simply call the "unity," of the mental states in question? It is not obvious to me that it does, given only what Kitcher has so far told us about synthesis. All that obviously follows from her principle is that A and B must each belong to a synthetically connected system; and from this it does not follow that A and B must belong to the *same* synthetically connected system. Of course, one could so define synthesis that the latter claim does follows; for example, one could stipulate that part of what it is for states to be synthetically connected is for it to be the case that when they are objects of inner sense (or of 'consciousness') at all, then inner sense will yield a judgment to the effect that they are synthetically connected. If synthesis were so defined, it would then of course need to be argued that any mental state (or perhaps any 'conscious' mental state) must belong to a system of mental states that are related by *this* sort of synthesis.

I am rather inclined to think that this can be argued. I am not suggesting, however, that we abandon the principle that consciousness involves self-consciousness in favor of the weaker claim that consciousness involves awareness of copersonality, or of unity of consciousness. For I suspect that any plausible argument for the latter claim will involve an argument for the former. What we really need is an account or synthesis from which it follows that when mental states A and B are states of a creature capable of forming any conception of itself and of its mental states, that creature's consciousness of A and B will necessarily be a consciousness of them as *its own* state, and *so* as states that are copersonal. A promising idea, I think, is that something like this is true in virtue of the fact that the relation of "contentual interconnectedness" that constitutes synthesis must be such as to bestow a considerable degree of *rationality* on the subject of the mental states, and that in creatures of any appreciable degree of conceptual sophistication, and more particularly those capable of conceiving of themselves, this rationality requires at least an appreciable degree of self-awareness. One reason for this is that it is only to the extent that a creature knows what its beliefs are that it is in a position to modify them in the light of new experience, in the ways required by rationality.[4] In any case, Kitcher writes as if the principle that consciousness implies self-consciousness follows from the principle of apperception even if no more is packed into the notion of synthesis than is included in her initial definition; and what I am suggesting is that if it follows at all, it does so because of details about the nature of synthesis that we have not yet been given.

[4]See Shoemaker, "Personal Identity," section 8. See also Colin McGinn, *The Character of Mind* (Oxford, 1982), pp. 20–21.

V

The 'Phenomenalisms' of
Berkeley and Kant

Margaret D. Wilson

BERKELEY AND KANT

Of all the major modern philosophical systems the views of George Berkeley have probably met with the most resistance, ridicule, and distortion. Among Berkeley's many detractors and distorters was Kant, who represented Berkeley as a "dogmatic idealist" who "degraded bodies to mere illusions." $(B71)^1$ As has frequently been pointed out, however, Kant's few direct remarks about Berkeley are not unrelievedly negative. In the *Prolegomena* particularly, Kant acknowledges a limited affinity with Berkeley, pointing out that they agree in treating space as ideal.[2] Kant goes on to indicate that he differs from Berkeley in regarding space as a priori rather than merely empirical, and for this reason is able to avoid Berkeley's illusionism. In the second edition of the *Critique of Pure Reason* Kant also points to his doctrine of space as the answer to dogmatic idealism—though the logic of his claim there is at least superficially quite different from that in the *Prolegomena* $(B274; cf. B69)$.[3]

---

[1] I use Kemp Smith's translation of the *Critique* but with some modifications.
[2] See the Appendix of the *Prolegomena*.
[3] I compare the *Critique* passages with the *Prolegomena* statement in my "Kant and 'the *Dogmatic* Idealism of Berkeley,' " cited in note 4.

Margaret D. Wilson

The historical and philosophical relations between Kant and Berkeley are topics of long debate among Kant scholars. It is generally acknowledged—at least by twentieth century critics— that Berkeley was far from considering himself an "illusionist." According to one strong tradition Kant's own position is in important respects quite close to Berkeley's *real* position.[4] Within this tradition one finds disagreement over whether Kant was simply ignorant of this fact, as a result of lacking firsthand knowledge of most of Berkeley's writings, or whether he deliberately misrepresented Berkeley's position to conceal an intellectual debt.[5] According to another, more recently developed, viewpoint Kant's empirical realism/transcendental idealism is in fact significantly different from Berkeley's position—and in approximately the ways Kant indicates that it is different.[6] Some commentators in arguing this viewpoint have presented rebuttals to their predecessors' claims that Berkeley's works would in general have been inaccessible to Kant, because he did not know English. (In fact, various works were available in Latin, French, and even German during Kant's lifetime.) Some recent writers further hold that Kant's system is philosophically superior to Berkeley's in at least some of the ways Kant took it to be.[7]

The earlier *and* the more recent critcs have tended to portray Kant and Berkeley as united by a common concern: that of vindicating the certainty of our knowledge of bodies in the wake of Cartesian doubt. Both philosophers, it is held, sought to achieve

[4]See Norman Kemp Smith's *A Commentary to Kant's Critique of Pure Reason* (New York, 1923), pp. 156–57; Colin M. Turbayne, "Kant's Refutation of Dogmatic Idealism," *Philosophical Quarterly* 5 (1955), 225–44. I critically discuss Kemp Smith's and Turbayne's views in "Kant and 'the *Dogmatic* Idealism of Berkeley,' " *Journal of the History of Philosophy* 9 (1971), 464–70.

[5]Kemp Smith maintains the former view, Turbayne the latter.

[6]See George Miller, "Kant and Berkeley: The Alternative Theories," *Kant-Studien* 64 (1973), 315–35; Henry E. Allison, "Kant's Critique of Berkeley," *Journal of the History of Philosophy* 11 (1973), 43–63; Richard E. Aquila, "Kant's Phenomenalism," *Idealistic Studies* 5 (1975), 108–126; G. D. Justin, "On Kant's Analysis of Berkeley," *Kant-Studien* 65 (1974), 20–32; and Wilson, "Kant and 'the *Dogmatic* Idealism of Berkeley.' " In "Berkeley's Immaterialism and Kant's Transcendental Idealism," M. R. Ayers defends and extends Allison's position (*Idealism—Past and Present*, ed. Godfrey Vesey [Cambridge, Eng., 1982], pp. 51–69). I have also seen unpublished work by William Harper on a similar theme.

[7]Aquila, "Kant's Phenomenalism," 125–26; Allison, "Kant's Critique of Berkeley," pp. 52 and 56; Miller, "Kant and Berkeley," 321–23; 334–35.

this result by denying the Cartesian (and Lockean) interpretation of physical objects as the mind-independent causes of our subjective perceptions. Berkeley responded with the theory that bodies *just are* sets of subjective sense-perceptions, which are presented in orderly fashion to human minds according to the well-disposed will of God. Therefore, our certain knowledge of our own subjective states in itself guarantees the certain knowledge of bodies: there is no need for a tenuous, extraexperiential causal inference that must inevitably succumb to skeptical challenge. Against the view that Kant's idealist solution to skepticism is essentially similar to Berkeley's, recent critics have held that Kant secures unproblematic knowledge of bodies while avoiding Berkeley's sensationalistic reductionism. Kant's position, in other words allows him to enjoy the sweets of phenomenalism without the bitters of subjectivism.[8] Kant's theory of space and time as a priori forms of intuition, together with the transcendental deduction of the categories (and the ensuing elaboration of the "principles" of causality and substance), allow him to hold that objects are as immediately known as the series of inner experiences. At the same time they allegedly allow him to preserve such essential features of objectivity as permanence, publicity, and the distinction between truth and illusion—results not achieved by Berkeley's cruder theory. It sometimes is also stressed that Kant's and Berkeley's idealisms have quite different implications for the interpretation of Newtonian science, and that the two philosophers do not take the same view of the primary–secondary quality distinction.[9]

In my opinion the earlier tradition that assimilated Berkeleyan and Kantian phenomenalism is clearly erroneous. Further, I grant that Kant's own view of his relation to Berkeley may be

---

[8]I use the term 'idealism' more or less alternatively to 'phenomenalism' to characterize Berkeley's system as well as Kant's. For expository purposes it is convenient to follow the practice of Kant and several of his commentators in this respect. I am aware that some Berkeley scholars vehemently oppose the characterization of his position as 'idealist', but I do not really accept their strictures, and in any case the issue is not crucial to the points I want to make.

[9]Allison, in particular, provides a perceptive discussion of these issues ("Kant's Critique of Berkeley").

accurately captured by some of the recent commentators. Nevertheless, the full difference between Kant's and Berkeley's position has still not been correctly expressed. For both Kant and his recent commentators (including myself) have tended to overlook a radical difference in the philosophical motivations of the two systems. It seems ot me that this difference of concern would give Berkeley good reason to regard Kant's position as alien to, rather than an improvement of, his own in a quite fundamental respect. It is therefore quite wrong to represent Berkeley as getting about halfway to a result that Kant finally achieved. Development of this idea leads me to touch on some features of Kant's theory of 'appearances' that I find rather strange. Without attempting to assess further the recent claims about Kant's philosophical superiority to Berkeley, I suggest that clarification of the differences between the two philosophers' goals is a necessary step towards such assessment.

BERKELEY ON THE REALITY OF SENSIBLE QUALITIES

The principal claim I want to defend is that Berkeley understood the challenge posed by Descartes's (and Locke's) transcendental realism very differently than did Kant. Berkeley's mission, at least in the great early works, was to vindicate the reality of the objects of ordinary sense experience, *as sensed*. The *primary* foe in this connection is not the historically somewhat fictitious position of "Cartesian skepticism." It is rather the historically quite real and (in modernized form) still current position of Cartesian scientific realism.[10] But Kant's empirical realism *is* a form of scientific realism. It is *not* a vindication of ordinary sense experience (or "common sense") as Berkeley conceived it. In other words, whatever Kant may have achieved in demonstrating the claims to reality of appearances as he understood them, he

[10]I defend this perspective on Cartesianism in my book, *Descartes* (London, 1978).

has not demonstrated (or tried to demonstrate) the reality of phenomena as Berkeley understood them. For Kant, what is empirically real is primarily the material world of the science of his time—a world that does not possess colors, tastes, and the like in any literal, irreducible sense.[11]

Berkeley, on the contrary, takes as empirically real the objects of ordinary sense experience, literally and richly endowed with colors, tastes, and the other 'secondary qualities'—and perhaps with aesthetic, religious, and emotive 'qualities,' too. This position of course leaves Berkeley with problems about how to accommodate the more esoteric concepts of contemporary mechanism, and the explanatory successes achieved through these concepts. Berkeley did make earnest efforts to confront these problems—at times taking refuge in instrumentalist accounts. I certainly do not claim that he was fully successful in these efforts. But the goal itself of vindicating the reality of the sensible world as concretely sensed and experienced, as against the "abstractions" of the scientists, is in my view a far from frivolous one. After citing some passages that show Berkeley doing just that, I shall consider a variety of passages from Kant's first *Critique* which seem to indicate the great difference between Berkeley's and Kant's position concerning the relations among real appearances, sensations, and the entities of science.

Consider the opening of Berkeley's first *Dialogue*. Berkeley's spokesman Philonous is in a garden, where he encounters his prospective antagonist, Hylas. Hylas has endured a night of intellectual unrest; and as a result he has risen early. In what superficially appears to be mere indulgence in scene setting, Philonous is made to respond with the following effusion:

It happened well, to let you see what innocent and agreeable pleasures you lose every morning. Can there be a pleasanter time of the day, or a more delightful season of the year? That purple sky, those wild but sweet notes of birds, the fragrant bloom upon the trees and flowers, the gentle influence of the rising sun, these and a thou-

[11]This use of the term 'literal' is borrowed from John Mackie, *Problems from Locke* (Oxford, 1976), pp. 14–15.

sand nameless beauties of nature inspire the soul with secret transports.[12]

But the passage is far from being as intellectually innocuous as the casual reader may suppose. Berkeley's citation of the beauties of nature (those, presumably, that are not "nameless") systematically touches on each of the commonly mentioned traditional 'secondary qualities,' omitting only taste. Thus we encounter in the garden color ("that purple sky"), sound ("those wild but sweet notes'), odor ("fragrant bloom"), and warmth ("gentle influence") of the rising sun. The emotive or affective aspects of the sensuously experienced natural scene are also lightly stressed.

Later, when the antagonist Hylas has been driven to concede that sensible objects have no reality "without the mind," and has thence concluded that there is no certain reality in nature, Philonous counters: "Look! are not the fields covered with a delightful verdure? Is there not something in the woods and groves, in the rivers and clear springs, that soothes, that delights, that transports the soul?"[13] And so on, at length. The speech concludes: "What treatment, then, do those philosophers deserve, who would deprive these noble and delightful scenes of all *reality*? How should those Principles be entertained that lead us to think all the visible beauty of the creation a false imaginary glare"?[14]

Elsewhere, in somewhat similar circumstances, Philonous emphasizes that the reality of the full range of the sensed qualities of a cherry is all that matters to us:

Hyl. . . . But, after all, Philonous, when I consider the substance of what you advance against *Scepticism*, it amounts to no more than this:—We are sure that we really see, hear, feel; in a word, that we are affected with sensible impressions.
Phil. And how are *we* concerned any farther? I see this cherry, I feel it, I taste it: and I am sure *nothing* cannot be seen, or felt, or tasted: it is therefore *real*. *Take away the sensations of softness, moisture, redness,*

---

[12]*Works* of George Berkeley, ed. A. A. Luce and T. E. Jessop, 9 vols. (London, 1948–51), vol. 2, p. 171.
[13]*Works*, vol. 2, p. 210.
[14]*Works*, vol. 2, p. 211.

tartness, and you take away the cherry, since it is not a being distinct from sensations. A cherry, I say, is nothing but a congeries of sensible impressions, or ideas perceived by various senses: which ideas are united into one thing (or have one name given them) by the mind, because they are observed to attend each other. Thus, when the palate is affected with such a particular taste, the sight is affected with a red colour, the touch with roundness, softness, [etc.]. Hence, when I see, and feel, and taste, in sundry certain manners, I am sure the cherry exists, or is real; its reality being in my opinion nothing abstracted from those sensations. But if by the word *cherry* you mean an unknown nature, distinct from *all those sensible qualities*, and by its *existence* something distinct from its being perceived; then, indeed, I own, neither you nor I, nor any one else, can be sure it exists.[15]

According to the common interpretation I have sketched, Berkeley is driven into empiricistic reductionism, and hence (unfortunately) into subjectivism, just because he supposes this is the only way to avoid the external world skepticism that is virtually built into Cartesian or Lockean scientific realism. I agree that there is clear evidence of this concern—for example at the end of the passage just quoted. Yet the several passages quoted indicate that Berkeley was not merely interested in affirming the reality of sensible appearances or qualities as a *means* to making a case for the reality of body in some form or other. It was precisely the reality of the world of experience, as experienced, that he was concerned to establish. Even if the Cartesian inference to *res extensa*, or the Lockean inference to (epistemologically indeterminate) real essences of physical substances were certain above all skeptical challenge, too much of reality as we conceive and experience it in ordinary life would have to be construed as "false imaginary glare." This at least is the reading I propose.

One further issue about Berkeley's conception of the reality of the world as we experience it is worth mentioning. Frequently in the *Dialogues* Hylas attempts the move of distinguishing the "real" sound or color or other quality (as the scientist understands it) from the mere sensation, with the aim of maintaining that the former at least is not simply "in the mind." Philonous

[15]*Works*, vol. 2, p. 249. Italics added.

in turn makes fun of the idea that real colors are unseen, real sounds unheard, and so forth. The following passage is representative.

Hyl. I own myself entirely satisfied, that [colors] are all equally apparent, and that there is no such thing as colour really inhering in external bodies, but that it is altogether in the light. And what confirms me in this opinion is, in proportion to the light colours are still more or less vivid; and if there be no light, then are no colours perceived. . . . It is immediately some contiguous substance, which, operating on the eye, occasions a perception of colours: and such is light.

Phil. How! Is light then a substance?

Hyl I tell you, Philonous, external light is nothing but a thin fluid substance, whose minute particles being agitated with a brisk motion, and in various manners reflected from the different surfaces of outward objects to the eyes, communicate different motions to the optic nerves; which, being propagated to the brain, cause therein various impressions; and these are attended with the sensations of red, blue, yellow, [etc.].

Phil. It seems then the light doth no more than shake the optic nerves.

Hyl. Nothing Else.

Phil. And consequent to each particular motion of the nerves, the mind is affected with a sensation, which is some particular colour.

Hyl. Right.

Phil. And these sensations have no existence without the mind.

Hyl. They have not.

Phil. How then do you affirm that colours are in the light: since by *light* you understand a corporeal substance external to the mind?

Hyl. Light and colours, as immediately perceived by us, I grant cannot exist without the mind. But in themselves they are only the motions and configurations of certain insensible particles of matter.

Phil. Colours, then, in the vulgar sense, or taken for the immediate objects of sight, cannot agree to any but a perceiving substance.

Having received Hylas's acquiescence in this restatement, Philonous concludes:

Phil. Well then, since you give up the point as to those sensible qualities which are alone thought colours by all mankind beside, you may hold what you please with regard to those invisible ones of the philosohers.

It is not my business to dispute about *them*; only I would advise you to bethink yourself, whether, considering the inquiry we are upon, it be prudent for you to affirm—*the red and blue which we see are not real colours, but certain unknown motions and figures which no man ever did or can see are truly so*. Are not these shocking notions, and are not they subject to as many ridiculous inferences, as those you were obliged to renounce before in the case of sounds?[16]

Viewed in one way, this passage of course shows Berkeley making a case for his general position that sensible objects have no existence without the mind. Roughly stated, a *sensible* color is a color as consciously experienced—not a stream of minute particles of which no one is directly aware in ordinary seeing. And Hylas admits that the *former* exists only in the mind. But at the same time, I suggest, the passage shows Berkeley insisting on the point that a *real color is* a color as consciously experienced—and that colors as consciously experienced are real colors, colors of things. Kant's position about perceptual reality is quite different, as we shall see.

KANT'S POSITION CONCERNING SENSIBLE QUALITIES

Throughout the first *Critique* Kant consistently seems to distinguish objects of experience or appearances (*Erscheinungen*) from sensations (*Empfindungen*). Sensations are the mere subjective results of the effects of "the real in appearances" on our peculiar organs of sense. The secondary qualities are assimilated by Kant to sensations. According to this complicated theory, then, bodies in space are transcendentally ideal because space is only the form of our sensibility, but their primary qualities are empirically real. Their perceived colors, odors, tastes, and so forth are not even *empirically* real.

Other commentators have pointed to this feature of Kant's

---

[16]*Works*, vol. 2, pp. 186–87.

position as an important difference between his idealism and Berkeley's.[17] I believe, however, that its profound significance for the difference in motivation and concern between the two philosophers has not yet been sufficiently appreciated.[18] Further, the attempt to affirm the primary–secondary quality distinction within an idealist or phenomenalist philosophy of body raises a perplexing issue about Kant's concept of appearance—an issue that surely deserves more consideration than it has received. Before articulating the problem I have in mind, I shall cite some relevant passages from three different parts of the *Critique of Pure Reason*: the Aesthetic, the Anticipations of Perception, and the Fourth Paralogism in the first edition (which has often been construed as an *especially* Berkeleyan passage.)

In *B*44–45 of the Transcendental Aesthetic Kant writes:

> With the sole exception of space there is no subjective representation, referring to something *outer*, which could be entitled objective *a priori*. For there is no other subjective representation from which we can derive *a priori* synthetic propositions, as we can from intuition in space. . . . Strictly speaking, therefore, these other representations have no ideality, although they agree with the representation of space in this respect, that they belong merely to the subjective constitution of our manner of sensibility, for instance, of sight, hearing, touch, as in the case of sensations of colors, sounds, and heat, which, since they are mere sensations and not intuitions, do not of themselves yield knowledge of any object, least of all any *a priori* knowledge.
>
> The above remark is intended only to guard anyone from supposing that the ideality of space as here asserted can be illustrated by examples so altogether insufficient as colors, taste, etc. For these cannot rightly be regarded as properties of things, but only as changes in the subject, changes which may, indeed, be different for different men.[19]

---

[17]Cf. Allison, *"Kant's Critique of Berkeley,"* pp. 52ff.

[18]I am aware of one important exception. In his Ph.D. thesis, "The Idealism of Kant and Berkeley" (University of Pittsburgh, 1979), George John Mattey stresses that Kant and Berkeley held quite different views on the primary–secondary quality distinction, and emphasizes the significance of this difference in comparing their idealisms.

[19]Allison also cites and discusses this passage and its predecessor in *A* ("Kant's Critique of Berkeley," pp. 56–56).

Part of the passage just quoted (toward the beginning) replaced a perhaps even more committed statement in the *A* edition, which includes the following sentences:

> The taste of a wine does not belong to the objective determinations of the wine, not even if by the wine as an object we mean the wine as appearance, but to the special constitution of sense in the subject that tastes it. Colors are not properties of the bodies to the intuition of which they are attached, but only modifications of the sense of sight, which is affected in a certain manner by light.[*A*28–29]

It may be noted that in this last passage Kant seems to agree with Berkeley that colors *are* sensations—not properties of light or nonsensational surfaces. But Kant is clearly distinguishing, in a most un-Berkeley-like way, between mere subjective effects of bodies, and objective properties of the bodies, considered as appearances.

In the Anticipations of Perception Kant's theory of perception comes through even more clearly. He reiterates the view that "sensation is not in itself an objective representation." (*A*166/*B*208). Appearances, however, besides intuition contain "the real of sensation as merely subjective representation, which gives us only the consciousness that the subject is affected, and which we relate to an object in general" (*A*166/*B*207–208). All sensation possesses intensity or degree, however, and this may be in turn taken to correspond to the "degree of influence on the sense." As Kant also says, "what corresponds in empirical intuition to sensation is reality [*realitas phaenomenon*]" (*A*168/*B*209). He continues:

> If this reality is viewed as cause, either of sensation or of some other reality in the appearance, such as change, the degree of the reality as cause is then entitled a moment, e.g., the moment of gravity. . . .
>
> Every sensation, therefore, and likewise every reality in the appearances, however small it may be, has a degree, that is, an intensive magnitude which can always be diminished. [*A*168–69/*B*210–11]

According to Kant's theory, then, physical causes (as understood by the scientist, such as gravity) affect our senses, giving rise to sensations which, while not resembling properties of the object, nevertheless bear some correspondence to the latter, owing to the proportionality of cause and effect.

The Fourth Paralogism of the first edition is a passage that has been cited by commentators as showing Kant at his most Berkleyan. Some have been held that Kant abandoned the argument of this passage in the second edition *because it was too Berkeleyan.*[20] There are in fact a few phrases in the passage that seem a bit discordant with Kant's distinction elsewhere between sensation on the one hand, and the real in space that gives rise to sensation on the other hand. We find, for example, the following statement: "All outer perception thus directly proves something real in space, *or is rather the real itself* . . ." (*A*375, italics added). But this very sentence continues; ". . . and in this way is empirical realism thus beyond doubt, i.e. *there corresponds to our outer intuitions something real in space*" (*A*373, italics added).[21] And other statements in the Paralogism in *A* seem completely consonant with the account of perception we have noted in the Aesthetic and the Anticipations of Perception. For instance, Kant writes:

Space and time are indeed *a priori* representations, which dwell in us as forms of our sensible intuition, before a real object has determined our sense through sensation, so as to represent the object under those sensible relations. Only this material or real, this something that is to be intuited in space, necessarily presupposes perception, and can not independently of it, which indicates (*anzeigt*) the reality of something in space, be composed and produced by any power of imagination. . . . It is unquestionably certain that whether one takes the sensations of pleasure and pain, or even the outer ones, such as colors, heat, etc., perception is that through which the stuff to think objects of sensible intuition must first be given. This perception thus represents . . . something real in space. [*A*373–7]

[20] Kemp Smith, for instance. See my discussion in "Kant and 'the *Dogmatic* Idealism of Berkeley,' " pp. 463ff. On the alleged "Berkeleyanism" of the Fourth Paralogism, see Allison, "Kant's Critique of Berkeley," pp. 45ff.

[21] Kemp Smith introduces a sentence break that is not in the German.

Here again the theory Kant is propounding appears to be a causal one, for all the "noninferential" or "direct" knowledge perception is said to afford us of "something real in space." Perception and sensation have a necessary dependence on such reality, which is not itself reducible to the mere *forms* of sensible intuition. The ideality of the forms assures that 'the real in space' will itself count as mind dependent, however. Kant seems to suppose that this fact is sufficient to counter the challenge of problematic idealism.

I will not attempt to assess here how strong a response to "external world skepticism" this theory really is. (Kant himself, as noted, did not stick by it.) What I do want to stress is that it is not a Berkeleyan response. The "something real in space" (*etwas Wirkliches im Raume*) is not in the least the same thing as, for instance, Philonous's cherry, *comprised of* the sensations of softness, moisture, redness, tartness. It is rather merely the *cause of* such sensations, shaking the optic and the other sensory nerves.

It follows, I think, that Kant's theory of the relation of perceptual experience and reality is much closer to Descartes's than it is to Berkeley's. Unlike Descartes, Kant thought that space had to be construed as ideal or mind–dependent, if we are to evade the skeptic's challenge concerning the reality of 'outer objects.'[22] And unlike Descartes *and* Berkeley, Kant seems completely untroubled by the discrepancy between the subjective world of 'sensation' (colors, tastes, warmth, and so on) and the world of bare matter (or forces) portrayed by scientific theory.[23] But like Descartes, and unlike Berkeley, Kant construes the world of science, and not the world of sensation, as empirically real. Like Descartes, and unlike Berkeley, Kant holds that our experiences

---

[22] Cf. A27–28. Amazingly, some commentators seem to take the view that Descartes's conception of material substance as mind-independent *logically bars* him from holding that we can have knowledge of matter: see, in this connection, Allison, "Kant's Critique of Berkeley," p. 47. As far as I can tell, this interpretation completely overlooks the theory of innate ideas and the "divine guarantee."

[23] In *Descartes* I argue that this discrepancy was a serious concern of Descartes's, relating closely to his preoccupations with the problem of God's veracity, and the respects in which the senses can be said to "deceive."

of colors, tastes, and so on are mere "subjective sensations" that do nothing to "determine an object."[24]

If my remarks on Kant's theory of perception are correct, Kant is a very peculiar sort of 'phenomenalist' indeed. He cannot think that things just are the way they appear in ordinary sense experience, for the secondary qualities with which they appear to be endowed are only subjective sensations, sensations caused by the objects. The "something real in space" must, it seems, retain its mystery until its true nature is revealed by sophisticated scientific–philosophical inquiry. The reality of this sensorily remote, mysterious 'matter' is, of course, just what Berkeley would want to deny. Granted, for Kant the fundamental concepts of scientific understanding of this matter are also implicit in the ordinary experiential ordering of the world. This concession does not affect the fact that Kant—like Descartes and Locke before him and numerous "scientific realists" after him, and very *un*like Berkeley—is a *critic* of what might be called the naive empiricist world view. Kant can be styled a phenomenalist not because he accords 'reality' to the ordinary 'image,' but only because the scientist's sophisticated reductive explanation of that image is, on Kant's view, elaborated within the framework of merely ideal 'forms of intuition.'

Thus, it may be that from one point of view Kant offers us the sweets of idealism without the bitters of subjectivism. From another point of view, I suggest, Kantianism yields the bitters of idealism, without the sweets of Berkeley's commonsense empiricism. In the Critical philosophy, as in the more naive materialism that Berkeley was attacking, a significant portion of our ordinary sense–world is rendered, in Berkeley's poignant expression, a false imaginary glare.

A corollary of this reading of Kant is that his conception of what constitutes 'experience' has to be, at best, somewhat recon-

---

[24]Cf. Descartes's discussion in *Principles of Philosophy*, part 2, 3–4; part 4, 197–9, in *Oeuvres de Descartes*, ed. Charles Adam and Paul Tannery, 12 vols. (Paris, 1957–), vol. 8–1, pp. 41–42; 320–23.

Here I assume the point of view argued earlier: that Berkeley was not merely concerned to refute the transcendental reality of matter, and correlatively to answer "Cartesian skepticism," but also to reinstate the reality of the sensible world as we experience it in ordinary life.

dite. The most interesting recent English–language commentaries—the works of P.F. Strawson and Jonathan Bennett—seem
to me to go wrong in completely overlooking this important
complexity.[25] Defense of this point would require, however, a
far more detailed discussion than is appropriate here.

CONCLUSION

If my interpretation is right, Berkeley and Kant are very far
apart in their views about physical reality, in relation to sense
experience and science. I would like to point out, though, one
widely overlooked point of apparent communality between the
two 'phenomenalists'; namely, their respective concepts of a *nonhuman* apprehension. Both Berkeley and Kant stress the passivity
of human sense experience, and contrast this way of experiencing objects with the wholly active, "archetypal" intelligence that
can be attributed to God.[26] Of course both philosophers introduce the latter notion in a quite sketchy way, and there is much
room for uncertainty about the exact nature of their views and
speculation about disanalogies between them. For example, it

[25]See Jonathan Bennett, *Kant's Analytic* (Cambridge, Eng., 1966), pp. 22; and
P. F. Strawson, *The Bounds of Sense* (London, 1966), p. 32. In the latter passage
I take Strawson to be interpreting Kantian phenomena in terms of
"ordinary reports" and "ordinary descriptions" of "what we see, feel, hear." On
pp. 40–41 of *The Bounds of Sense* Strawson rather startlingly *contrasts* Kant with
"the scientifically-minded philosopher"!
[26]Berkeley discusses the archetypal-sensible distinction in *Works*, vol. 2, pp.
241, 254, and in his 1729–30 correspondence with Samuel Johnson (*Works*, vol.
2, pp. 271–94). See also Russell A. Lascola,"Ideas and Archetypes: Appearances
and Reality in Berkeley's Philosophy," *The Personalist*, 54 (1973), 42–59 (especially
pp. 52ff) and George H. Thomas, "Berkeley's God Does Not Perceive," *Journal
of the History of Philosophy* 14 (1976), 163–68. At *B*72 Kant contrasts our sensible
intuition, to which objects have to be *given*, with "original" intuition, "which so
far as we can judge, can belong only to the primordial being." Elsewhere, notably
in Phenomena and Noumena, Kant does claim that we cannot even comprehend
the possibility of an original intuition. (If Thomas's thesis as stated in his title is
correct, then Berkeley's "to be is to be perceived (or to perceive)" thesis seems
to require fundamental rephrasing. For it is surely Berkeley's view that both
God and the archetypes in his mind have being.)

Margaret D. Wilson

will immediately be noted that Berkeley is dogmatically assertive where Kant is critically circumspect in observations about the relation between God's mind and its 'objects'. Further, Berkeley succumbs to the temptation to appeal to archetypal intelligence as a basis for resolving objectivity problems that arise within his phenomenalist account of things: the problem of their continuous existence in particular. (Things are always in God's mind, even though human perceptions are intermittent.)[27]

Kant, on the contrary, evidently construes the resolution of such problems as an essential and integral requirement of the phenomenalist enterprise itself. All the same, Kant notoriously does hint that the appearances which for us constitute "empirical reality" are in some sense grounded in the things in themselves— where the latter may be at least speculatively identified with the objects of (God's) nonsensible intuition (See Bxxvi–vii). On the other hand, Berkeley's casual attempt to *integrate* the flow of human sense perceptions with the divine archetypal apprehension is surely undercut by his acknowledgment of the radical discrepancy between the two modes of apprehension.[28] To this extent, it seems, Berkeley as well as Kant must be attributed a qualified empiricism: a position that ultimately acknowledges

[27]Berkeley, in his youthful works, tried to use God's archetypes to ground the permanence and perhaps the "publicity" of the objects of outer sense: see *Works*, vol. 2, pp. 212; 230–31. Perhaps he later gave up on this idea. He makes hardly any reply to Samuel Johnson's queries about archetypes—especially in relation to the issue of permanence—even though Johnson expresses his questions clearly and rather persistently (*Works*, vol. 2, pp. 274–76; 285–86). (Berkeley does reply appositely to most of Johnson's other inquiries.) Allison, "Kant's Critique of Berkeley," p. 61, quotes a striking, often overlooked passage in Kant's *Gesammelte Schriften* in which Kant comments on Berkeley's recourse to "the mystical [intuition] of God's ideas." Although the passage is obscure, I take Kant to be saying that he, unlike Berkeley, does not need to call on the divine understanding to provide for the connection of appearances. The passage is also cited by Graham Bird in a different connection in *Kant's Theory of Knowledge* (New York, 1962), p. 37.
[28]According to Berkeley, "God perceives nothing by sense as we do" (*Works*, vol. 2, p. 241, and Thomas, "Berkeley's God Does Not Perceive," p. 166). Of course, the assimilation of Berkeleyan archetypes to nonsensible *intuitions* (in the Kantian sense) will not hold fully if the former are understood platonically, as universal forms—as Johnson *may* be understanding them in section 1 of his second letter (Berkeley's *Works*, vol. 2, pp. 285–86). I conjecture God's archetypes must be particulars for Berkeley's purposes in the early works—from which it would follow that their relation to our ideas is not one of form to instances.

172

that ordinary human sense perception is not the very last authority on the truth about things. And both philosophers, by introducing at least the possibility of a strictly active apprehension, leave room for the relative "mereness" of appearances to us.[29]

[29]This paper was completed under a grant from the American Council of Learned Societies, through a program funded by the National Endowment for the Humanities.

Kant's Scientific Rationalism

Elizabeth Potter

Against commonsense physics and science, critics have argued that commonsense science generates certain contradictions and absurdities. Against Aristotelian physics, for example, it was argued that if we accept the commonsense assumption that things are as they appear in our best sensory observations, then things have contradictory properties; for example, a basin of water is both cool and warm when it feels cool to my left hand and warm to my right.

Against rationalist or mathematical physics and science, advocates of common sense have argued that rationalist science generates theories that conflict in absurd ways with our best sensory observations—that if we accept rationalist scientific theories, we lose what our senses tell us is obvious. This objection appears as early as Zeno's arguments against the Pythagorean mathematical physics; namely, if mathematics really applied to the sensory world, then motion and change, two phenomena that we clearly observe, would be impossible.

As Margaret D. Wilson has pointed out so convincingly in the preceding essay, Berkeley places himself squarely on the side of commonsense science against rationalistic science. The primary question I want to address is whether Berkeley and Wilson are right in their charge that, on the rationalist physical view adopted by Locke and Kant, something essential is lost, that half of what we experience through our senses is rendered, in Berkeley's phrase, a "false, imaginary glare." I suggest that on Locke's view nothing is rendered a false, imaginary glare, and although I shall not attempt to defend Kant's identification of secondary properties with sensations, I do not view his error as a very interesting one. His error was one of mistaking the reference of secondary quality terms, not of inconsistency in holding to the primary/secondary quality distinction. In my arguments for this claim, I will, therefore, also address Wilson's suggestion that as a phenomenalist (even a transcendental one) Kant is not entitled to a distinction between primary and secondary qualities, and that his account of experience is a recondite one.

My initial argument rests in part upon the thesis that the distinction Locke really wanted between primary and secondary qualities was between the intrinsic properties of the elementary particles that constitute bodies and all the other properties of bodies, which turn out in fact to be relative to (a) the properties of the particles, (b) our sense organs, and (c) factors in the environment such as light and air.

Locke did not make the distinction in this way, of course; he distinguished between those properties that resemble our ideas of them and those that do not, but which are somehow adequately represented by our ideas of them. The temptation to make the distinction in this way was, I believe, overwhelming to Locke because he held the following views.

I. The Gassendi-Boyle atomic theory was correct, therefore:
1. Bodies are comprised of insensible particles.
2. These particles are essentially extremely small bodies.
3. Both particles and sensible bodies have extension, shape, motion or rest, solidity, existence, duration, and number.
4. The properties of bodies, such as color, weight, taste, odor, sound, temperatures, hardness or softness, and so on, are merely dispositions of the configurations of the small particles in those bodies to cause certain sensations in us.
5. Our sensations of these properties are caused by an interaction of the small particles, environmental factors, and our sense organs.

And

II. We have simple ideas that include existence, duration, number, extension, shape, solidity, motion or rest, colors, tastes, odors, sounds, temperatures, textures, and so on.

I will not offer textual support for all these claims, but I will argue for the more controversial ones. I support claim (3) here and claim (4) in my defense of Locke against Berkeley and Wilson. Locke says that primary qualities are "such as sense constantly finds in every article of matter which has bulk enough to be perceived [so they are properties of sensible bodies] and the mind finds inseparable from every article of matter, though less than to make itself singly be perceived by our senses [so they are properties of the elementary particles]."[1] It seems, then, that Locke (and Boyle) took primary qualities to be the same qualities in both minute particles and sensible bodies; that is, the shape of a particle is no different in kind from the shape of a sensible body, and so on. And as properties of sensible bodies, these properties are powers to produce primary ideas in us.

Given the two sets of beliefs just mentioned, it is, as Locke remarks, "easy to draw this observation," that some of our simple ideas are *the same* as the properties of bodies and of the small particles comprising them. This is very exciting, for it follows that those ideas accurately picture or resemble (Locke says, "as in a mirror") these properties of the bodies and elementary particles.

We should note here that "drawing observations" is not arguing; that is, Locke does not *argue* for his view that primary ideas resemble certain properties of bodies. Close attention to the text reveals that in sections 7–8 Locke makes the distinction between qualities and ideas, in section 9 defines primary qualities, in section 10 defines secondary qualities, in sections 11–13 establishes how primary and secondary qualities produce ideas in us, in section 14 reiterates the list of secondary qualities and their definition, and then, without further ado, begins section 15 with the "observation" that ideas of primary qualities resemble

[1]John Locke, *An Essay Concerning Human Understanding*, ed. P. H. Nidditch (Oxford, 1975), vol. 2, viii; 9.

them. On the other hand, what he is at pains to show throughout the rest of the chapter is that secondary qualities are quite different from primary ones and that we are wrong in supposing them to be the same, and further wrong if we suppose that secondary ideas resemble anything in bodies—that is, if we think they ought to. Throughout, Locke's arguments turn on showing that if the atomic theory of Boyle is correct, then we ought not be surprised that secondary ideas do not resemble secondary qualities, any more than we are that ideas of the "powers" of bodies do not resemble those powers, as for example, the idea of 'melting wax' is not taken to resemble the sun's power to melt wax.

Once Locke has convinced us that secondary qualities are not to be supposed primary qualities, then we can see that secondary ideas are not supposed to be like primary ideas and are not, therefore, second-rate ideas or failed primary ideas. Instead, they represent certain of the properties of bodies in ways fully explicable by physics, optics, and so on. Although secondary ideas do not, according to Locke, resemble anything in bodies, he does not take secondary qualities to be merely ideas or sensations. I argue that, *contra* Berkeley, Locke does not take secondary quality terms, such as 'color', 'taste', and so on, to refer to sensations or ideas.

Berkeley is correct in pointing out that if Locke's arguments do prove that secondary qualities are not in bodies themselves, but are merely ideas in the mind, those same arguments also prove that primary qualities are merely ideas in the mind. Berkeley says:

> They who assert that figure, motion and the rest of the primary or original qualities do exist without the mind, in unthinking substances, do at the same time acknowledge that colors, sounds, heat, cold, and such-like secondary qualities, do not; which they tell us are sensations, existing in the mind alone, that depend on and are occasioned by the different size, texture, and motion of the minute particles of matter.[2]

---

[2]*The Principles of Human Knowledge, Works of George Berkeley*, ed. A. A. Luce and T. E. Jessop (London and New York, 1948–51), section 10.

This remark is immediately followed by the argument that primary and secondary qualities are conceptually dependent, that the concept of 'body' entails both sets of qualities, and so, since one set exists in the mind only, the other set must as well.

The text of Locke's *Essay* does not, in my judgment, support the claim that Locke acknowledges secondary qualities to be sensations. He says secondary qualities are "in truth nothing in the objects themselves but powers to produce various sensations in us by their primary qualities, i.e., by the bulk, figure, texture, and motion of their insensible parts" (2, viii, 10). This is not to acknowledge that secondary qualities do not "exist without the mind." It is to reduce them to the bulk, figure, texture, and motion of the elementary particles, or to the disposition of the bulk, figures, texture, and motion of the particles to produce sensations in us.

Other passages may be more problematic for this interpretation of Locke. For example, he says plainly that porphyry "has no color in the dark." In the next sentence, however, he says, "It has, indeed, such a configuration of particles, both night and day, as are apt, by the rays of light rebounding from some parts of that hard stone, to produce in us the idea of redness, and from others the idea of whiteness; but whiteness and redness are not in it at any time, *but such a texture that hath the power to produce such a sensation in us.*"[3] Thus, for Locke, secondary qualities are powers, due to configurations of the elementary particles, to produce secondary ideas.

I believe Locke was wrong, even given his own premises, in failing to see that the bulk, figure, texture, and motion of the particles in a body are the ground of the powers to produce not only secondary ideas, but primary ideas as well. The extension, shape, situation, motion, and so on of sensible bodies, which are what produce primary ideas, are due to the configuration of the particles. And this is no different from the color, taste, and so on of sensible bodies being due to the configuration of particles which causes secondary ideas. Both the primary and secondary properties of *sensible* bodies are due to the configurations of their

---

[3]Locke, *Essay Concerning Human Understanding*, vol. 2, viii, 19, italics added.

elementary particles. Therefore, the distinction Locke wanted was between the intrinsic properties of the elementary particles and the properties of sensible bodies, which are relative to the elementary particles.

If the foregoing interpretation of Locke is correct, then it is untrue to say that on his view colors, for example, are a false, imaginary glare. In the first place, colors are not "false" because it is not false, on his view, to say that "color is an intrinsic property of bodies" or that "bodies have color." Yet it has seemed to Locke's readers that, because he holds a resemblance theory of some ideas, and because our color sensations do not resemble the surface particles of bodies, colors are an "imaginary glare." But that would be so only if color sensations or color ideas were supposed somehow, were somehow intended, to be pictures of the colors in bodies. However, as shown earlier, Locke is at great pains to argue that science tells us that this is not what color sensations and ideas are supposed to be. On the Boyle-Locke view, secondary ideas are not failed primary ideas nor are they imaginary ideas. They would be an imaginary glare, they would be second-rate or failed ideas (and color statements would be false), if color sensations were not systematically caused by anything in bodies; if, for example, an evil genie caused color sensations in us in such a way that we mistakenly took bodies to have color when in fact they did not.

Some of Kant's remarks make clear his belief that secondary qualities reduce to sensations. He says, "Colors are not properties of the bodies to the intuition of which they are attached, but only modifications of the sense of sight, which is affected in a certain manner by light" (A28–29). So, although he accepted a causal account of color sensations in which they are caused by light, or by an interaction between light and our eyes, Kant takes the term 'color' to refer to the sensation, not to the light or to any property in the body.

Can we rescue Kant from Berkeley's charge? On Kant's view, the statement, "Color is an intrinsic property of bodies," is false, though it is not false, for him, to say that "Bodies have color," since he would take that statement as biconditional with "Some properties in bodies interact with light which can interact with our eyes and cause color sensations in us." But if one takes color sensations to be colors, are not colors after all just an imaginary glare?

Certainly colors are not an imaginary glare in the sense that they are illusions, caused by an evil genie and causally unrelated to bodies. Even if Kant accepted a resemblance theory of primary ideas on which secondary qualities might be thought to be secondary ideas and thus imaginary and unreal because they do not resemble anything in bodies, his acceptance of a rationalist physical theory of matter and account of perception means that he understood secondary ideas to be systematically caused by certain properties of bodies. Although Kant's rejection of empty space (*A*172–73/*B*214) leads him to reject the Boyle-Locke view that sensations of colors are caused by an interaction between the surface particles of bodies, light, and our eyes, his remarks in the Anticipations of Perception show that he took secondary sensations to be caused by something in bodies. His way of making the point is to say that something real in the object of perception causes sensations in us:

> Corresponding to this intensity of sensation, an *intensive magnitude*, that is, a degree of influence on the sense ... must be ascribed to all objects of perception. [*A*166/*B*208, Kant's emphasis]

> Every reality in the [field of] appearance has therefore intensive magnitude or degree. If *this reality is viewed as cause, either of sensation* or of some other reality in the [field of] appearance, such as change, the degree of the reality as cause is then entitled a moment. [*A*168/*B*210, italics added]

And finally:

> Every sensation, therefore, and likewise every reality in the [field of] appearance ... has a degree.... Every color, as for instance red, has a degree. [*A*169/*B*211]

Precisely because he understood sensations to be systematically caused by something real in bodies, I do not believe that Kant is obliged to assent to the claim that colors are imaginary, not real. Not even his belief that colors are sensations makes color an imaginary glare, because not all sensations are false or imaginary. Some are, but some—those systematically caused by bodies in ways explicable by science—are not. Rationalist science offers Kant a clear way to distinguish imaginary from real sensations.

Admittedly, Kant does say that colors are subjective and relative to individuals; this admission follows from his identification of colors with sensations. But the force of this admission is not to reduce being to seeming or color sensations to imaginary sensations because, as we have seen, he has a clear way to distinguish in principle veridical from nonveridical sensations. Colors and other secondary properties are not subjective, on Kant's view, in the sense that it is impossible in principle to determine what property a body actually has that causes the color sensations in us.

I expect Kant would say that the sentence, "Apples are red," is true because the intrinsic properties of apples make them seem red to most people most of the time; however, apples seem red to us, not by chance, but because of an intrinsic property the apples possess. And it is just this fact that prevents our saying that on Kant's view colors are a false, imaginary glare. In my judgment, he is wrong about the reference of the terms, 'color', 'taste', 'sound', and so on. It is false to say that "color is not an intrinsic property of bodies," but because Kant accepts a causal account of perception offered by rationalist science, it is open to him to follow Locke and take 'color' to refer to some physical property of bodies. In any case, on his view, color attributions are not false, nor are colors imaginary.

Assuming that he can distinguish imaginary from veridical sensations by an appeal to material properties of bodies, to bodily sense organs, and so on, is Kant entitled to a distinction between sensations (veridical or nonveridical) and material properties? After all, on his view, the material world is simply an appearance, a world of phenomena, presumably the way things in themselves *appear* to us.

If his arguments in support of transcendental idealism were sound, Kant would be entitled to the distinction. I will not attack or defend these arguments here, but will defend an interpretation of what they are supposed to prove. On this interpretation, his distinction between veridical sensations and material properties can be seen to be a valid one. If one accepts an ontology that includes sensations, the individual mind that has them, a community of such minds, and something independent of all minds that appears to them in a systematic way, then one can make a distinction between an individual's sensations, and a world, independent of one's mind, which causes those sensations. This world might, however, be dependent upon the community of minds in either of two ways: it might be purely a construction of those minds (in which case conventionalist or linguistic idealism is the correct ontology) or it might be constructed by those minds (partially or totally) on the basis of how reality in itself appears to them. In either case, however, that world is not reducible to an individual's ideas, and there are grounds for making a distinction between an individual's sensations or ideas and material properties, that is, properties independent of the individual's sensations. Does Kant's transcendental idealist ontology include (a) sensations and the individual mind that has them, (b) a community of such minds, (c) an objective world constructed by those minds either independently of or in response to (d) reality?

(a) and (c). For our purposes, the most important distinction is the one between (a) and (c). We see in many passages from various of Kant's works that he intended to distinguish the individual mind and its ideas from a world independent of that mind. Perhaps the Refutation of Idealism is among the clearest on this point. Laying aside the question of whether his proof for it works, Kant's thesis is plain: "The mere, but empirically determined consciousness of my own existence proves the existence of objects in space outside me" (*B*275). Thus Kant takes (a), the fact that I have a mind and sensations, as given and attempts to demonstrate (c), that a world of actual things exists outside me.

(b). There are very few texts in which Kant explicitly argues for a community of minds or for its necessity. A most intriguing text, therefore, is the following: "Cognitions and judgments must, along with the conviction which accompanies them, allow uni-

versal communicability, for otherwise there would be no harmony between them and the object, and they would be collectively
a mere subjective play of the representative powers just as scepticism claims" (*KU* 21).[4] Here we see that for Kant the objectivity
of our judgments requires that they be public, or as he puts it,
"universally communicable." The point is even more explicit in
the *Prolegomena*:

> There would be no reason for the judgments of other men nec-
> essarily agreeing with mine if it were not the unity of the object to
> which they all refer and with which they accord; hence they must
> all agree with one another.
>
> Therefore objective validity and necessary universality (for every-
> body) are equivalent terms. [*P*19]

Whether or not Kant has a succcessful argument for these claims,
clearly he holds that our judgments are universally communicable, which entails that there exists more than one mind and
that communication can (necessarily) occur between them.[5]

(*d*). That Kant believed the phenomenal world to be constructed
by us is made clear in his numerous remarks about the dependence of nature upon our minds. For example, he says that "the
order and regularity in the appearances, which we entitled *nature*, we ourselves introduce. We could never find them in appearances, had not we ourselves, or the nature of our mind,
originally set them there" (*A*125). And finally, that Kant is not
a linguistic idealist, that he never believed we construct or create
the world *ex nihilo*, is revealed in those passages in which he
mentions things in themselves. He says, for example, that

> Things in themselves would necessarily, apart from any under-
> standing that knows them, conform to laws of their own. But ap-

[4]My translation.
[5]Jane E. Kneller argues that Kant does prove the claims at *P* 19 in "Objective
and Intersubjective Validity in the Critique of Pure Reason," *Akten des 5. Internationalen Kant-Kongresses*, ed. Gerhard Funke, Teil I.1, pp. 164–70. Thomas J.
Nenon, on the other hand, claims that for Kant communicability to others is not
a necessary condition for the objectivity of a judgment, but is merely a reliable
indicator of objectivity. See his "Konsensus and Objektivität: Hat Kant seine
Position aus der Kritik der reinen Vernunft nachträglich revidiert?" in *Akten*,
ed. Funke, pp. 171–78.

pearances are only representations of things which are unknown as regards what they may be in themselves. As mere representations, they are subject to no law of connection save that which the connecting faculty [the understanding] prescribes.[*B*164]

It seems clear from these passages that Kant was arguing (with whatever success) for an ontology including distinctions between individual minds, the community of minds, the world constructed by these minds, and reality as it is in itself, which probably appears to those minds in systematic ways. He was also claiming that both other minds and a public world independent of the individual mind provide ways to distinguish subjective ideas and sensations from external bodies and properties.

It might well be argued that Berkeley actually held an ontology similar in the relevant respects to Kant as just described; that is, one in which God and the individual mind constitute a community of minds which constructs a public, shared world. In this case, Berkeley, too, could make a distinction between sensations and properties "external" to the mind. The philosopher who *cannot* make such a distinction is the one who holds an ontology that includes only ideas and sensations and one mind that has them; namely, the philosophical solipsist. Perhaps Berkeley was misread, by Kant among others, as holding such an ontology. Berkeley may not be, as Margaret Wilson suggests at the end of her essay, any more than Kant is, a pure 'phenomenalist' or solipsist.

VI

Kant's Philosophy of Science

Philip Kitcher

Contemporary philosophers are not usually enthusiastic about Kant's philosophy of science. It is easy to understand why Kant's discussions of science meet with a lukewarm reception. In the first place, Kant seems to be committed to the idea that some substantive scientific principles can be known a priori. Second, his apparent attempt to do a priori science, the *Metaphysical Foundations of Natural Science*, contains some very unpromising arguments; moreover, its relation to the first *Critique* is quite obscure. In this essay, I shall explore some of Kant's ideas about science, with the aims of understanding whether he is really an advocate of a priori science and of exposing the intended relation between the *Critique* and the *Metaphysical Foundations*. I also want to see if there is anything we can learn from Kant's doctrines about science.

A PRIORI SCIENCE?

Kant's apparent commitment to the existence of a priori science is expressed in the early pages of the *Critique* (and in parallel sections in the *Prolegomena*). Despite the fact that his assertion that synthetic a priori judgments exist in natural science is more outré than the companion claim about mathematics, Kant offers little by way of defense or explanation. He states bluntly that two propositions are necessary and a priori, and that this status is evident. Kant's propositions recall general truths of physics: "in all changes of the material world the quantity of matter remains unchanged" and "in all communication of motion, action and reaction must always be equal" (*B*17–18).

Later in the *Critique* some passages seem to retract this bold doctrine. At the height of the Deductions, Kant declares that only laws "which are involved in a *nature in general*" are knowable a priori (*B*165; also *A*127–28). The Antinomies section is more forthright. Drawing an invidious contrast with pure mathematics and pure ethics, Kant declares: "In natural science...there is endless conjecture, and certainty is not to be counted upon" (*A*480*B*508). As he firmly believes that all a priori knowledge is certain, this passage implies that natural science is not a priori.

We can easily reconcile the contrary indications by drawing a distinction that Kant sometimes makes explicitly. Perhaps *most* of natural science is empirical, and Kant's remarks in the Deductions and the Antinomies are prompted by consideration of empirical natural science. What is distinctive about Kant's philosophy of science is the idea that natural science contains a pure part; the Introduction to the *Critique* is intended to advertise the existence of pure natural science.

It is evident that Kant does not believe all natural science to be a priori, so this distinction must be drawn. Yet it does not resolve all our problems. Does Kant's a priori science include any more than the very general propositions about nature he tries to prove in the Transcendental Analytic? If not, then Kant's doctrine loses its provocative character, and the claim that there is a priori science is exposed as based on a dull pun. The Introduction to the *Critique* suggests a way to restore the excitement. Kant's examples resemble central laws of Newtonian physics; we might attribute to Kant the view that central parts of Newtonian physics belong to a priori science.

This attribution has been popular. It rests on three pieces of evidence. Besides the Introduction to the *Critique*, there is a section in the *Prolegomena* that appears to sketch an a priori route to the law of universal gravitation (*P* §36), and an entire work, the *Metaphysical Foundations of Natural Science*, is seemingly devoted to the task of proving many basic Newtonian principles. Taken individually, however, these three pieces of evidence are inconclusive; taken collectively, internal tensions exist among them.

Kant's use of the terms 'matter', 'action', and 'reaction' is not clearly explained in the *Critique*. Although the propositions enunciated in the Introduction resemble principles of Newtonian science, we might easily reinterpret them as the more general claims for which Kant argues in the Analogies. In the *Prolegomena*, Kant does indeed outline what resembles an attempt at a priori argument for the law of universal gravitation (*P* §36). But he characterizes the argument by saying that it explains why the law "is usually propounded as capable of being known a priori." This characterization stops short of endorsing the argument as an a priori proof. Finally, despite the fact that the *Metaphysical Foundations* does claim that there is a pure part of natural science to which basic Newtonian principles belong, Kant clearly distinguishes between the status of those principles and the propositions established in the *Critique*. Indeed, the more detailed articulation of his views about science given in the later work suggests that we *must* reinterpret those parts of the *Critique* and the *Prolegomena* that seem to claim the apriority of Newtonian science. Kant maintains that *some* general Newtonian principles are knowable a priori, *given the empirical concept of matter*, but his discussion of the law of gravitation does not even attribute this status to it.

These jumbled doctrines about Newtonian science are best understood if we adopt an interpretative hypothesis. Kant does not believe that principles such as that of the conservation of matter and that of the equality of action and reaction are fully a priori. Nor does he hold that these principles are best described simply by declaring them to be empirical. Instead he takes them to admit to *something like* a priori proof. Introducing a label, let us say that for Kant parts of Newtonian science are *quasi a priori*, and that the *Metaphysical Foundations* is his attempt to display their quasi apriority. Perhaps we can give sense to the idea of quasi apriority in a way that illuminates what Kant says about Newtonian science.

Quasi A Priority

Our chief clue for quasi-apriority comes from the announcement of his project that Kant provides at the beginning of the *Metaphysical Foundations*. After attempting to explain why there can be no "natural science proper" without a pure part, Kant continues by elaborating on the nature of this "pure part."

> [It] must indeed always contain nothing but principles which are not empirical (for that reason it bears the name of a metaphysics). But either it can treat of the laws which make possible the concept of a nature in general even without reference to any determinate object of experience, and therefore undetermined regarding the nature of this or that thing of the sense-world—and in this case it is the transcendental part of the metaphysics of nature—or it occupies itself with the special nature of this or that kind of things, of which an empirical concept is given in such a way that besides what lies in this concept, no other empirical principle is needed for cognizing the things. [*MN* 469g 6e]

This passage presents a division of labor between the *Critique* and the *Metaphysical Foundations*. The task of the *Critique* is to set forth those principles that apply to nature in general. The later work is to expound those quasi a priori principles, obtained by introducing an empirically grounded concept.

What exactly does this mean? There is an obvious, and trivial, way to relativize the notion of apriority. We can say that a proposition is a priori relative to a theory if, given knowledge of the theory, we can obtain knowledge of the proposition without further reliance on experience. This is trivial because most empiricists concede that any theorem of any knowable theory is a priori relative to that theory. However, Kant seems to be after something different. He does not say that the law of conservation of matter is a priori relative to Newtonian theory, but that this (and other Newtonian principles) is a priori relative to an empirical concept.

The trivial relativization of apriority just considered presupposes a particular way of thinking about science that is deeply embedded in contemporary empiricist philosophy of science but at odds with Kant's approach. We find it natural to view science as a collection of theories and to identify a theory as a deductively organized set of propositions. Although Kant does not explicitly consider the question, What is a scientific theory? I believe he would reject the standard empiricist idea that the epistemologically interesting questions about science should be addressed by taking theories to be organized sets of propositions.[1] By understanding how an alternative approach to theories might be developed, we can obtain a clearer view of that relativization of the notion of apriority Kant intends to employ.

Let me begin obliquely. We standardly use two different notions of scientific theory. In our more restrictive usage, we talk about theories as short-lived entities; thus we might speak of Newtonian theory, intending to refer to the particular set of propositions put forward by Newton in a particular work (*Principia*). I shall call such entities *theory versions*. We also talk of theories as enduring entities, and identify different, incompatible theory versions as belonging to the same theory. In this usage we envisage something that stands behind the sets of propositions accepted by successive generations of scientists, that unites those sets of propositions as versions of a single theory.[2]

At any stage in the history of a scientific field, we can identify the set of statements that practitioners of the field accept. For

---

[1]This is a *minimal* empiricist view, shorn of all the standard claims about the theory-observation distinction(s), axiomatizability, and so forth. Even though many philosophers have abandoned those extra claims, the minimal view remains very popular.

[2]I take it that Kuhn's concept of a paradigm, Lakatos's notion of a research program, and Laudan's idea of a research tradition attempt to do justice to this usage. (See T. S. Kuhn, *The Structure of Scientific Revolutions* [Chicago, 1970]; Imre Lakatos, *Philosophical Papers*, vol. 1 [Cambridge, Eng., 1978]; Larry Laudan, *Progress and Its Problems* [Berkeley, 1977]). Whatever the difficulties of these particular notions, I believe there are genuine philosophical problems that require us to introduce some similar notion.

some epistemological purposes, it may be useful to axiomatize (a subset of) these statements. I believe that there are some epistemological inquiries and some fields of science, however, for which the focus on statements (rather than on questions, or on procedures for answering questions) is inappropriate. But, even if we concede the traditional idea that epistemological questions about the science of a time can take the set of accepted statements as an index of the state of science, the question still remains of what unites the sets of accepted statements (theory versions). What is the larger entity, the one theory that embraces the different versions? One approach is to identify a set of core propositions which persists through the sequence of theory versions. Another answer—the answer I attribute to Kant—is that a temporally enduring theory is constituted by a *projected order of nature*.[3]

A projected order of nature is a scheme for classifying and explaining natural phenomena. Kant's presentation develops the idea in a particular way. Think of a concept as a rule for marking out a set of things (the extension of the concept) by specifying certain properties that the members of the extension are to have. A theory, or projected order of nature, presents a hierarchy of concepts. At the top of the hierarchy is a concept, whose extension is the set of *fundamental entities* with which the theory is concerned, and which marks out those entities according to their *fundamental properties*. As we move down the hierarchy, we encounter concepts that apply to *derivative entities* (or perhaps to subsets of the fundamental entities) and that identify those entities by *derivative properties*. This means that if a concept C_{n+1} occurs immediately below a concept C_n, then the fact that the entities actually belonging to the extension of C_{n+1} have the properties that C_{n+1} attributes to them is to be explained by appealing to the fact that the entities in the extension of C_n have the properties C_n attributes to them. On this account, a theory is taken to be that which tells us how to group things together and which presents the skeletal structure of explanations.

[3]The principal passages in which Kant advances this answer occur in the Appendix to the *Ideal* and in the Introduction to the *Critique of Judgment*. For a striking discussion, see p. 21 of the Bernard translation of the latter work.

It is easy to see that a theory, or projected order of nature, can give rise to different theory versions. The theory may tell us that a particular property (or set of properties) is dependent on another property (or set of properties). The exact form of the dependence need not be specified. So, for example, Dalton's atomic theory proposed to explain chemical reactions in terms of molecular rearrangements. This theory generated a number of different versions, each of which was characterized by precise claims about how the molecules combine in particular cases.

I claim that if Kant had addressed the question What is a scientific theory? his answer would have been "a projected order of nature." In introducing this answer, I began with a problem that has interested many modern philosophers of science, the problem of how to understand scientific change. This is not an issue that would have motivated Kant. He would have been concerned to emphasize two respects in which the account of theory just sketched is superior to the standard empiricist analysis: (a) it provides a more accurate picture of the methodology of empirical science; and (b) it allows us to understand how pure natural science—quasi a priori science—is possible. I shall elaborate both points concentrating primarily on the second.

CONFIRMATION OF THEORIES

Kant's discussions of the confirmation of theories hardly amount to a systematic treatment. Nevertheless, his remarks indicate that he views theories as subject to judgment according to a number of different criteria. Most obvious is an emphasis on the predictive success of theory versions. Indeed, Kant sometimes sounds like a proponent of twentieth-century hypothetico-deductivist orthodoxy: we support our theory versions by verifying their observational consequences (*B*xii–iii; *A*646–47/*B*674–75). Yet there are more distinctive suggestions about confirmation. Kant appears to believe that there are principles we can use to assess the merits of theories directly, prior to our enunciation of theory versions. One principle enjoins us to prefer theories that give rise to theory versions that are more subject to test. Others, presented in the Appendix to the Ideal of Pure Reason, direct us to choose theories with special properties: for example, we are to search for unified theories. I believe these principles can be understood if we attribute to Kant the perspective on theories I indicated above.

Toward the end of the second chapter of the *Metaphysical Foundations*, Kant considers the merits of two rival explanatory schemes.[4] One of these, the "mechanical way," proposes that the phenomena of nature are to be understood by tracing them to the interactions among atoms, each of which is viewed as having certain fundamental properties, including impenetrability. The alternative, which Kant favors, is the "dynamical way." On this conception, we are to understand natural phenomena by regarding them as the results of the distribution of centers of fundamental forces. As Kant puts it, the goal of science lies in "explicating all varieties of matter through the mere variety in the combination of the original forces of repulsion and attraction" (*MN* 532g 90e). Although the details of this proposal are far from clear, it is not difficult to identify the merits that Kant takes it to enjoy. He is worried that it is too easy to construct theory versions that conform to the "mechanical philosophy." The use of the concepts of "absolute density" and "absolute emptiness" allows too much freedom to the scientific imagination (*MN* 532g 90e). As he puts it positively, "a dynamical mode of explication . . . [is] more favorable to experimental philosophy inasmuch as it leads directly to the discovery of the moving forces proper to matters and the laws of such forces, but restricts the freedom of assuming empty intermediate spaces and fundamental particles of determinate shapes, neither of which can be

---

[4]These two schemes have an obvious connection to the two major Newtonian traditions of the eighteenth century: the corpuscularian program and the movement to develop field theories. For discussion, see Mary Hesse, *Forces and Fields* (London, 1961), and, especially, R. E. Schofield, *Mechanism and Materialism* (Princeton, N.J., 1969).

discovered or determined by any experiment" (*MN* 533g 91-2e).[5]

Because the "dynamical mode of explication" is a cloudy notion, it is not easy to evaluate Kant's application of the criterion invoked here. However, what concerns me is the criterion rather than its employment. The rival hypotheses are both projected orders of nature. We are invited to compare them, independent of the specific versions of them that may be available. Kant envisages a situation in which, given one account of the hierarchy of concepts, we see how to proceed experimentally to identify precise versions of the relations of dependence, while, on the other account, we have no similar experimental procedure for isolating the correct version. The methodological directive is to prefer those explanatory schemes that focus our explanation-seeking questions, making them accessible to empirical investigation. To use Kant's famous terminology from the Preface to the second edition of the *Critique*, some projected orders of nature teach us how to interrogate nature, and such theories are intrinsically more worthy of acceptance than those that do not.

The idea of comparing theories, rather than theory versions, is also fundamental to the Appendix to the Ideal. Kant identifies three "regulative principles," the principles of "*homogeneity, specification*, and *continuity* of forms" (*A*658/*B*686). Neither the content of these principles nor their intended status is made particularly clear by Kant's remarks. However, both kinds of obscurity can be lessened if we understand this section to be concerned with criteria for judging theories. Consider first the maxim on which Kant places most emphasis, the directive to "bring . . . systematic unity into our knowledge" (*A*650/*B*678).[6] I interpret this as enjoining us to prefer theories that put forward a smaller number of fundamental entities and properties. (How

[5]Given the history of the corpuscularian program in the eighteenth century, Kant's judgment is hardly unfounded! Here, as elsewhere, quotations from the *MN* are from the James Ellington translation.

[6]Kant's terminology in the Appendix is somewhat ambiguous. "Systematic unity" is usually employed to cover the maxim that requires us to reduce fundamental entities. But sometimes the term is used to identify what we achieve by following all three maxims in conjunction.

precisely the accounting is to be done is a tricky business; I shall not explore this issue here.)[7] The second maxim directs us to "attend to the diversity no less than to the identity." Here, Kant seems to be insisting that the bottom level of the hierarchy must be sufficiently fine to accommodate the variety of natural phenomena. Finally, he adds a law of "the *affinity* of all concepts," directing us to group together concepts into families at each level of our conceptual hierarchy, so that "all the manifold differences are then related to one another, inasmuch as they one and all spring from one highest genus, through all degrees of a more and more widely extended determination" (*A*658/*B*686). When we combine the three principles, we can easily obtain a picture of the type of theory (projected order of nature) that is intrinsically worthy of acceptance.

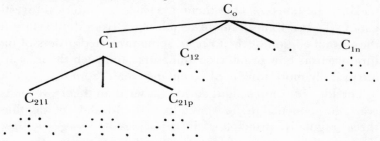

(The numbers n, p are large, so that the tree branches considerably at each node.)

Kant's own summation itself suggests this picture (*A*660/*B*688).

I believe that the account of theories attributed to Kant makes sense of his attempts to explain how theories are confirmed. Kant thinks of a theory as something like a taxonomy. A theory is a hierarchy of concepts which exposes the direction of explanation. The passages cited articulate this conception in terms of the Aristotelian logic that Kant knew. As I shall suggest in the final section, contemporary logical views may enable us to provide a more sophisticated development of the basic Kantian idea. First, however, I want to show how Kant's views about the meth-

---

[7] For one way to analyze the notion of systematic unification, see Philip Kitcher, "Explanatory Unification," *Philosophy of Science* 48 (1981), 507–531.

ods of empirical science provide a framework within which his conception of quasi a priori science can be set.

A PRIORI PROCEDURES: EMPIRICAL LEGITIMIZATION OF CONCEPTS

Two related definitions of quasi a priori science present themselves. The first begins from the apparent possibility that, having adopted a theory, we might be able to proceed, without any further assistance from experience, to arrive at a particular theory version. The second involves an even more ambitious procedure. Suppose that we had empirical reason to believe that it is appropriate to conceptualize the entities we are interested in investigating as having certain properties (not necessarily fundamental properties). Then on the basis of this, but using no further empirical information, we might be able to construct parts of a projected order of nature and even to arrive at parts of a particular theory version. I maintain that Kant conceives of this possibility as genuine, and that he takes it to be realized in Newtonian science. The *Metaphysical Foundations* is his attempt to display how quasi a priori science, in the more ambitious sense, is possible.

It will be useful to have a more precise characterization of the bolder notion. I begin from the ideas of an *a priori procedure* and of an *empirically legitimized concept*. Quasi a priori science consists of two types of activity: (a) using a priori procedures to construct a hierarchy of concepts which will include the empirically legitimized concept; acceptance of this hierarchy is justified by the empirical evidence which supports the concept and the a priori procedures employed; (b) using a priori procedures to reason from the hierarchy of concepts constructed in (a) to a determinate theory version. We shall see that in the *Metaphysical Foundation* Kant tries to engage in both kinds of activity.

Two central Kantian themes need to be tackled before this project is fully comprehensible. Consider first the notion of a

Philip Kitcher

priori procedure.[8] Early in the *Critique*, Kant identifies a priori knowledge as knowledge that is independent of experience. His definition is best understood by supposing that a priori knowledge is knowledge obtained by following an a priori procedure and focusing on the concept of a priori procedure. An a priori procedure for a proposition is a type of process such that, given any experience sufficiently rich to enable someone to entertain the proposition, a process of the type would be available to the agent and, if it were followed, would generate knowledge of the proposition. The function of the restriction to "sufficiently rich experiences" is to allow for the possibility that we know a priori propositions involving concepts that are not innate. Kant plainly wants to allow that there are a priori propositions containing concepts that we can only acquire with the aid of experience. (See, for example, his characterization of the proposition that every alteration has its cause as impure but a priori [*B3*].)

The basic idea of this notion of a priori procedure is easily explained. Picture a person as a device endowed with a set of cognitive capacities. Consider all the possible streams of experience the person could have. Some of these will be long and complicated; others will be very short. With respect to any proposition, we restrict our attention to those streams of experience that would enable the person, constituted as she is, to entertain the proposition. A type of process is an a priori procedure for the proposition, if, given any experience in the restricted class, the person could undergo some process of the type, and, if she were to undergo such a process, she would achieve knowledge of the proposition.

What kinds of procedures might count as a priori? In the *Critique*, Kant divides a priori procedures into three main types. Conceptual analysis is a procedure (about which Kant says very little) that is supposed to yield knowledge of analytic truths. Two procedures give us a priori knowledge of synthetic truths. Construction in pure intuition is the route to a priori mathematical knowledge. So, for example, Kant believes that by constructing

[8]The account that follows recapitulates the analysis given in my paper "A Priori Knowledge," *Philosophical Review* 89 (1980), 3–23.

196

geometrical figures and inspecting them with the mind's eye we expose to ourselves the features of space, and thus gain a priori knowledge of geometrical truths. A different kind of a priori procedure consists in analysis of the conditions of possible experience. The arguments advanced in the Principles chapter of the Analytic are intended to exemplify this kind of procedure: they are attempts to show that certain conclusions must be true if experience is to be possible for us. Furthermore, Kant seems to believe that they supply routes to those conclusions which would yield knowledge of them whatever (sufficiently rich) experience we might have.[9] There is an obvious difference between the theses about a priori procedures advanced in the Aesthetic and the Analytic. Whereas the process of pure intuition is *described*, and its epistemological credentials are analyzed, the procedure of analysis of the conditions of possible experience is *displayed*, and Kant does not examine carefully whether it will really satisfy his constraints on a priori procedures.

Let us now turn to the issue of conceptual legitimacy. Throughout the *Critique*, Kant insists on the importance of establishing that the concepts we use are rightfully employed. How does this inquiry arise? Kant's basic idea is that concepts of certain kinds are so deficient, that if a person believes a proposition involving such concepts then that person's belief is *ipso facto* unjustified. Consider a simple example. If I maintain that all round squares are round, you might be willing to credit me with a piece of knowledge, even a piece of a priori knowledge, on the grounds that I have followed an a priori procedure, analysis of concepts, to obtain a true belief. Kant would deny that this attribution is correct. Concepts, such as that of a round square, which cannot be exemplified, are not constituents of propositions one can justifiably believe. Analysis of a *legitimate* concept counts as an a priori procedure, but not every concept is legitimate.

It is important to note that there are two separate questions Kant would be prepared to ask about a given concept. We could

---

[9]Thus, in two places, Kant hails the conditions of possible experience as the "third thing" that enables us to link subject and predicate to arrive at a priori knowledge of a synthetic truth. See $A156–57/B195–56$, and $A216–18/B263–65$.

inquire whether some experience of a particular kind is needed to *acquire* a particular concept. Or we could inquire whether some experience of a particular kind is needed to *justify our use* of a particular concept. Kant allows for a priori knowledge of propositions containing concepts that can only be acquired on the basis of particular kinds of experience. But I take him to deny that we know a priori propositions containing concepts whose use could be undermined by experience. Part of his doctrine about mathematics, the part that gives point to the Axioms of Intuition, is that we cannot have empirical justification for abandoning the concepts involved in mathematical judgments. (These concepts are a priori concepts.)

Kant's interest in the issue of conceptual legitimacy (so prominent in the Analytic) makes his views about the a priori much more complicated that they are often taken to be. Allowing that a priori knowledge is knowledge obtainable given any *sufficiently rich* experience opens the possibility of a priori knowledge of propositions including concepts that can only be acquired empirically. Demanding that the concepts that figure in items of knowledge be legitimized means we cannot know a priori those propositions which contain concepts that experience could justify us in discarding. Implicit in the *Critique* is the denial that all analytic propositions are a priori. Kant is working his way toward a Quinean insight. Experience can undermine our beliefs by showing that we should abandon a particular way of thinking about the phenomena.[10]

In the *Critique*, Kant's touchstone for conceptual legitimacy is possible exemplification in experience. Although this test is adequate to his principal epistemological purposes, it does not really capture his central insight. Kant sees that it is possible to employ crazy concepts, and that someone who does so makes no con-

[10]I would thus argue that Kant recognizes that analyticity is not the key to solving the problem of a priori knowledge. For passages that support this attribution, see note a to *A*242, *A*252–54, *B*308–310, and especially Kant's reply to Eberhard. (Henry Allison, ed., *The Kant-Eberhard Controversy* [Baltimore, 1973], p. 175; see also L. W. Beck, "Can Kant's Synthetic Judgments Be Made Analytic?" in R. P. Wolff, ed., *Kant* [Doubleday, 1967], pp. 3–22.) I have defended the attribution at some length in "How Kant Almost Wrote 'Two Dogmas of Empiricism' (and Why He Didn't)," *Philosophical Topics* 12 (1981), 217–49.

tribution to human inquiry. But instantiation in actual experience (or in possible experience) is neither necessary nor sufficient for conceptual sanity. Idealizations are properly employed in our investigations. Concepts that intersect natural kinds in bizarre ways are not.

There is a brief discussion of the use of idealization in science in the Appendix to the Ideal, a discussion that indicates an improved criterion for conceptual legitimacy. Kant suggests that the drive for a unified system of knowledge warrants us in abstracting from some of the conditions we encounter in experience (A645–46/B673–74). Generalizing this suggestion, we may propose that a concept is legitimate if and only if it belongs to (or further extends) a well-confirmed theory, that is, to a well-confirmed projected order of nature.

This proposal will help us to explicate the notion of an empirically legitimized concept and also to see why Kant stresses the importance of the "pure part" of natural science. Consider a responsible scientist. She will want to use the evidence available to her to assess the adequacy of the concepts she employs. Can she succeed without having at her disposal a well-confirmed theory? I believe that Kant's answer would be that it depends on the concepts in question. *Some* concepts, the more special ones, may not be subject to legitimization except by noting that they belong to a successful theory. Kant would claim, however, that the credentials of some concepts can be established even prior to our articulation of a full theory. The idea would be that, even before we have developed a projected order of nature, we may be able to recognize, empirically, that certain concepts must figure in any successful theory. So, for example, experience might teach us that *all* the entities with which our science will be concerned will have particular properties. Thus the concept that marks them out as having these properties must find some place in our theory—though not necessarily as a fundamental concept.[11] Let us call concepts whose use can be justified by expe-

---

[11]Thus a concept that is universally instantiated would be assured a place in our projected order of nature because it would be immune from the two most obvious ways in which concepts fail to be legitimate; namely, by not being instantiated and by cutting across natural kinds.

rience prior to the articulation of a theory *empirically legitimized* concepts.

The doctrine that natural science must have a pure part can now be explained. Kant would suggest that proper scientific investigation should exemplify the following pattern. One begins by using experience to legitimize certain concepts. On the basis of these concepts, one uses a priori procedures to construct a theory and, possibly, even parts of a theory version. Once this stage has been reached, one has achieved a framework within which the experimental interrogation of nature can profitably begin. *Pure natural science is important because it takes us from a position in which naive observation teaches us that some concepts are legitimate to a situation in which we can propose and test precise technical hypotheses.*

In developing my interpretation of Kant's thesis that natural science must have a pure part, I have adopted a particular construal of the Kantian notions of a priori knowledge and a priori concepts. An alternative approach to these notions, which can justifiably be traced to the first *Critique*, is outlined in the remainder of this section. I shall contrast this approach with my own, and suggest why my construal offers a more promising reading of Kant's philosophy of science.

Like Kant's own introduction of the concept of apriority, I have begun with the idea of a priori *knowledge*.[12] It is quite apparent, however, that the Transcendental Analytic is primarily concerned with a priori *concepts* and with a priori principles involving those concepts. If one begins with Kant's remarks in the Analytic, taking these usages as primary, a different picture of apriority emerges. This view has been sketched by Hilary Putnam and Manley Thompson.[13] On the Putnam-Thompson account, *a priori propositions* are those propositions that cannot be defeated by experience because, given any possible experience,

[12]In this I follow the approach taken by Saul Kripke. See his *Naming and Necessity* (Cambridge, Mass., 1980), p. 34.

[13]Hilary Putnam, "There Is at Least One A Priori Truth," *Erkenntnis* 13 (1978), 153–70; Hilary Putnam, "Analyticity and Apriority: Beyond Wittgenstein and Quine," *Midwest Studies in Philosophy* 4 (1979), 423–41; Manley Thompson, "On A Priori Truth," *Journal of Philosophy* 78 (1981), 458-82.

we must believe those propositions if we are to be capable of rational thought at all. *A priori concepts* are concepts that must figure in our beliefs if rational thought is to be possible for us. It is relatively easy to discern these conceptions of a priori proposition and a priori concepts in some of the discussions of the Transcendental Deductions and the Principles chapter of the Analytic.

Let me note first that the Putnam-Thompson characterization of a priori propositions does not seem to be equivalent to mine. My approach allows in principle for the apriority of propositions that are, as it were, luxuries of our belief system. Thus, on my account, it would be possible to hold that a recondite logical or mathematical truth is a priori, in that there is a procedure we can follow which will warrant belief in it, given any sufficiently rich experience, even though it is acknowledged that it is not a prerequisite of rational thought that one believes the logical or mathematical truth in question. We can simultaneously hold, for example, that Gödel's theorems for elementary arithmetic can be known a priori, and that people (such as Hilbert) who believed propositions incompatible with those theorems are capable of rational thought. (This is not to maintain that, on my account, Gödel's theorems will turn out to be a priori truths. My point is just that, on the approach to apriority I have developed, the conclusion that Gödel's theorems are not a priori does not follow from the premises that Hilbert believed a proposition inconsistent with the theorems and that Hilbert engaged in rational thought.)

The Putnam-Thompson criterion for a priori propositions diverges from mine in a different respect. It is possible that a person may not be justified in believing a proposition that is a prerequisite of rational thought. Consider the following scenario. Humans come into contact with a race of aliens who seem quickly to learn to communicate with us. The aliens teach us many remarkable things, clear up long-standing problems in mathematics and science, and introduce us to concepts that make it possible for us to develop entirely new fields of inquiry. One day they tell us that the time has arrived to correct a fundamental misapprehension. Our standard logical system, including a principle that we (rightly) take to be a fundamental prerequisite of rational thought, should be abandoned. The aliens explain that our old system has foundations that are conceptually flawed, and they offer to teach us something better. Unfortunately, when we are shown their "logic," we find it incomprehensible. The aliens profess disappointment, and provide apparently conclusive demonstrations that their "logical" perspective has led them to solve important problems. Yet we are still unable to learn.

Would we be justified in believing the propositions of our logic—including those that are indeed prerequisites for rational thought—given the type of experience that I have described? The first point is that the mere fact that the propositions we are asked to abandon are prerequisites of rational thought does not make us justified in continuing to believe them. A lazy dogmatist among us, someone who simply ignored the alien challenge, would not be justified in his belief. As in more mundane cases, whether we are justified depends on how our belief is generated.[14] Now a second point arises. It is conceivable that there is no procedure we can use to turn back all the challenges that the aliens can muster. They may offer excellent reasons for believing that our inability to learn their "logic" reflects the same psychological difficulties encountered by our ancestors in coping with non-Euclidean geometry or quantum physics. Perhaps they may dupe us into thinking that members of our species have been able to gain entry to their logical system with remarkably liberating results. Under these circumstances, though we might have no option but to continue using our old system, we would not be justified in believing its principles. Our position would be an extreme version of predicaments in which human inquirers have sometimes found themselves: we would feel compelled to carry out our investigations within a system that, quite reasonably, we believe to suffer from serious defects.

If these arguments are correct, then the Putnam-Thompson conception of apriority will identify as a priori a rather different

---

[14]For a defense of this general point about justification, see Gilbert Harman, *Thought* (Princeton, N.J., 1973), chapter 2. I draw the moral for a priori knowledge in "A Priori Knowledge," pp. 21–23.

class of propositions than those countenanced by my analysis. I have already noted the existence of both notions in Kant's *Critique*. It is likely that Kant took the two conceptions to be equivalent, and when he claims that the principles of the Analytic are a priori, he apparently believes that they are both items of a priori knowledge (in my sense) and that they are prerequisites of rational thought. (Of course, given his early linking of the notions of necessity and apriority, he also contends that the principles are necessary truths. As Kripke and others have argued, this equivalence is also faulty.)[15] The question that now confronts us is whether, in Kant's discussions of pure natural science, we should read him as maintaining that the propositions hailed as a priori are being celebrated as items of a priori knowledge or as prerequisites of rational thought.[16]

An interpretation of Kant's claims along Putnam-Thompson lines could proceed as follows. What Kant asserts is that any rational investigator who forms judgments involving particular concepts must have certain beliefs. In particular, to form judgments involving the concept of matter—(more exactly, the concept(s) of matter articulated in the *Metaphysical Foundations*)—one must believe that there are attractive forces that act at a distance, that matter obeys Newton's laws of motion, and so forth. This interpretation appears extremely implausible. The Putnam-Thompson conception of apriority is geared to the explanation of the status of beliefs so fundamental to our thinking that they appear undeniable. It is not well adapted to understanding the status of scientifically controversial propositions. Kant would be hard pressed to defend the idea that Leibniz,

---

[15]Kripke, *Naming and Necessity*, pp. 55–57, 97–105. I have tried to extend Kripke's argument in Philip Kitcher, "Apriority and Necessity," *Australasian Journal of Philosophy* 58 (1980), 89–101.

[16]I should note explicitly that many traditional interpretations of Kant's epistemology and philosophy of science seem to err in failing to give any adequate analysis of what Kant might have meant in hailing a particular proposition as a priori. Kant's conception of apriority may be muddled or ambiguous, but I do not believe that one can understand his doctrines about pure natural science (for example) by refusing to analyze it. Hence I believe that a crucial step in interpreting Kant's philosophy of science is to identify the relevant notion of apriority, and, to the best of my knowledge, the Putnam-Thompson approach and my own treatment in "A Priori Knowledge" provide the only clear analyses currently available.

and other opponents of Newtonian principles, opponents who advanced judgments about matter, had abandoned prerequisites for rational thought. My rival interpretation appears far more likely. Given their acceptance of the concept of matter, Newton's detractors ought to have withdrawn their criticisms. For, on Kant's view (as I construe him), there are procedures that can be followed independently of experience which will lead from acceptance of the concept of matter to endorsement of Newtonian judgments. Rather than being scientific analogues of those who try to flout the principle of noncontradiction (or Putnam's "minimal principle of non-contradiction"),[17] anti-Newtonians are like those who fail to appreciate the subtle consequences of their beliefs. (They do not recognize the presuppositions of their own criticisms.)

The characterization of quasi a priori science that I have given can best be defended by showing how it illuminates the enterprise of the *Metaphysical Foundations*. Kant claims that certain concepts of matter are legitimized by experience. Spatial objects that are to affect us must have certain properties; we learn this by discovering very general facts about how our senses are affected (*MN* 4 76fg 13e; see also *MN* 481fg 28e). The properties in question are known on the basis of experience to apply to all objects of outer experience. If one supposes that a concept that applies to all objects which fall within the domain of physical science must find a place within our physical theory, then it is possible to conclude that the concepts that ascribe the relevant properties are empirically legitimized.

What are the properties Kant selects? The concept of matter is developed in sequence through the chapters of the *Metaphysical Foundations*. Kant begins with the concept of matter as "the movable in space," arguing forthrightly that what is not movable cannot affect the "external senses" (*MN* 477g 4e). Subsequent chapters add the properties of "filling a space" (glossed as the property of resisting instrusion) and of "having a moving force"

[17]Putnam, "Analyticity and Apriority: Beyond Wittgenstein and Quine," pp. 440–41.

(construed as a power to impart motion). In the final chapter Kant adds the definition of matter as that which "can as such be an object of experience," but this characterization seems redundant. The earlier chapters appear to be an attempt to specify the conditions that must be met if something is to be an object of experience. I shall henceforth ignore the final chapter, which, like the Postulates section of the Principles chapter of the *Critique* to which it corresponds, seems to have been introduced solely to fill a vacant gap in Kant's all-too-tidy system.

Whatever the merits of Kant's reasons for thinking that the concepts of matter he chooses are empirically legitimized, the central doctrine of the *Metaphysical Foundations* is an interesting one. Given that it is appropriate to characterize the objects of physical science as movable, as able to fill space and to transmit motion in impact, we are to construct a priori a projected order of nature and to justify a priori certain Newtonian principles. Specifically, we are to show a priori that diverse natural phenomena are to be understood by advancing hypotheses about the distribution of centers of fundamental forces, that the impenetrability of matter is explained by the fact that matter is endowed with a fundamental repulsive force, and that gravitational phenomena result from the fact that matter has a fundamental attractive force. Further, we are to reason a priori to the truth of a principle of mass conservation, and of Newton's first and third laws. This is quite an agenda.

Kant has a clear conception of how the conclusions are to be reached. The *Critique* identifies two types of a priori procedures for synthetic truths. Believing that one of these, the analysis of the conditions of possible experience, takes precedence over the other, the construction of concepts in pure intuition, Kant asserts that the initial state of pure natural science must consist in "metaphysical constructions." Hence, even though the *Metaphysical Foundations* attempts a very ambitious task, Kant restricts himself to using only part of his arsenal of a priori procedures, namely, the procedures of the Transcendental Analytic. Throughout the work, Kant is faithful to the self-imposed prohibition against the use of mathematics. I shall argue later that his policy leads him into serious errors.[18] Kant does not succeed in restricting himself to applying the conclusions of the Analytic, since the regulative principles of the Appendix to the Ideal play an important part in developing his explanatory scheme (see *MN* 503g, 48e, 532–35g 90–94e).

When we look at seventeenth- and eighteenth-century speculative natural philosophy, examining the writings of Descartes, Leibniz, Euler, Boscovich, or Kant, there is a strong temptation to dismiss the enterprise as thoroughly confused. However, Kant offers an interesting theory of a type of scientific activity in vogue among his predecessors, and the *Metaphysical Foundations* represents his own attempt to practice it. (Given his belief that the critical machinery provides a detailed account of the activity, he was also confident that he could do it properly.) I suggest that the activity is as much a part of our own science as it was of the science of Kant's day. Anyone who has taken a standard college course in special relativity, electromagnetic theory, or fundamental particle physics will have heard arguments which, beginning from a particular conceptualization of the phenomena, proceed, by steps that make no obvious reference to empirical findings, to striking conclusions. Similarly, derivations of the central equations of population biology seem to adopt a particular description of the situation to be studied and then to advance to the enunciation of precise laws without further recourse to experience. In the "thought-experiments" of contemporary physicists and the "modeling" of contemporary biologists and social scientists, we find the present versions of the part of sci-

---

[18]As Michael Friedman pointed out to me, there is one place in the *Metaphysical Foundations* where the prohibition seems to be relaxed. In the first part of the work, Kant appears to try to prove a mathematical result, the parallelogram law for the composition of velocities (*MN* 492g 34e). As I interpret this discussion, however, the main point is to establish a proposition that will make the application of mathematics to experience possible. Kant's goal appears to be that of showing how we have to represent composite velocities to ourselves (*MN* 490g 31fe) and he introduces geometrical notions only insofar as they are needed to classify the possible forms that the representations can take. Thus I construe his argument not as a mathematical proof of a mathematical result, but as drawing on mathematical concepts to formulate what he views as a metaphysical argument. The status of this argument would be parallel to the treatment in the Axioms of Intuition, where methematical notions are discussed but mathematics is not done.

entific activity that Kant's account of pure natural science tries to characterize.

Empiricists are likely to respond either by denying that the activity has any epistemological significance or by proposing an alternative account of it. In the final section I shall take a brief look at this empiricist response. First, however, I want to show that Kant's execution of the project of quasi a priori science in the *Metaphysical Foundations* is a disaster. In trying simultaneously to exemplify his philosophical theory and to resolve substantive scientific questions, Kant fails to achieve either goal.

KANT ON GRAVITATIONAL FORCE

The scope of the intended conclusions of the *Metaphysical Foundations* makes it impossible to examine in detail here all the arguments Kant offers. I shall focus on one example which represents both the merits of the work and its shortcomings. The example is Kant's treatment of attractive force.

The main direction of argument of chapter 2 of the *Metaphysical Foundations* is as follows. Kant begins with the definition of matter as the movable which fills a space. On the basis of this conception, he argues that we should attribute as a fundamental property of matter the property of being a seat of repulsive force. This argument endeavors to move from a concept to a projected order of nature. It is presented briefly early in the chapter (*MN* 498g 42e, 502g 48e) and in a more extended form in the concluding General Observation (*MN* 523–35g 77–94e). After a sequence of propositions characterizing this fundamental force, Kant claims that "the possibility of matter requires a force of attraction, as the second fundamental force of matter" (proposition 5, *MN* 508g 56e). He believes that he can not only prove quasi a priori the existence of this attractive force, but that he can establish some of its general properties, in particular that it acts at a distance. Kant denies, however that he can demonstrate quasi a priori the specific mathematical form of the law of gravitation. On his account, to show that the attractive force is inversely as the square of the distance requires further assumptions.

Let us consider one step in this sequence of arguments, the attempt to show that matter must be a seat of attractive force. The proof of proposition 5 begins as follows:

> Impenetrability, as the fundamental property of matter whereby it first reveals itself as something real in the space of our external senses, is nothing but matter's capacity of extension (Proposition 2). Now, an essential moving force by which parts of matter recede from each other cannot, firstly, be limited by itself, because matter is impelled by such a force to continuously expand the space that it occupies, and cannot, secondly, be fixed by space alone at a certain limit of extension. This second is so because even though space can indeed contain the ground of the fact that with the increase in the volume of matter extending itself, the extensive force becomes weaker in inverse proportion; yet inasmuch as smaller degrees of every moving force are possible to infinity, space cannot anywhere contain the ground of the ceasing of such a force. Therefore, matter by its repulsive force alone (which contains the ground of its impenetrability), and if no other moving force counteracted this repulsive one, would be held within no limits of extension, i.e., would disperse itself to infinity, and no assignable quantity of matter would be found in any assignable space. Consequently, with merely repulsive forces of matter, all spaces would be empty; and hence, strictly speaking, there would be no matter at all. [*MN* 508fg 56fe]

Kant then goes on to argue that the dispersal of matter could only be prevented if matter were endowed with a fundamental attractive force.

Like most of the attempts at proof in the *Metaphysical Foundations*, this argument is a failure. Instead of reveling in its inadequacies, I shall try to understand why Kant produced so misguided a piece of reasoning. Let us begin by noting that, notwithstanding the reference to the theory of space in the opening sentence, Kant does not use his favored a priori procedures to reach his conclusion. The argument belies the advertisement for "pure natural science" that we find in the Preface to the

Metaphysical Foundations. Kant appears to be engaging in a clumsy thought experiment. We are asked to imagine a situation in which matter, endowed only with repulsive force, is present; Kant tries to show us that the situation must develop into a state in which space is empty.

The trouble is that the original situation is hopelessly under-described. Kant has forbidden himself the use of mathematics, and his qualitative formulations permit him to neglect a myriad of alternative possibilities. The claim that matter is the seat of repulsive force seems to amount to supposing that, when a particular volume of space is occupied by matter, a field of repulsive force takes on nonzero values through the volume. Kant apparently makes the following assumptions: (a) the field is uniform through the volume; (b) because the force is repulsive, at later times the matter will be dispersed and the associated force field will take on nonzero values on a larger volume; (c) the intensity of the repulsive force varies inversely as the volume occupied; and (d) the sequence of volumes occupied at successive time is not bounded above. Lacking a precise specification of his premises, Kant produces the sketch of an argument instead of a proof.[19]

It is interesting to compare the proof of proposition 5 with the far more explicit discussion of the law of universal gravitation. Kant emphasizes that we cannot attempt to establish precise quantitative force laws in the same way that we can prove the existence of a fundamental attractive force (*MN* 518g 69e; 529g 76e). His argument for the inverse square law of gravitation is supposed to have a second-rate status. Ironically, because this argument is liberated from the theoretical constraints on quasi

[19]If we were to continue with the proof we discover that Kant's qualitative formulations disguise even more assumptions. For example, when he investigates the possibility that the dispersal of matter might be checked by a balance of repulsive forces, he writes as though pieces of matter would have to be introduced one by one, and would be subject to instantaneous dissipation. It would be interesting to try to mathematize Kant's "dynamical conception of matter" and see what further premises are needed to make the sequence of arguments of chapter 2 succeed. Some of Kant's claims about "filling" and "occupying" space are difficult to construe on any simple field theory of matter, however.

a priori proofs, he is able to expose more clearly the assumptions on which his reasoning depends.

I suggest that Kant's efforts at thought experimentation go awry because of his belief that he must operate in purely qualitative terms. Operating in vague and general terms, he smuggles in assumptions galore. However, this does not explain the fact that, in the proof of proposition 5, and in many other parts of the *Metaphysical Foundations*, the principles and procedures of the Analytic are conspicuously absent.[20] To see why Kant compromises his official theory of quasi a priori science, we must recognize that he intends not merely to reconstruct but to *advance* Newtonian science. The long General Observation on Dynamics, which ends chapter 2 of the *Metaphysical Foundations*, sets forth a program for extending physical science. Here Kant outlines proposals for explaining phenomena in several fields (for example, hydrodynamics, the theory of elasticity, and chemistry).

Besides these suggestions about how Newtonian science should develop, Kant believes that he has advanced beyond Newton in laying to rest certain misguided criticisms. Specifically, the popular objection that action at a distance is inconceivable is to be met by a typical Kantian strategy. The objector believes that the concept of matter as that which fills a space is legitimate. When we apply correct methodological principles, however, we find that the concept commits us to a theory that attributes to matter a fundamental repulsive force. This commitment brings others in its train. Matter must be endowed not only with a fundamental repulsive force, but also with an equally fundamental attractive force which acts at a distance. Hence, like so many of the skeptics Kant wants to refute, the envisaged objector finds himself attacking a doctrine that is presupposed by his own formulation

---

[20]The link between the *Metaphysical Foundations* and the Analytic is most evident in chapter 3. Here Kant does try to apply the principles of the Analogies to derive substantive laws. So, for example, the principle of the First Analogy serves as a premise for a law of mass conservation. This argument fails to fit the format of quasi a priori science for a slightly different reason: Kant seems to make no use of the specific property of matter attributed in the definition that begins chapter 3. The argument deserves analysis, but I do not have space to investigate it here.

of the objection. To worry whether *matter* can act at a distance is confused because matter, to fill a space, *must* act at a distance.

PROSPECTS FOR A KANTIAN PHILOSOPHY OF SCIENCE

Despite the failure of the *Metaphysical Foundations*, Kant's philosophy of science contains insights relevant to modern thinking about science. Kant offers an interesting approach to scientific justification which recognizes features of scientific practice often neglected by his empiricist successors. His basic insights are developed by adding two more dubious theses: (a) the justification of specific versions of scientific theories involves the use of a priori procedures; and (b) the *Critique* provides an exhaustive account of our a priori procedures and of their interdependencies.

Fundamental to Kant's philosophy of science is his view of a scientific theory as a *projected order of nature*. Many twentieth-century philosophers of science have debated the possibility of axiomatizing various pieces of science. When we turn away from the standard examples from physics, however, and consider theories in biology or geology, the issue of axiomatizability frequently appears irrelevant. A more fundamental problem is to decide what corpus of statements we are trying to axiomatize. Biological and geological theories do not come neatly presented as collections of displayed formulas—as do Newton's laws of motion or Maxwell's equations. Attempts to force contemporary evolutionary theory or plate tectonics, for example, into the standard empiricist mold inevitably strike practitioners of the theories as producing caricatures. They do so not because of sophisticated worries about the observation-theoretic distinction, but because the theory is not adequately represented as a set of statements.

Kant's approach to theories fares better. If we think of scientific theories as schemes for classifying and ordering phenomena, then we can make sense of theories that appear problematic when viewed from the empiricist perspective. We can think of contemporary plate tectonics, for example, as a collection of strategies for answering questions about a variety of geological phenomena—such as mountain building, sea-floor spreading, and earthquakes—by tracing those phenomena to the motions of plates. What is fundamental to the theory of plate tectonics is its classificatory and explanatory scheme, the way in which it formulates geological questions and the way in which it directs us to answer such questions.

Kant's own presentation of the idea of a theory as a scheme for classification and explanation is not readily adapted to reconstructing contemporary science. In the Appendix to the Ideal, the fundamental idea of theories as directives for describing and explaining is transmuted into the view of theories as conceptual hierarchies. Perhaps this metamorphosis is to be understood in terms of the influence of Aristotelian logic on Kant's thought. In any case, we can achieve a more flexible presentation of the fundamental insight. Theories can be identified by the questions they address and the patterns of reasoning they use to answer those questions. The classification of natural phenomena is reflected in the questions posed, while the patterns of reasoning used in giving answers reflects the projected dependencies of phenomena on one another.

The Kantian approach to scientific theories just sketched serves as the basis for a Kantian account of scientific justification. Kant's minimal claim is that, given empirical justification for using a particular concept within a field of science, there are procedures for justifiably adopting a particular theory and for accepting specific principles, procedures that can be carried out in advance of testing those principles. On Kant's account, there is a rationale for embryonic science.

I believe that this minimal claim is correct. Scientists working in fields as diverse as fundamental particle physics and population ecology frequently advance arguments that justify the acceptance of particular methods of problem solving, and even of particular conclusions, on the basis of an initial acceptance of some conceptualization of the phenomena under study. Kant's philosophy of science is motivated by his awareness of the eighteenth-century versions of this practice (primarily in the development of Newtonianism). His thesis is that the gathering of experimental evidence presupposes a framework which is rationally adopted before the work of experimentation is begun.

Some empiricists might deny that the *Gedankenexperimente* of the physicist or the "model building" of the population ecologist serve anything more than a heuristic function. The heuristics merely induce us to fancy certain theories which receive their support only from the subsequent experiments. I believe that this version of empiricism is incorrect. Embryonic theories are rationally adopted, and it would be foolish to condemn as unreasonable those who were persuaded by Darwin's "long argument" for his programmatic theory or those who were convinced by Einstein's thought-experiments in advance of the experimental determinations.

Kant adds to his minimal claim two further suggestions about the rationale of immature science. The first is the idea that there are methodological directives, such as the directive to obtain "systematic unity in our knowledge," which enable us to evaluate scientific proposals even before those proposals can be put to the test. Darwin's argument for the theory of evolution by natural selection illustrates two of the methodological canons to which Kant draws attention: Darwin is justly proud of the unifying power that the explanatory scheme of the *Origin of Species* supplies, and he defends his view by pointing out how it gives direction to biological research, by identifying the ways in which we should interrogate nature.

More problematic is the contention that there are a priori procedures that play a critical role in the rational genesis of theories. Kant supposes that a proper reconstruction of the scientific arguments for proposals justified in advance of experimentation will reveal the operation of those a priori procedures whose workings are described in the *Critique*. As we have seen, his efforts to resolve some scientific controversies of his day by applying this general thesis about scientific justification succeed neither in confirming his own philosophical theory nor in settling the scientific issues. I suggest that the fundamental flaw is the imposition of the apriorist machinery of the *Critique* on the sensible idea that the rational acceptance of theories—that is, schemes

for classification and explanation—is a crucial step in the justification of scientific claims through *subsequent* experimental
investigation.

Some philosophers and historians of science are drawn to the
idea that experimental confirmation of hypotheses presupposes
acceptance of a framework and that decisions to accept such
frameworks cannot be understood as completely rational. Kant's
philosophy of science is built upon endorsing the first part of
this idea, and providing a particular way of denying the second,
skeptical, claim. The choice of a framework (or of a projected
order of nature) can be completely rational because scientists
can use a priori procedures to arrive at their choices. A thoughtful empiricist should accept neither of these accounts. When the
arguments that figure in embryonic science are analyzed they
are seen to turn on very general considerations about the world
which have been inherited from previous pieces of successful
science. The physicists who appeal to symmetries in nature, or
the population biologists who propose that the differential equation for the growth of a population will take a particular form,
are neither making assumptions that involve "leaps of faith" nor
appealing to a priori principles about the universe. Their arguments extend the findings of previous scientists—including
scientists working in apparently unrelated areas—to justify a new
scheme for problems and problem solving within their field. It
may be that such principles are *relatively* immune to disconfir-
mation. But they do not meet the conditions that Kant requires
of the a priori.

This evaluation is admittedly short and speculative. I have
tried to outline a view of scientific justification that has some
affinity with Kant's, and to motivate some of its elements. Quite
evidently, my remarks do not amount to a defense. Yet if I am
correct, then traditional appraisals of Kant's philosophy of science are almost exactly backwards. Orthodox Kantians are wrong
to dismiss Kant's views about science as an embarrassing adden-
dum to the central achievements of the *Critique*.[21] Taking the

[21]Of course, some commentators have tried to reconstruct Kant's ideas about
science. Scholarly discussions of the *Metaphysical Foundations* and its relation to
the *Critique* include those by Jules Vuillemin, *Physique et Métaphysique Kantienne*

project of isolating items of a priori knowledge to be worthwhile, they suppose that assigning substantive scientific principles to the category of the a priori is misguided. Although I doubt that there is much that answers to Kant's conception of the a priori, the approach to scientific justification on which Kant imposes his apriorist views—the approach I have indicated in this section—is both interesting and important. Furthermore, the general assumptions about nature that scientists so frequently use in justifying embryonic theories may come as close to the ideal of the a priori as anything in which we are likely to be interested.[22]

(Paris, 1955); Hansgeorg Hoppe, *Kants Theorie der Physik* (Frankfurt, 1969); Peter Plaass, *Kants Theorie der Naturwissenschaft* (Göttingen, 1965). Unfortunately, none of these works succeeds either in making clear what the project of pure natural science is supposed to be or in identifying any Kantian insight about science. More successful, to my mind, are two recent works in English. In the long final chapter of his *Metaphysics and the Philosophy of Science* (1969), Gerd Buchdahl gives a sympathetic exposition of many of Kant's discussions of science. Buchdahl is very clear in his contention that Kant does not believe he can deduce Newtonian science a priori. Buchdahl proposes that there is a "looser relation" between the *Critique* and Newtonian science, although he has not given any clear account of this relation. In *Kant's Theory of Science* (Princeton, N.J., 1978), Gordon Brittan is more forthright. He maintains that the goal of the *Metaphysical Foundations* is to show that certain concepts must be instantiated in any world in which science is to be possible. Although Brittan's discussions, like Buchdahl's, are sometimes illuminating, I do not believe he achieves a satisfactory view either of Kant's project or of Kant's practice of it. The trouble stems from Brittan's explicit dismissal of some of Kant's central epistemological notions (for example, *Kant's Theory of Science*, p. 24, n. 43).

[22] I am grateful to Patricia Kitcher for many valuable criticisms of drafts of this paper. Earlier versions were read at Temple University and at Cornell University, and a number of people made helpful suggestions. In particular, I thank Charles Parsons (who commented on the version read at Cornell), Richard Burian, Michael Friedman, and Ralf Meerbote for comments that have caused me to abandon or to amplify previous formulations. This is not, of course, to imply that *anyone* accepts my interpretation of Kant's philosophy of science or my assessment of its importance.

Remarks on Pure Natural Science

Charles Parsons

In attempting to crack the hardest nut in Kant's philosophy of science, his conception of an a priori or "pure" part of science, Philip Kitcher shows both courage and an appreciation of what is central to Kant's philosophy (see preceding essay). The issues that in the *Critique of Pure Reason* are the subject of the Transcendental Analytic are discussed in the *Prolegomena* under the heading, "How is pure natural science possible?" Some of the most difficult issues faced by interpreters of Kant could thus be represented as concerning how Kant answers that question. But what does the question itself mean? What part of natural science is pure? 'Pure' is clearly closely related to 'a priori', but are they the same, and if not, how do they differ? What principles in or about science are a priori? Writers on Kant's philosophy of physics do not agree on such questions. The issues are not resolved by turning to the *Metaphysical Foundations of Natural Science*, a work that raises as many questions of interpretation as it answers.

The distinction Kant makes in the Introduction to the *Critique of Pure Reason* (*B*3) between *a priori* and *pure* knowledge is obviously relevant to the *Metaphysical Foundations*, but it turns out to be not nearly so straightforward as it seems. The idea seems to be that a proposition is pure only if there is nothing empirical in its *content*, so that a paradigm example of an impure proposition would be an analytic one involving empirical concepts, such as "Gold is yellow" (at least for the first of the two men referred to at *A*728 *B*756). Then one can see how *synthetic* a priori propositions that are not pure can arise: a logical model for the notion would characterize them as propositions that can be proved by arguments whose premises are either a priori propositions involving only pure concepts, or logical truths, or analytic propositions, in which evidently only the third can involve empirical concepts essentially.

'Pure natural science' must on any account involve essentially concepts that are in some sense empirical. About matter, the subject of the *Metaphysical Foundations*, Kant could hardly be more explicit. In explaining in the Preface what he means by calling his investigation metaphysical, Kant contrasts the "transcendental part of the metaphysics of nature" with metaphysics of nature in a more special sense. His remarks about the latter suggest the model of nonpure a priori knowledge I have just sketched: it "occupies itself with the special nature of this or that kind of things, of which an empirical concept is given in such a way that, besides what lies in this concept, no other empirical principle is needed for cognizing the things" (*MN* 470g 7e). In the next sentence he mentions the "empirical concept of matter." Whatever Kant means by 'pure natural science,' in the case of physical science (which seems to be the only genuine case), it will be a development of the special metaphysics of physical nature that is the official subject of the *Metaphysical Foundations* and is based on the empirical concept of matter.

The sense in which the concept of matter is empirical is controversial, as we will see. Even if we do not disturb the apparent straightforwardness of Kant's account, a terminological inconsistency emerges, in that 'pure natural science' either itself contains or depends on propositions that in the sense of $B3$ are *not* pure.[1] One might be tempted to suppose that the distinction Kant makes between "transcendental" and "special" metaphysics

---

[1] It is well known that this inconsistency surfaces in the Introduction itself: Kant's example of an impure a priori proposition is "Every alteration has a cause." But that very statement is referred to soon after as a "pure a priori proposition" ($B4$–5). In replying to a critic who pointed out the inconsistency, Kant says that "pure" is ambiguous, and that in $B3$ it meant "with no admixture of anything empirical" and in $B5$ "dependent on nothing empirical" (*GT* 183–84, my translation). I do not find the second characterization at all clear. At all events Kant's emphasis in $B4$–5 is on necessity and strict universality.

of nature turns on the absence in the former and presence in the latter of empirical concepts. This would seem to contradict *B3*, where the example proposition, "Every alteration has a cause," is said to be not pure because "alteration is a concept that can only be drawn from experience." This would suggest that containing empirical concepts essentially is a feature that the propositions of the *Metaphysical Foundations* share with some of those of the first *Critique*, presumably at least the Dynamical Principles. Nevertheless, this admission is certainly not made clearly in the *Critique*.

One of the merits of Philip Kitcher's essay is that he examines how concepts that are in some way empirical can figure in a priori knowledge. He does not take the empirical/a priori contrast for granted, as one may be tempted to do with Kant even if one does not in one's own philosophy. With respect to the propositions of the *Metaphysical Foundations*, at least those closest to Newtonian laws, Kitcher sees Kant as taking them to be a priori only in an attenuated sense; they "admit of something like an a priori proof."

It is worth noting that the question whether and in what sense Kant holds basic Newtonian principles to be a priori has received rather divergent answers in recent commentary. Kitcher's reading of Kant is in fact definitely more aprioristic than that of the two recent writers in English who have discussed the *Metaphysical Foundations* most extensively, Gerd Buchdahl and Gordon Brittan (see Kitcher's note 21). The general tendency of German writers seems to be the opposite; they tend to take Kant at his word and assume that the statement from the Preface quoted above applies at least to the formal content of the *Metaphysical Foundations*, for example, the Propositions (*Lehrsätze*) which in the Mechanics include the conservation of matter, the law of inertia, and the equality of action and reaction.[2] Kant's explicit

---

[2] See also *B*17–18. The German writers I have in mind are Peter Plaass, *Kants Theorie der Naturwissenschaft* (Göttingen, 1965); Lothar Schäfer, *Kants Metaphysik der Natur* (Berlin, 1966); Hansgeorg Hoppe, *Kants Theorie der Physik: Eine Untersuchung über das Opus Postumum von Kant* (Frankfurt, 1969). (I am indebted to

statements about what he is doing certainly favor the German view.

Kitcher offers a systematic reason, which, however, seems to apply to any principles that contain empirical concepts essentially. A proposition, even if true, does not express knowledge of objects unless the "objective reality" of the concepts constituting it has been established. In the case of empirical concepts, this can only be by experience. It follows that any proposition containing empirical concepts essentially will have an empirical presupposition for its expressing knowledge of objects. It is chiefly by emphasizing this rather simple point that Kitcher differs from the more aprioristic commentators. Kitcher's notion of "conceptual legitimacy," however, departs consciously from Kant's explicit notion of objective reality as possible exemplification in experience, in order to account for the role of idealization in science.

In the case at hand, we must consider what is meant by saying that the concept of matter is empirical. Kant's basic conception of matter is of "the movable in space"; because the representation of space is certainly a priori, anything empirical in its content would have to come from the concept of motion (*P*295g 39e). What would be empirical in the content of this notion is not any more clear, as it seems to involve merely the notion of an object's changing its location in space, and thus the categories, space, and time. This consideration lends support to the hypothesis of Peter Plaass that in its *content* the notion of matter is in fact a priori; experience is needed only to establish its objective reality.[3]

Ralf Meerbote for calling the latter two works to my attention and correcting my all-too-uncritical reliance on Plaass.) German writers have stressed the connection between the *Metaphysical Foundations* and the *Opus Postumum*; in addition to Hoppe I might mention the very interesting article by Burkhard Tuschling, "Kants 'Metaphysische Anfangsgründe der Naturwissenschaft' und das Opus postumum," in Gerold Prauss, ed., *Kant: Zur Deutung seiner Lehre von Erkennen und Handeln* (Köln, 1973), pp. 175–91. Tuschling maintains that early in the work reported in the *Opus Postumum* Kant abandoned some of the central theses of the *Metaphysical Foundations*. In preparing this essay, I have not attempted the enormous task of delving into such matters.

[3]Plaass, *Kants Theorie der Naturwissenschaft*, chapters 4 and 5.

A similar hypothesis would deal with the empirical character of the concept of change or alteration (*Veränderung*), which Kant mentions among the "predicables" or "pure, but derived concepts of understanding" in the *Critique* (*A*82/*B*108).[4] Plaass's view seems to me much the clearest view that has been offered of how the empirical enters into the formal content of the *Metaphysical Foundations*.

Plaass apparently holds that the role of experience in establishing the objective reality of the concept of matter is almost trivial: "for, that a concept has objective reality, can be completely proved by a single example."[5] Kitcher can criticize this view effectively even without appealing to his extension of the notion of objective reality to that of empirical legitimization. To establish any example of motion, we would have to make the distinction between real and apparent motion. Even granted the relativity of this distinction to a frame of reference, it seems we would need to set up such a frame, thus applying a theory to the world. Of course, descriptions of motion have implications about acceleration and therefore about the distribution of forces. Thus, even if the role of the empirical is minimized, as it is on Plaass's hypothesis, some significant attenuation of the a priori character of fundamental physics seems unavoidable, along the lines Kitcher suggests.

At this point we might mention Kitcher's suggestion that the "empirically legitimized concepts" that enter into what he calls "quasi a priori" knowledge might be concepts we have *prior* to the construction of theories, and thus—unless one supposes them to be innate—concepts of a commonsense character. I confess this seems un-Kantian in spirit and at odds with Kant's explanations of the concepts of matter and motion, which tend rather to connect them with technical notions of his philosophy. The picture Kitcher suggests is probably an improvement on Kant's, in that one begins theory construction with rough and ready concepts, which are modified as theory construction proceeds.

Kitcher's notion of the "quasi a priori" has another difficulty,

---

[4]Plaass, *Kants Theorie*, p. 84.
[5]Plaass, *Kants Theorie*, p. 89.

of a kind faced by many interpretations of the relation of the *Critique* and the *Metaphysical Principles*. For it is not easy to see how the attenuation of apriority that Kitcher discerns in the latter work is completely escaped by the Dynamical Principles of the *Critique*. As we have seen, Kant holds that the objective reality of the concept of alteration which occurs in his principle of causality can only be established by experience. Again, it may seem that the empirical element is trivial, in that virtually any experience will reveal change. But what Kant specifically means is alteration of the state of a substance; he is actually operating with a distinction like that between a "real" and a "mere Cambridge" change.[6] But then the identification of objective changes is a theory-laden matter; in particular, uniform motion in a straight line is not a change of the state of the moving body and therefore does not require a cause, while acceleration is a change of state ($A207n/B252n$). The consideration involved is quite general: in order to identify objective change, we must "categorize" what is given so that the states of the objects that are said to change are singled out.

At this point one might object that on the basis of a single experience we can be sure that *something* alters; what is then more "theory-laden" is the identification of the object that changes, its location in one substratum rather than another. I am not sure how to spell this out in Kantian terms without making the objective reality of the concept of alteration a priori, because the only presupposition of its objective reality would be that experience really is possible.

If we consider the same question in the more specific case of motion, we encounter new puzzles. In a single experience we can certainly discern *motion*, even if latitude is left as to what is said to move and what is said to be at rest. Kant's statement that "the fundamental determination of a something that is to be an object of the external senses must be motion, for thereby only can these senses be affected" (MN 476g 13e) seems to imply that *any* experience will contain motion, but Kant's view of the status of this proposition is unclear. Plaass attempts an a priori proof

---

[6]Plaass, *Kants Theorie*, p. 97.

of the statement just quoted, which he calls a "metaphysical deduction" of the concept of motion.[7] If this proof captures Kant's intention, Kant took it to be a priori true that any outer experience would contain motion, thus placing motion on the same plane as alteration, except for the qualification "outer" (which is discussed below).

Plaass's argument seems to me fallacious. One can perhaps accept his assertion that an object of the outer senses must contain "an objective connection" of spatial and temporal determinations and that this connection is made by the concept of motion; however, he offers no argument that this role must be played by the concept of motion rather than some other. Moreover, the question remains whether Kant intended this statement with the generality that Plaass gives it or even as an a priori truth; one could object with Ralph Walker that the statement only says "what must be so for *us*, because of the way our sense-organs are constituted."[8]

I do not know whether Plaass or Walker is right concerning Kant's meaning. The dispute reveals an unclarity in Kant's statement on the relation of the *Critique* and the *Metaphysical Foundations*, which is in my opinion bound up with problems of the interpretation of the *Critique* itself. At the beginning of the *Foundations* Kant distinguishes the "transcendental part of the metaphysics of nature," evidently what is contained in the Analytic of Principles, from metaphysics that "occupies itself with the special nature of this or that kind of things" (*MN*470g 7e), which he then identifies as metaphysics of "corporeal or thinking" nature. The fact that the categories are schematized only in terms of time is supposed to give the Analytic of Principles an abstract generality that cuts across distinctions in the sensible world, such as that between the physical and the mental.

But the matter is in fact not so neat, as Kant admits in the second edition of the *Critique*, when he says that *outer* intuitions

---

[7]Plaass, *Kants Theorie*, pp. 98–99.

[8]Ralph C.S. Walker, "The Status of Kant's Theory of Matter," in L. W. Beck, ed., *Proceedings of the Third International Kant Congress* (Dordrecht, 1972), pp. 591–96, at 593. Hoppe regards the statement we are considering here as "not at all a critical result, but rather a residue of tradition, not overcome by transcendental philosophy" (*Kants Theorie der Physik*, p. 64, my translation).

are needed to establish the objective reality of the categories
(*B*291). He goes on to say: "In order to exhibit *alteration* as the
intuition corresponding to the concept of *causality*, we must take
as our example motion, that is, alteration in space.... The intuition required is the intuition of the movement of a point in
space" (*B*291–92). The last remark complicates the issue, because, as Kant makes clear at *B*155n, this "intuition" is not of
motion in the physical sense. Although it does indeed give in-
tuitive content to the concept of alteration, it falls short of establishing its objective reality.

The dispute between Plaass and Walker would arise concerning the meaning of "we must" in the passage just cited. Kant's
appeal to a purely geometrical notion of movement seems to
give some support to Plaass. At the same time it also seems to
be a confusion; clearly only the real possibility of physical motion
would establish in this way the objective reality of the concept
of alteration. Walker is, in my view, quite convincing in arguing
that outer experience as such does not require physical motion.

Before leaving the subject of the sense in which the content
of the *Metaphysical Foundations* is a priori, we might comment on
the notion of a priori knowledge Kitcher uses in his reconstruction. The fact that the interpretation was originally devised for
the purpose of incorporating a notion of a priori knowledge into
naturalistic epistemology makes one suspicious about its application to Kant.[9] In fact, Kitcher seems to understand his notion
of a priori procedure in causal terms: "An a priori procedure
for a proposition is a type of process such that...if it *were* followed, *would* generate knowledge of the proposition" (italics
added).[10] Kant himself lays himself open to such a causal inter-

[9]See Philip Kitcher, "A Priori Knowledge," *Philosophical Review* 89 (1980), 3–
23, at 4.
[10]Cf. Philip Kitcher, "How Kant Almost Wrote 'Two Dogmas of Empiricism'
(and Why He Didn't)" *Philosophical Topics* 12 (1981), 217–49, at 218. Kitcher is
more explicitly psychologistic and causal in "A Priori Knowledge," where, however, he is not primarily concerned to interpret Kant. He does refer to the
explication there offered as having "Kantian psychologistic" underpinnings. Historically, Kant has been appealed to both for and against psychologism; my own
inclination, in contrast to Kitcher's, is toward an antipsychologistic interpretation.
In view of the attention Kitcher pays in "How Kant Almost Wrote Two Dogmas"
to Kant's equation of the necessary and the a priori and the difficulties that gives
rise to, I might hazard the conjecture that it is just to escape a psychologistic
causal interpretation of the a priori that Kant gives so much emphasis to this

pretation of the a priori in characterizing a priori knowledge as knowledge that is *independent* of experience (see for example, *B*3). Pressing a causal interpretation would wreak havoc with transcendental philosophy as Kant understands it. I believe that this aspect of Kitcher's understanding of the a priori does little work in his preceding essay. What matters is the identification of certain key conceptions and modes of argumentation as a priori.

In finding the argument of the *Metaphysical Foundations* mainly unsuccessful, Kitcher is in agreement with many earlier commentators.[11] Although I do not intend to challenge this conclusion. I believe a more positive account of the relation of the Analytic of Principles and the main parts of the *Foundations* is possible. I also take issue with portions of Kitcher's diagnosis of the weaknesses of Kant's argument.

In any sustained attempt at Kantian reconstruction, there is a risk that one of the main actors in the drama of Kant's philosophy will be left out. In Kitcher's reconstruction I miss the *categories*. Kitcher chooses the Dynamics for detailed discussion. Architectonically, the categories that should be at work there are those of quality. These are murky notions even in the *Critique*; it is not too surprising that Kitcher does not find the connection.[12] If we turn to the Mechanics, however, we find a clear enough connection of the propositions with principles for the categories of relation. On the other hand, we find a more fundamental source of weakness in the arguments than a mere architectonic prohibition of the use of mathematics.

The conservation of matter (Proposition 2 of the Mechanics) is obviously an application of the First Analogy, the law of inertia

---

equation. Consider the following passage, which closely anticipates the definition of a priori truth given by Frege at the beginning of the *Grundlagen*: "If we have a proposition which in being thought is thought as *necessary*, it is an *a priori* judgment; and if, besides, it is not derived from any proposition except one which also has the validity of a necessary judgment, it is an absolutely *a priori* judgment" (*B*3).

[11]And, if Tuschling is right (see note 2), with Kant himself.

[12]A more positive account of this connection is given by Schäfer, *Kants Metaphysik der Natur*.

(Proposition 3) of the Second Analogy, and the equality of action and reaction in the communication of motion (Proposition 4) of the Third Analogy. The force of "application" in this context is problematic. In each case, Kant's argument rests on a particular interpretation of a categorial concept.

The key step in Kant's proof of the conservation of matter is this passage: "Hence the quantity of the matter according to its substance is nothing but the multitude of the substances of which it consists. Therefore the quantity of matter cannot be increased or diminished except by the arising or perishing of new substance of matter" (*MN*542g 98e). Kant has already identified quantity of matter with the number (*Menge*) of its movable parts (*MN* 537g 93e), and undertaken to motivate this interpretation by appeal to the notion of substance. He emphatically rejects (*MN* 539–40g 95e) the notion that matter should have a "degree of moving force with given velocity" (that is, momentum) which can be taken as an *intensive* quantity. This idea in turn seems to rest on the identification of matter as substance in space:

> But the fact that the moving force which matter possesses in its proper motion alone manifests its quantity of substance rests on the concept of substance as the ultimate subject (which is not a further predicate of another subject) in space; for this reason this subject can have no other quantity than that of the multitude of its homogeneous parts, being external to one another.[*MN*541g 97e]

We may see Kant as dealing with the following sort of problem: How are we to make sense of the notion of substance in space—that is, to make judgments involving this category in application to our actual outer intuitions? The schematization of the category in terms of time does only part of the work. Even if one takes as inevitable the identification of substance in space (Descartes's extended substance) with matter, it is another step to think of an extended portion of matter as consisting of parts that are *themselves* substances. Kant may have had in mind arguing that they must be substances because they are subjects of motion; that is, once one has identified extended substance as the movable in space, it will follow that the subject of motion must be a substance. But the best result this consideration can accomplish is to force the question back to one concerning the idea that motion must be the fundamental determination of something that affects the outer senses (see above). Indeed, there seems to be a factor in the interpretation of the category of substance in the context of space that is not deduced from the pure category and the nature of space itself. Where time instead of space is involved, this is exactly what happens in the schematism of the categories; Kant's argument requires something like a second schematization of the category in terms of space.

This point is perhaps clearer when we turn to the connection between the Second Analogy and the law of inertia. In Kant's proof (*MN* 543g 104–5e) he simply assumes that motion (in effect, uniform motion in a straight line) is a *state* and that therefore only acceleration is an alteration in the sense of a change of state (as he explicitly states in the *Critique*, A207n/B252n). Without some such assumption there is no way to advance from the principle of causality to Kant's conclusion. Without an assumption of this general form, we are unable to apply the category of causality to matter and motion.

Commentators often represent Kant as concerned in the *Metaphysical Foundations* with the "mathematizability" of phenomena, in other words, concerned with showing that a mathematical theory of the physical world can be constructed and elaborating a philosophical account of how this is possible. In so doing, Kant interprets the categories of substance and causality in quantitative and spatial terms. 'Pure natural science' might develop what Kitcher calls a "projected order of nature" in the form of a mathematical model of a world in space and time conforming to the Kantian categories. On any interpretation, Kant's conception of a scheme of this kind leaves much to experience. But Kant did not show convincingly that even his basic interpretations of the categories were not optional.

Here is a brief sketch of a picture of 'a priori science' somewhat different from Kitcher's. One might single out certain *concepts* because they involve only space, time, very general categories, and fundamental and abstract notions concerning our cognitive faculties. Obviously, a theory sketched in terms of such concepts has highly general application *if* it even approximates the truth. Indeed, a problem with such a theory might be finding a "handle" for empirical verification and falsification. If the theory has a high degree of intrinsic plausibility, it may resemble logic and mathematics from an epistemological point of view. If a theory so developed turns out to be false, it may well require some revision in our notions of the relation of our cognitive faculties to the world. In fact, the revision of classical physics early in this century exhibited this character.

Contributors

LEWIS WHITE BECK is Burbank Professor of Intellectual and Moral Philosophy Emeritus, The University of Rochester.

JONATHAN BENNETT is Professor of Philosophy, Syracuse University.

TERENCE IRWIN is Professor of Philosophy, Cornell University.

PATRICIA KITCHER is Associate Professor of Philosophy, University of Minnesota.

PHILIP KITCHER is Professor of Philosophy, University of Minnesota.

RALF MEERBOTE is Associate Professor of Philosophy, University of Rochester.

CHARLES PARSONS is Professor of Philosophy, Columbia University.

ELIZABETH POTTER is Associate Professor of Philosophy, Hamilton College.

SYDNEY SHOEMAKER is Susan Linn Sage Professor of Philosophy, Cornell University.

MARGARET D. WILSON is Professor of Philosophy, Princeton University.

ALLEN W. WOOD is Professor of Philosophy, Cornell University.

Index

Library of Congress Cataloging in Publication Data

Main entry under title:

Self and nature in Kant's philosophy.

   Includes index.
   1. Kant, Immanuel, 1724-1804—Addresses, essays, lectures.   I. Wood,
Allen W.
B2798.S39 1984   193   84-7678
ISBN 0-8014-1610-8